A CLOAK
OF LIGHT

BOOKS BY WRIGHT MORRIS

NOVELS

Plains Song
The Fork River Space Project
A Life
War Games
Fire Sermon
In Orbit
One Day
Cause for Wonder
What a Way to Go
Ceremony in Lone Tree
Love Among the Cannibals
The Field of Vision
The Huge Season
The Deep Sleep
The Works of Love
Man and Boy
The World in the Attic
The Man Who Was There
My Uncle Dudley

PHOTO-TEXT

Photographs & Words
Love Affair: A Venetian Journal

God's Country and My People
The Home Place
The Inhabitants

ESSAYS

Earthly Delights, Unearthly
 Adornments
About Fiction
A Bill of Rites, A Bill of Wrongs,
 A Bill of Goods
The Territory Ahead

ANTHOLOGY

Wright Morris: A Reader

SHORT STORIES

Real Losses, Imaginary Gains

MEMOIRS

Will's Boy
Solo
A Cloak of Light

A CLOAK OF LIGHT

Writing My Life

by WRIGHT MORRIS

1817

HARPER & ROW, PUBLISHERS, New York
Cambridge, Philadelphia, San Francisco, London
Mexico City, São Paulo, Singapore, Sydney

A signed first edition of this book has been privately printed by The Franklin Library.

Portions of the author's description of his photographic trip in 1940 were excerpted from *Photographs & Words*, published by The Friends of Photography in 1982.

FIRST HARPER & ROW EDITION

Designed by Ruth Bornschlegel

Photo layouts by Barbara DuPree Knowles

Library of Congress Cataloging in Publication Data

Morris, Wright, 1910-1998
   A cloak of light.

   1. Morris, Wright, 1910-   —Biography.
2. Novelists, American—20th century—Biography.
I. Title.
PS3525.07475Z464   1985   813'.52 [B]   84-48182
ISBN 0-06-015399-7

85 86 87 88 10 9 8 7 6 5 4 3 2 1

FOR JO

Photographs follow pages 84 and 276

FOREWORD

The circus posters on the barns and sheds of my boyhood, vivid as flames over the long, hot summer, peeled away over the winter to leave enticing glimpses of the leaping tiger, the girl on the flying trapeze, more enticing than the circus itself.

Filling in what has vanished, filling out what is puzzling, is one of the prerogatives of the writer. Among the gifts reserved for his age, one above all is both welcome and unexampled. He is empowered, if he so wills it, to gift himself with a rerun of the life he has discarded, some of it as fresh as the paint on a park bench. It is the writer's nature and his talent to restore to the present much presumed to be lost. Even those candles he recklessly burned at both ends may prove, on examination, to have cast shadows in which he now sees forms from which he once averted his eyes. The faculty of image-making, of time retrieval, to which he has given the labor of a lifetime, is now at his disposal to evoke his own likeness. In this image there may well be more of a conscience than a resemblance. The emotions generated in this act of repossession may also exceed those he felt at the time, evidence that the past is never so much a part of the present as at this moment of recovery. If there is the risk that something of what he recovers will prove to be more trivia than treasure, it is one he has often run as a writer. He dips into his own life, as into others, at his own peril.

A CLOAK
OF LIGHT

*N*o word in my life is so charged with sentiment as *dream.* Not the dreams concerned with the phantoms of sleep, but American dreams, such as mine, concerned with the prevailing fictions of the wakeful mind. I had lived most of my life in their presence, and on their energy. For the person under the spell of these expectations, the time of one's life was the best of times, and that is how I found them.

In the spring of my sophomore year in college I proposed to a girl I had known for three days.

She sat at the cool north window of my Chaucer class, the light frosting her flaxen hair and mouse-colored lashes. I thought her more beautiful full-face than in profile, but I confess her weak chin troubled me a little. Not that I wanted a *strong* chin, but I wanted one not quite so retiring. I liked her best with her gaze slightly averted. I spoke to her on the creaky hall stairs on Wednesday, and on Friday evening I proposed. And not in my sleep. This was a dream of my wakeful mind. On the grid of my memory I see her glowing in the shadow of a tree that dripped fragrance. As the three-piece band played "Good Night, Sweetheart," we pledged our troth.

What you have to remember is that the expectations of my sophomore year lacked a transcendent object. For two years straight they had been rising. I was ignorant of the past, optimistic about the future, and took my cues about the present from Hoagy Carmichael's "Stardust." It was hardly the best tune for my voice, but it was my song.

On the following weekend, in her brother's sporty Ford roadster—he was a junior at Caltech—she drove me to Redlands to meet her family. At that time I knew nothing whatsoever about "old" money, or "new" money. Money was money. I was open to its persuasion, but I lacked experience with it. A chauffeur, in his shirtsleeves, hosed down the family Pierce-Arrow while chatting with a plump matronly woman who proved to be her mother. They were discussing flower arrangements. Her father, who came off the porch to greet me, wore a faded yachting cap and old tennis sneakers. All of the family, including her younger sister and older brother, had assembled at dinner to see me. I saw, for the first time, a raw oyster served on the half shell.

Her father was a reader of Henri Bergson, and probed me as to what I thought of his writings. I would not read much Bergson for another ten years, but this was not the place for me to admit it. We discussed time and memory. I thought I did pretty good on time. In the questions he began to ask me, however, I was able to see that my remarkable early life and bizarre adventures had not impressed him as much as they had his daughter. What did I plan to do with my life? he asked me. In what manner had I chipped one of my front teeth? This incident had not been narrated to his daughter, so I went into it, fully, while we were having coffee. None of them, it seemed, had ever seen or heard of an Irish Mail.

I'll call this young woman Joan Harwood, since her brief engagement to me was not one of her memorable triumphs. She took a seat on the porch swing beside her mother, who was winding up balls of wool yarn while she gave her daughter tips on the sweater she was knitting for me. I was asked to

2

stand up and be measured for the sleeves. Never before had it been pointed out to me that my right arm was longer than my left. How explain it? Thinking pretty fast, considering the situation, I said that I had recently been playing a lot of tennis, and stretching for the serve had probably lengthened my arm. Her brother took exception to that, but it turned out that he didn't play much tennis. I pointed out that my serve was one of the strong points of my game.

There were no dishes to be washed by the guests in this family, and at an early hour my girl drove us back to college. The sky to the west still flamed with the sunset. The gems of the dashboard light were reflected in the windshield. We drove without any music rather than have an argument as to who was the best female vocalist.

One of the very special aspects of our romance was that my girl, at the time I wooed her, had come down with a pretty bad case of trench mouth. So had most of her dormitory. All of the kissable girls I happened to know seemed to me more upset about it than Joan. My own emotions were so rarefied, however, that this sort of deprivation actually increased my affection for her. All in good time, I said—and what did we have but time? At the door to her dormitory, the air fragrant with the perfume of flowering shrubs, I would gently put my lips to her hair—so much like corn silk, it always struck me— or the nape of her lilac-scented neck. I burned with such a fever of chaste desire it often filmed my eyes.

In June her family moved from Redlands to their summer home in Balboa. To be near her, I accepted a job I wouldn't ordinarily have considered. Some work was being done on the new slip for the Balboa ferry, and I was the one they hired to do the work under the water. I had to wear one of the heavy one-eyed divers' helmets, but not much else. It paid a dollar an hour, more than I'd ever made, and it had simply never occurred to me what things might be like when you saw them under water.

In the evening, if the ferry wasn't running, I would swim the channel to be with my girl. If the tide was strong, as it often was, there were times I wondered if I would make it. I had some close calls with boys in catboats, and old men with

3

outboard motors. Since my girl had spent the day on the beach, playing with her friends, she didn't feel up to much in the evening. Most of the time I played caroms or Parcheesi with her sister, who liked to win.

One evening on the porch, her mother, who liked me, hinted that maybe I had come on too strong for a girl like Joan. There simply weren't many world-beater types among the young men to whom she was accustomed. They were more easygoing, as Joan was herself. I hadn't thought of myself as a world-beater type, and I used some of the time I spent under water to think about it. Some world-beater I was, eyeball to eyeball with a bunch of queer fish! It hadn't even crossed my mind, until her mother pointed it out, that Joan already had most of the things I planned to give her, except myself.

I put off for so long asking Joan about her trench mouth, I found it harder and harder to bring the matter up. Did it ever cross my mind that back in Chicago I had lost a great girl because her mother liked me? It should have, but I don't think it did.

Her brother had gone east for the summer, but he was back in time to darken up his tan and play me his new Mills Brothers records. One day, out in his catboat, we had a long talk. He could see what was happening, he said, but from his own inside, knowledgeable point of view, he felt I should consider myself lucky. Speaking man to man, he thought his sister was a real pain in the ass. Take just one thing—had she finished the sweater she was knitting for me? And I could be thankful she hadn't.

I thanked him for his opinion, but I had never before heard a brother speak that way about his sister, and it shocked me. Whatever her shortcomings—like the small flaw in her profile, and the unusually persistent case of trench mouth—she was not so dumb she failed to perceive I was a bit of a pain in the ass myself. In myself, indeed, I seemed to have found a subject adequate to my expectations. I had been eager to share my life with my girls, but this girl had soon tired of it. I had been so full of myself that that small point had gone unnoticed. I had not yet become an object of my own study (all

4

in due time, as time would reveal), but neither did I prove to be a subject she felt compelled to master. Her nature, as little as I had plumbed it, probably recoiled from the self-made, true-grit, plucky sort of suitor I had unconsciously taken as my model. When I later read that the rich were different from us, I had some personal knowledge of this distinction. My solemn, tireless, relentless wooing, the eagerness with which I would prove myself worthy, the manner of my indifference to her snubs, all of this must have bored her profoundly. If I would only go away! If it disturbed me to learn that she was a pain in the derriere—as attractive as I found it—it did excuse me from my commitment to carry on a losing battle. For a woman like that, should I continue to make a fool of myself?

I had known from the first—a guilty, burdensome knowledge, troubling the surface of my self-esteem—that her family had both class and money, but I felt that in learning what a paragon I was they would make a place for me in the family, and maybe even in the firm. That, too, was pretty dumb on my part, since the trucks they manufactured were all back in Ohio. Once happily married, we would live in La Jolla, or perhaps in Hawaii, where they sometimes vacationed in the winter. As unlikely as it seemed, for a girl of her type, or her attitude to trench mouth, I had once seen her, at one of our dances, do a hula that I couldn't believe. She had all of the great movements really down pat. I think she truly did like to listen to me talk, but when I wasn't talking I could see she was restless. Another thing she didn't like was the sort of young man who was always doing handstands. What it all added up to was that it undermined the pride I took in the way I hung in there, which was pretty much the opposite of what I really was. If I wasn't really crazy about her, would I ever behave like that?

I had already lost a great girl in Chicago because I had been such a hit with her mother—had she wanted me to be unfriendly with her mother? yes, that was what she wanted—and now I was losing another because I was such a hit with myself, too full of the self in which I was learning to take pride. It seemed to me I had led an interesting life, and I was eager to share it with a good listener. For almost three weeks she had been one—then most of what she heard made her restless. I remember all that. I remember the way she would clasp and unclasp her hands.

At the end of the summer her mother offered me a ride back to Redlands with the rest of the family, but I was too embarrassed to accept when I learned that Joan wouldn't be with them. If there had been anywhere else for me to go, I would have gone there. I felt like a fool going back to college. I thought of going to Chicago, on one of my father's railroad passes, but the mother of the girl I had lost, depending on what else had happened, might no longer want to see me. I had made a real mistake. How do you unmake a real mistake? On the other hand, if I hadn't made it, I would be working in the lobby of the Y or as an usher in one of the North Side movies, until the girl was old enough to get married. She had been fourteen. I still can't believe it, but that's what she had been.

Back in the spring, before I'd met Joan Harwood, and had nothing on my mind but summer vacation, I'd been asked by the mother of one of my classmates to come and live with her son, to serve as a good example. He was having problems with his courses in English, which happened to be my best subject. The two of us would live in a studio apartment at the rear of a house big enough for parties.

What I planned to do, once I got back to Pomona College, was lose myself in work. I would first write up what had happened between me and Joan, in case I might someday actually want to read about it. Parts of it I did read, to this boy I was living with, but he was too inexperienced to appreciate it.

One day I happened to take from a shelf in the college library the two-volume edition of *The Decline of the West*, I've no idea why. Once I got past the long introduction, I couldn't put it down. The boy's mother, who liked me, gave me a copy of the one-volume edition of Spengler's book for Christmas. On my second close reading, which took me about a month, I underlined what I found of particular interest in red. On my third reading, which took me even longer, I underlined the main points in green. While reading Spengler I was referred to a graduate student who had spent the previous year in a garret, in Paris. Another winter he had spent in Mallorca, as the guest of a woman who liked young people, especially Americans.

I was about to read Spengler one more time, when I made up my mind to take off for Europe. Joan Harwood may have had something to do with this, since she had told me, back when we were talking, that I was one of those people who would end up doing what I said I would do. What I had said was that I was thinking about taking off for Europe.

At the Oxy-Pomona annual football game, I happened to see Joan with a Sigma Tau playboy who drove an Auburn roadster with disk wheels. He wasn't a bad type, really, and better-looking than most girls, with tight curly blond hair and long dark lashes. One thing I remember is how he always dressed for breakfast, and only troubled to attend his afternoon classes. From the way he smiled, some people thought he was tipsy, but that was just how he was.

My ex-girl was there at the Oxy game with him, clasping and unclasping her hands the way I remembered. During the whole game she sat with her knees pressed together, but when the fog came in and seemed to tangle in her hair I really couldn't have cared less what a pain in the ass she was.

In late May, just as I had planned, I took off for Europe. Five or six years later, making a sharp right turn in Alexandria, Virginia, I glanced up to see a woman standing on the curb, her hands gripping the handle of a big perambulator. In a clutter of grocery bags and returnable bottles, a very black child was squatted, a clothespin corking its mouth. The woman was hardly black at all, more a golden peanut-brittle color, and about her broad shoulders she wore a ratty fur piece that dangled a grinning shrunken fox head. In her face, like a sunburst, I swear that what I saw was my own salvation. It was all right there in her face, as if the window of the car framed my conversion. In the rearview mirror I caught a glimpse of her figure tilted way back, as if to see me better. She waved first, then I waved. I just drove along with no interest at all in where I was going. This was in the fall of 1939, and may have been the first of my real losses and imaginary gains.

What she saw in my face, and maybe what Joan saw, and others too, that I haven't mentioned, was one of those fools who persists in his folly, never mind what. It seems clear to me now that I was that kind of fool.

In one of the books I happened to read in Paris, the author said: "Scoroncocolo, fetch me my cloak of light!" I've no idea why that seemed so magical to me. Without any idea what the author meant, I knew I was the reader he had in mind. In the best of times, in the worst of times, the writer has within him his own cloak of light, and he travels with it wrapped around him. That lady on the corner in Alexandria, Virginia, recognized in me one of those fools, and the good news is that she both liked and pitied what she saw.

When I came back from Europe I took a bus to Cleveland, where my new girl met me at the station. I had a silky-type moustache she hadn't previously seen, and a more serious demeanor, but she was nervous and flustered to be driving a car on which her brother still owed three payments. Another thing was that the ring with the college seal I had given her when I left for Europe she had left in a washroom.

My new girl and her family lived on a big shaded lot, great for squirrels and birds. A dog named Sox barked and clawed at the screen when we came up the driveway. Her father, a law school professor, was sitting on the steps of the back porch, husking sweet corn. The day was a hot one, the windows of the house were open, the curtains tied back. From the window above the porch, a woman wearing a shower cap put out her head and spoke to all of us in a voice so calm it seemed disembodied. She hadn't expected a houseguest so early, she said, and leaned far out the window to shake a small rug.

My girl led me through the cool, dark house, taking the route that bypassed the kitchen, where the linoleum was covered with newspapers. Just the year before, I had come in through the kitchen, where her mother had been crouched, her backside to me, taking up the old papers and putting down new ones. Her parents had made the Grand Tour in the early twenties, coming back with the Dresden plates stored in the sideboard along with the goblets made in Venice. That day the dog, Sox, was waiting for me on the stairs, making vertical jumps as if he were on springs. He was put into the room on the left, while I was shown the room that had once been my girl's, but was now her brother's. He had put up his tennis racquet, some Dartmouth pennants, and an Arabian sword in a scabbard. We stood facing the rear dormer window, where a big fierce blue jay was hammering at the feed tray. The one thing I remember her saying to me was that she had lived most of her life in this room—could I imagine that? All I could think of at the time was how lucky she had been. That's how dumb I was.

Although I had been away for more than a year, my rucksack bulging with her letters, I had managed to return from Paris without even a bottle of perfume. I had brought her a poem, offering her the gift of myself. She mistook my confusion and embarrassment for a deep understanding of what she had said. What I did happen to have, right there in my pocket, were little chips of marble I had picked up along the grassy paths of the Roman Forum. She was too touched and moved to thank me. Impulsively, I put my arms around her. We were both speechless, and a good thing. Her mother left the bathroom just in time to catch us in this compromising situation, but she had her own problems, flushed from her shower, with her nightgown peeping at the throat of her bathrobe. It was enough to remind us all that from this point on the game was for keeps. I was twenty-four, older than Alexander at the time of his greatest triumphs, and I had seen more of the world than he had, yet I still knew little or nothing of expectations that were not my own.

Two days later, with one of her Scripps school friends, we were headed west by car for California. Her friend dropped us off in Williams, Arizona, so we could have a few days alone together at the Grand Canyon. I signed the register with a bold but untried hand. I finally read her that poem, and she didn't much like it. She was a reader of "The Waste Land," a poem I had not as yet read.

A few days later we were on the night bus to Claremont, where I carried her bag through the mist of the sprinklers to Browning Hall at Scripps College, where she still had another year. I had another year to go myself, but I had returned determined to be a writer. In one of the comfortable shacks on Hogan's Alley, rented to seniors who were eager to save money, I installed myself with several notebooks of unlined paper and a radio loaned to me by my girl. She had also offered me the use of her typewriter, but first I had to learn to type.

Fifteen months after leaving Claremont, I was back where I had started, with another girl I would soon propose to. What, I had been asked, did I intend to do with my life? Was it sense or folly that led me to feel that this was one of the things I would learn by writing, one of the features of my untried cloak of light. So I was hoping. So, in my ignorance, I told myself.

Although I had gone to Europe for the great adventures writers went in search of, and found them, they did not turn up in what I found myself writing. In their place were scenes and incidents from my boyhood that I had all but forgotten. My Chicago years had proved to be so eventful it had not occurred to me to look behind them. If asked where I was from, I would reply California. Joan Harwood had heard about my life in Chicago, and my trips to California, but nothing about my boyhood in Nebraska. What had it been like? I had put it all behind me. The year I spent in Europe, especially the long summer in Paris, where I found time to ponder what I was up to, led me to reflect on the separate lives I had lived as a boy. It seemed to me I had had a marvelous childhood, even better than Tom Sawyer's, but what did I know? Something about being an exile, traveling around alone, had aroused in me a curiosity about who I was, and where I was from. Yet my reflections did not reach a conscious level until I found myself seated with pen and paper, my mind a blank until I began to write.

After a few weeks of rambling, I found a form, even a style, that seemed to come naturally to me. Seldom more than a paragraph, the language simple, compact, the writer straining to evoke an incident from his boyhood. What he wanted above all was a *specific* time, and a *specific* place. One might have reasoned that he described a picture that he saw through a window before him.

Through the vines was Bickel's General Store and a brown dog drinking at the fountain. Sparrows dropped from the trees to the wires and then from the wires to the ditch grass. A pigeon dropped from the belfry to the roof of the barn. He went along the tin roof to the hole for pigeons, dropped inside. More sparrows dropped from the wires, stirred the grass near the road. Mrs. Riddlemosher stopped picking currants and turned with her pan. Jewel's Tea wagon passed and the dust came up and went by. Behind the feed store Mr. Cole's mare whinnied and Mr. Bickel smoothed the front of his apron, stopped shooing flies. Tipping her sunbonnet back, Mrs. Riddlemosher looked toward the square, where the dust came marching down the road with the rain. (The Inhabitants, 1946)

This writer seems to feel that one word too many would break the spell that he, and the reader, should be under. Time had not actually stopped, but the movements were slow enough to be photographed. The scene had the characteristics of a still life. The writer sought a distillation, a decisive moment, that was both visual and verbal. The narration itself introduced a movement he seemed at pains to minimize. I had a sheaf of such pieces before it crossed my mind that one might actually "take" the pictures I was describing. On occasion I had seen similar pictures in magazines.

While I was having these reflections, I received a bequest, of almost five hundred dollars, from the will of my Seventh-Day Adventist grandfather, who had just died in Boise, Idaho. With part of this money I bought a secondhand Rolleiflex camera, and began to take some of the details I had tried to describe. My instincts led me to artifacts, rather than people. The people I would conjure up with words (I was not lacking in assurance), but the power of the photograph to capture the concrete detail, the visible reality, seemed to me even then, as ignorant as I was, matchless.

In the alleys and backyards of small California towns I found all that I had left in the Platte Valley of Nebraska, and occasionally more. Fences and gates, the steps and stoops of back doors, the clutter around porches, the yards strewn with the ruins and costs of living, the machinery, the junk, and the haunting presence of wrecked, battered and abandoned cars. I put the writing aside to concentrate on the pictures. The first few photographs I managed to enlarge astonished me with their power, their confirmation of what I saw. These were days of excitement I would continue to feel as my experience with the camera broadened, but it did not, at the time, occur to me to relate the visual images to what I had written.

Neither did it occur to me that these photographs, appropriate as they were to my intentions, did not displace, for the writer, the image he sought to describe on his mind's eye. They were collaborating, and reassuring, but not at all the same thing. They also proved expensive to enlarge. For the time being I put the photographs aside and went back to work on a novel about a boy, quite a bit like myself, growing up. Like other boys, he started young:

In a room of lampglow, where the shadows waver on a low ceiling, I lie full of longing at the side of a woman whose bosom heaves, but she is faceless. Not knowing the nature of the longing I felt, would it persist and reappear as poignant yearning for what it is in the past that eludes me? (Will's Boy, 1981)

It would be years before I read *A Portrait of the Artist as a Young Man*, where these matters are given their due, and brief, recognition.

Once upon a time and a very good time it was there was a moocow coming down along the road and this moocow that was down along the road met a nicens little boy named baby tuckoo.

One thing at a time was more than enough for this young writer, who figured, and rightly, he would get to reading later.

My girl came to visit me on weekends, and I might visit her during the week and sit in the visitors' lounge of her dormitory. On the grand piano in the lounge she would often play for me Cyril Scott's "Lotus Land," a piece to my taste. I had also grown to like the *Symphonic Variations* of César Franck, played on the Victrola. At school in England she had met celebrated pianists, and on one occasion, with Myra Hess, she had played a composition for four hands by Mozart. Even more than the music my girl liked to play, I loved to see her seated at the piano, her body swaying slightly, as she was carried away by the music. At these moments I liked to fancy myself at her side, turning the pages of the music, waiting for that moment when she would turn, gaze into my eyes, and I would embrace her. An embrace was a good deal more than a kiss. I had seen it done properly, in my opinion, in a painting I had seen somewhere in Europe, the man embracing the woman as well as he could while still holding his violin. My girl had her mother's dark, remarkable eyes, one feature being how they went so long without blinking, and it had not escaped my attention, at those Scripps dances where she never wore her glasses, that she had a lot of boyfriends I had not previously met. For a girl, she played a good game of tennis, and when we played catch with an indoor ball she threw it with a zip that sometimes led to an argument. It was never really clear to me where it got the zip.

We were both so busy we didn't often get around to discussing marriage. One of the chief attractions of marriage for me would be that when she visited me on weekends she could spend the night. Another thing would be that her mother would finally understand that I was serious. She was suspicious of would-be writers. Her father didn't want to rush us, but my girl felt that anytime we took the leap he would give us a nest egg to start with, perhaps as much as three hundred dollars. The part-time job I had with the WPA was already paying me about thirty a month.

With the winter rains we had the most beautiful clouds I had ever seen. Great towering cumulus masses backed up against the mountains as they did in the paintings of Maxfield Parrish. I took some pictures of them, and won a second prize in a contest held by Marshall Field, in Chicago. They hung it on its side, as if they didn't know what cumulus clouds looked like. The photograph that won the prize we called *Les Nuages*, after much thought.

Early in the spring, feeling the way we did, an old friend who had loaned us all of his Brahms records drove us to San Bernardino, where we were married by the justice of the peace. My girl was a knockout in her blue knit suit and perky red hat. I had to borrow a suit coat from one of my friends, since the one I'd worn to Europe was no longer fit to be married in.

When the word got around that we had been married—one of the cooks at Scripps read it in the San Berdoo paper—there was hell to pay at Scripps, where married women were not allowed to enroll in the college, or live in the dorms. One of her teachers felt the marriage should be annulled. Another, a very prominent scholar, felt that she had betrayed him personally, and questioned the morals of a society that let young people behave in this manner. Even then I could see that he had a point. My wife's father, however, just as she said he would, wired us a money order for two hundred and fifty dollars, with another hundred dollars in the kitty if we needed it. We found a two-room guesthouse; the rooms weren't so large, but there was space in the kitchen for an upright piano, which we bought from Bekins Storage for thirty-five dollars, including delivery. Our rent was eleven dollars a month. I already had a job with the WPA, and my wife found work teaching the piano at a local private school. We really didn't need the money in the kitty, but we took it. More than two years would pass before Scripps College would allow my wife to take her degree, but that's the way it should be if the place has standards. It just so happened she did it magna cum laude, because once she was married, her mind was free for study.

I thought it strange, as I worked on my novel, that in all my college years I had not once thought of my life prior to Chicago, until I found myself on the top of a freight car rattling downgrade in the Platte Valley of Nebraska. From that elevation, which I had enjoyed as a boy, I had a quick, blurred impression of the town I was born in. I applied myself to this challenge five and six hours a day, sometimes working in the

cool of the Pomona library basement. I shared Joyce's sentiments about nicens baby tuckoo and the moocow, but I
lacked his crafty example. Several hundred single-spaced
pages had accumulated by the time the narrator had reached
his ninth year. This volume I titled "So He . . . ," from Robert
Browning's "Caliban upon Setebos," and sent off to Saxe
Commins of Random House, who published books I liked the
looks of. In due time I received it back with a civil, instruc-
tive, encouraging letter, suggesting that I send him my next
book. This I did. In those confident years it seemed obvious to
me that when I wrote a novel that was good enough to publish, it would be published.

I worked a few hours a day giving drawing lessons to some
of my wife's music students, and our income rose to ninety
dollars a month, more than enough to cover the basics. We
bought a record player. We bought our first books. We joined
the record rental plan at the college, and our first album of
records, *Death and the Maiden*, was one I managed to sit on.
On occasion I rode with a friend to Los Angeles and spent the
day browsing in secondhand bookstores. The clerk at the Ar-
gonaut, on Sixth Street, soon became one of my friends. From
him I bought my first Faulkner, *The Sound and the Fury*,
which cost me a dollar, being a clean, mint copy. We talked
books at lunch. We talked books while I browsed. It interested
him to learn that I was a writer. Archer had already begun his
Faulkner collection, and he invited me to his home to look it
over. His wife, Margot, had a droll and sophisticated humor,
and a taste for writers like Carl Van Vechten. She introduced
me to *Peter Whiffle*, a wonderful book about Paris before the
war, wherein the author pointed out a lot of things I had
missed. If there was a sale at Dawson's, around the corner on
Wilshire, Archer would tip me off with a postcard. Mr.
Dawson's specialty was incunabula, and he would buy a lot of
modern stuff just to get the old and rare items. He considered
Arthur Machen a modern writer, and was puzzled that so few
people read him. I bought my first signed, limited editions
from Dawson, for one dollar apiece. He had them all out on
tables at the front of his shop and I was out of my mind trying
to choose between a thin book of Ezra Pound and a thicker

one of Yeats. I borrowed eight dollars from Archer on that occasion, and before lunch I had spent all of it.

Our two-room guesthouse on the alley off Dartmouth was soon crowded with books and records. We hung our clothes on wires across the bathtub. My friend Lorne Ward, whom I had left in Italy when I went to Paris, would bring bags of avocados and oranges when he paid us a visit. We didn't entertain much since we simply didn't have the room. My wife had not had much experience with cooking, but she quickly caught on to casseroles, especially with tuna fish. We could have our milk fresh daily at twenty cents a gallon if I would cycle the four miles out and back for it. The cream was so heavy once it set that we had to spoon it off. I was also good for government handouts, a leg of lamb or a pot roast, but we needed a car to make the pickups, so we usually got along without it. Just a few blocks away we could pick the oranges off the trees. I didn't want to tell my wife I'd seldom had it so good, since she might wonder whom she had married, but except for the three great years in college, and my life with the Mulligans in Omaha, that was a fact. I had arrived back in Claremont with about eight of the twenty dollars I had borrowed from my wife's brother, and here we were, just a year later, living about as well as anybody, with the credit to buy an electric refrigerator.

Sometimes we hiked to Johnson's pasture, in the foothills, from where we could see for miles in three directions, and away to the east, at sunset, the snow-capped peak of San Jac made me think of the Alps. The voices of children, the yapping of dogs, seemed to swell like balloons as they rose toward us, just the way it had been at Schloss Ranna. My wife had not seen as much of the world as I had, but most of the time she agreed with me that there was nothing like California. Neither of us would choose to live anywhere else, even if we could.

After the purchase of an electric refrigerator that would not kill us both if a leak occurred in the freezing unit, we moved to more expansive quarters. The green-shingled cottage was actually pretty crummy, set up on concrete blocks so cats and dogs would fight beneath it, but we had two big bedrooms and a garage at the back we might be able to rent. In the room I used as a study, I kept the cracked green blinds drawn at the window to screen out the light. On the hot days I would begin to perspire about ten o'clock. Our house sat on a corner, under a street light, and one summer evening two high school boys stopped to sit on our curb and have a big discussion. The night was warm and all our windows stood open. This discussion went on until about three o'clock in the morning. I got up to ask them to please move on, but one of them might have been a freshman at the college, since he was wearing a green freshman dink, with the yellow button at the crown. I fell to listening to what was being said, and they were having a literary conversation. One had just read *Magnificent Obsession*, a religious-type novel, and he was explaining it all to his friend. On the strength of what I heard, and how he seemed to feel about it, I later read the book.

The need I felt to have a car in our garage was one reason I decided to buy one. On Figueroa Street, in L.A., I found a '29 Model A coupe, with yellow wire wheels, for forty-five dollars. It also had a bearing knock in the motor. I got the friend who had driven me to L.A. to follow me all the way back to Claremont in case what I expected to happen happened. Nothing did, however, but driving more than forty miles with a defective oil pump finished off the motor. It locked up so tight the crank wouldn't turn it. The wheels would turn, however, and we were able to coast and push it down the incline to a garage. There it sat for about a month while I figured out what to do next. My wife's father had written, some weeks before, that now we were married we should pay them a visit. To this end, they would pay our railroad fare both ways. When I learned what the fares would come to, I had an idea. The local mechanic, a wizard named Zeke, would swap and install a rebuilt motor for sixty-five dollars, which was less than our one-way passage. We also needed a set of new tires and a top, since the roadster had come without one. Ten months of the year you can do pretty well without a top in California, but not if you're driving to Cleveland in the summer. The motor, the tires, the top, and five quarts of oil came to less than our fare on the Santa Fe *Chief*.

17

There was one other little problem. One of our neighbors, who taught at Scripps College, had boarded out his dog, Pat, with us for the summer while he went to Europe. Pat was a lapdog-type police dog. He loved us so much he preferred to live with us, so boarding was no problem. There was no one to leave him with, so he had to go to Cleveland with us. He was a big dog and he panted a lot. Around Claremont he liked to ride in our rumble seat, his head thrust up above our new sporty top. If he saw anything coming toward him he loved to bark. Claremont people got accustomed to him, but out on the highway, with the traffic coming toward us, people might get the idea that the dog was driving. My hope was that with the wind in his face, he would soon get tired.

We got away about sunrise, early in June, to get as far as we could before crossing the desert, but going over the pass to Victorville, I noticed that Pat's eyes were red and watering. At every gas station we had to find some shade and try to hose him down with water. It was my idea, in Barstow, to buy him a pair of goggles: racing goggles, with the fur lining, and a piece of elastic to slip behind his ears. He pawed them off unless he was distracted by a passing car. Once the car was in motion, however, in his excitement he failed to notice he had the goggles on. Over in Utah, on the narrow blacktop road approaching St. George, many of the cars coming toward us would pull off the road to watch us go by. Everything went pretty well until my wife noticed that Pat seemed to be missing. We thought we might have lost him on one of the turns, but when we stopped we found him curled up asleep on the floor of the rumble seat. There he stayed. We got him to lap up some water now and then, but he refused to eat. We drove straight through to Cleveland without stopping, and when we pulled into the yard he was still groggy. In the driveway at the back of the yard we hoisted him from the rumble, but he was so dazed and shaky he could hardly stand up. At that moment the family dog, Sox, came out of nowhere and hit him full tilt from the side. The racket was deafening, and I thought it would surely be the end of Sox. My father-in-law came out of the house in his B.V.D.s—it had been a hot day—got a hand on one dog, a firm grip on the other, and held Sox out at his side like a trophy. I got the leash on Pat, and Sox was put in an upstairs bedroom. We hadn't even had the time to greet each other, but when it was over and quiet there was no need to. We all just sat around the yard drinking ice-cold root beer and watching the fireflies rise out of the grass.

The weeks we were in Cleveland we had an airtight system of signals to keep one dog upstairs and one down. It was a big deal for Sox, and he made the most of it. Late in the evening, my father-in-law and I took Pat for a walk to the local drugstore, where we had double-chocolate Cokes. I think Mr. Finfrock liked me well enough, but he regretted the fact that I couldn't play bridge. We saw two Yankee-Cleveland baseball games together, and I met some of the young lawyers who had been his students. They all called him "Fin." He was a big man in Ohio, and since we did the shopping together, I met a lot of influential bird-watching people. "My son-in-law is a writer," he would say as he introduced me, and none of these young lawyers had met a real working writer. I hadn't been published, but they figured, as I did, that I would be in time.

During that summer I had worked my way up from the past to where I was thinking more and more about Schloss Ranna, the castle in Austria where I had spent the winter. Already it seemed farther away than any other part of my life. In a sense of course it was, going back to the Middle Ages, but I was puzzled by the way the nature of time seemed to apportion and dominate my life. It was all in my head, but in such a cunning manner I accepted it as a fact.

My wife's brother, Charles, was doing some law teaching that summer, but he came up for a visit just before we left. I liked the way he would come to the door of our room and stand there, like a dancer, his fingers poised on his hips. His wisecracks were so good I was slow to get them. Some years later, I saw a photograph of T. E. Lawrence standing poised yet casual, his fingers at his hips. I felt a similar concern for them both.

Charles had been a sprinter on the Dartmouth track team, and liked to discuss with me the strategy of sprinting. He saw most things, including the girls he knew, in terms of strategy.

It all sounded pretty good to me since I had no strategy whatsoever, except to sit and write. When we played doubles together on the public courts, the time we spent on strategy really riled our opponents. The one occasion we played for money we each won sixty-five cents.

Charles felt his sister was right in settling for me, and that the three of us made a great team. He was smarter than I was, an all-A student in law, but I dimly perceived he had some curious hang-ups. If something impressed him as amusing, it might bring on a fit of chortling glee. When he learned that Robert Taylor had been one of my classmates, a young man from Nebraska named Arlington Brugh, it almost broke him up. When I went on to explain that while he was in college I used to have to arrange his blind dates for him, since the girls were ill at ease with a guy so good-looking, he turned and walked into his room, where I could hear him almost gasping with laughter. It was never anything he would discuss with me later, once he'd had his laugh.

What we had come back for was to reassure his mother that I was a proper son-in-law, and she seemed to accept it. When I spoke to my wife about her mother's feelings, she said to me, "Mother doesn't have feelings." My own impressions of her mother were contradictory. Unless we were going somewhere, she was always in her bathrobe, tidying up. When I came down to breakfast in the morning, I might find her spreading newspapers on the linoleum in the kitchen. That summer her big problem was a new icebox. She was reconciled to the fact that it should be electric, but how could she be sure it was the latest model? Already she had seen the models change twice while she had been weighing their virtues. The old ice chest she had had for twenty-three years was full of jars growing mold on stuff that had rotted. When it began to look as if they might explode, she had taken them out and buried them in the compost pit. Her advice to my wife was that she put her faith in how things smelled, not in how they tasted. At dinner, Mother, wearing her pearl earrings, her beautiful eyes as large and unblinking as an owl's, would solemnly gaze at me while she peeled and sliced an orange. I sometimes wondered if her husband ever wondered, as I did, what it would be like to really kiss her. Would it be at the risk that his sleeping beauty would wake from her sleep?

We drove back to California in August, but not with Pat. He was packed into a crate the size of a playhouse, and shipped back on the *Zephyr*. When the crate finally arrived in Claremont, and we pried the boards loose to let him escape, he ran around and around it, moaning and whimpering, as if he might be mad. Then he stopped to greedily lap up the bucket of water I had brought him. After that he was more or less his same old self, a great lapdog.

*I*n my college years, the town of Claremont was a green tranquil oasis in a surround of orange groves and desert wash. Mist from the sprinklers softened the blaze of summer heat and light. A few miles to the north, the San Gabriel Mountains rose abruptly from the soft contours of the foothills to the summit of Old Baldy, capped by snow most of the year. In the crisp' shimmering light of winter, the mountains, framed by my dormitory window, seemed near enough to touch. This was what I had dreamed about in Chicago, and to actually be there was the very heaven—a poetic way of putting it I soon picked up.

Over Christmas vacation, the school cafeteria closed, I would live pretty well on the oranges my professor Leon Howard and I would glean from the neighboring groves. We would sneak out at night, with a couple of pillowcases, and come back with a haul of oranges. Professor Howard was only five or six years my senior, but he proved to be several decades wiser. He had recently married a very pretty young woman with an attractive Baltimore accent. His own Southern accent was very pronounced, and one of the things I liked about him. I was not his favorite student, however, being one of the serious types he frowned on. I couldn't seem to get enough of what he was saying, or whatever it was I was reading. Leon preferred the witty girls at Scripps who had already read and liked the censored books, and loved to play charades at the Howards' in the evening. God, how I disliked charades! In Omaha, as a boy, we had called it "New Orleans," and played it with the girls under the street light, but to watch a grown-up Scripps girl crawling around on the floor like a baby was a taste I had not developed.

Leon was one of the first to encourage me to think I might have some sort of talent—he was reluctant to say, however, what it might be for. When my story about my winter at Schloss Ranna began to take shape, I showed some of it to him. I don't know how he managed to read it.

It was written in the manner of blank verse and a hundred or more pages of this cost me a great effort. Was it readable? Leon said that it was. Not much more than that, really, just that it was. With this reassurance, I would get up early, before the heat, to sit in the room where the screened light was green as pond water, and peck away on a Remington typewriter older than the one used by my father. I was a two-finger typist, and the cuticles of these fingers were usually ragged. But in the fall of that year (1937) I had reached a stage where I thought even a writer like myself should be published. The next book I sent off would be with the understanding that the publisher should not reject it. So I was slow to send it off.

At Scripps College that semester, Magdalene Schindelin, from Vassar, was an exchange teacher in the German Department. My wife had met her in one way or another, and brought her home to meet a real living flesh-and-blood writer. Miss Schindelin was a small, buoyant, assured, radiantly liberated young woman. Her specialties were Thomas Mann and Rainer Maria Rilke. She wore practical shoes, and walked with the stride of a long-practiced grain sower.

"Look here!" she said to me. "What do you write?"

I read her some of my short, compact sketches. I was now

smart enough to speak of them as epiphanies, "a showing forth." I showed forth for a good hour or more, and she hailed them as a new art form. I myself accepted that as good. She was not so sure. As a new art form, it would take my readers longer to know what I was up to. And how were readers to do that if I was not published?

"Patience!" she cried, her knitting needles flashing, and she paused to check over the stitches. A woman of profound enthusiasms, she was naturally opinionated. "Look here!" she would cry, often meaning "Look out!" I was quick to return as good as I got. Her eyes would flash, her cheeks puff out, and my wife would say, "It's time to eat!"

Schindy's office at Scripps was just a block way, so we often saw her for lunch. She would arrive with her knitting, and perhaps a sack of apples. Plugged into her energy, my tiring batteries were soon recharged. I was reluctant, however, to send off a book so much in advance of the reading public, in particular the publisher. So I would continue to be patient and try to finish the book in hand. It would be called *The Madmen of Ranna*, and be all about the winter I had spent there. Nothing much had happened, actually, but it had left on me a profound impression. Would it leave a similar one on its readers? I was a bit skeptical.

I did not spring any of this on our Miss Schindelin, fearing she might not get the bloom of it. She adapted to our life style, our diet, our taste in movies, and her place straddling the gearshift in the Ford. At this time a young woman from England, a classmate of my wife's at her progressive prep school (the mixing of boys and girls together) near London, had arrived on a freighter from Australia, and bedded down with her sleeping bag in our front room. She was a lean, intense, sober-minded young woman with a beautiful complexion and Virginia Woolf's profile. To walk about our town she wore a pair of soiled lederhosen, a rucksack and a green beret. During a visit to our friends the Howards, Leon's wife jokingly said, "Would you like a shower?" to point up the hot weather we were having.

Crumb replied, "I don't mind if I do," and followed her hostess to the bathroom. Her name was Brenda, but at school she was known as Crumb. She proved to play a wicked game of Ping-Pong on one of the tables in a Scripps dormitory. As a rule, she did not like the food we were eating, and prepared her own meals out of her rucksack. She had been away from England, at the time, for a year and a half. She came close to driving us both crazy the five weeks she spent as our guest, but when I got around to reading the letters of Gertrude Bell, I felt I had come to know one of her kind: a British woman of extreme independence and self-sufficiency. On a trip to the Big Sur country, which included Schindy and a young English poet, who was writing a novel, we stopped to have a look at the sea at Point Lobos.

"There's nothing like this anywhere!" I exclaimed, with some passion.

Everyone agreed to that but Crumb. She was silent until we got back to the car. From there she had another look, then soberly said, "Imagine my having been there!"

Was it worth all the trouble she gave us? We decided it was. I am confident she is now somewhere in England making her way, line by line, through Doughty's *Arabia Deserta*, which she will justly admire, but not excessively. After all, he was English. And the making of an Englishman does take time.

My wife had many women friends in Claremont, and with a husband like me she needed them. The friendship of older women had come naturally to her, and they appreciated her for both her qualities and her attention. She welcomed the affectionate concern she received from housemothers and teachers. One of these was Mrs. Snyder, a housemother at Scripps, very responsive and attractive, who had recently lost a daughter my wife's age in a car accident. These women were also very appreciative of a young man who applied himself so seriously to the writing of books it was high time somebody published.

There were also those, of course, who thought it was more than high time that I got a job and supported my wife (how long had it been—almost three years?), but she was not herself unhappy with what she was doing and rather enjoyed the contribution she was making. In the meantime, given the continuing Depression, what sort of job would I find even if I looked? The Great Depression was many writers' ace in the hole.

From our friend Schindelin I heard the startling news that California was not the best place for a writer. There was too much easy living, too much light and heat. There was too much driving to the sea and the mountains, and too much running around on the highways. The life of the mind suffered. The young had no curiosity. They were like young gods in their sunny, open natures, but she felt in them a troubling blandness. They would never write *Death in Venice*. They would probably never read the *Duino Elegies*. The reading of Thomas Mann's *Joseph in Egypt* had led her to reflect about such matters. The life of the mind, of the arts, should experience the nurturing cycle of the seasons! She urged us to consider a new life in the East, where, among other things, I would find my readers. The California people she had met browsed in a book, but they did not read it. Why, indeed, should they? It was hot in the study and the library. Outside, the light sparkled, and the sea washed the beaches. Thomas Mann knew all about it, and saw this life of the body as intoxicating. The sun lulled the mind and the spirit into a languor. If I would forgive her for speaking so frankly, she saw it in the way I was fighting the sunlight. Look how I drew the cracked blinds and sat brooding in the dark! Look how I suffered from eyestrain, a sore back and headaches! This was no place for a truly creative person. It was too much of the outdoors and the outer life, of the desert and the sun.

"But what about the Greeks?" said I, and read her some great lines from Pindar, but a lot of good it did me. What she said was, after needling her brows, "You are not a Greek."

A person like myself, she said (and she had given it some thought), a young person from the new world, not the old world, who felt the forces of the new world rising in him, who should have had better sense than to waste his time on Spengler—such a person should be back where there were seasons like those they had around Poughkeepsie, in Dutchess County. Did I know what it was like around Poughkeepsie? I did not. Therefore I should be quiet until I did.

27

When she herself got back there, next summer, she would invite us for a visit, to see for ourselves.

That was just talk, of course, but I sat there listening. I do a lot of talking myself, and I'm responsive to it.

"What sort of springs are there in Nebraska?" she said.

What sort indeed. Spring came when the winter ended, and we took off our shoes and ran around like crazy. That was spring. By the time we stopped running it was summer, with the asphalt melting, then it was winter and Christmas.

"You've no idea what is spring," she said, reading my mind. "Not just green, but green in all colors. So many greens one didn't need any colors!" How I loved to hear her say that! What a poet she was. With her needles clicking, she said, "You come back to Dutchess County and I show you! You can come back and live in California later, when you are old."

My experience of American life had been varied, intense, disorderly, uncritical. I accepted the world as I found it, and as it found me. The serene insularity of college life, a sheltered haven of peace, plenty and promise, I had interrupted with a year of adventure that deprived me of the fruits of my academic labor, the Bachelor of Arts degree that might have provided me a job. With it I might have been part of the future; without it I had thus far been a public burden. A deep frown creased the brow of one of my classmates—secure in his cage at the local bank, trim in his wrinkled summer seersucker—when he cashed my monthly WPA voucher. He flicked the new bills with his rubber-tipped finger, crisp with his contempt. Nevertheless, I envied him the seersucker jacket. What had briefly been my own life, to do with as I pleased (his wife had discussed this with *my* wife), I had immediately complicated in this unacceptable manner. My request for a small loan had been turned down. Nor did I question the wisdom of this judgment, since it was on such hallowed unquestioned principles that I ran boldly at streams too broad for leaping. When my book was finally published, it would be clear (among the other details on the back of the jacket) that my actions were in the interest and spirit of the virtues carved on the stone gates of the college. The one puzzlement to both the college and myself was that I had come back—to our mutual embarrassment. The very least I might have done was go to another country, and marry another girl.

On occasion, some straggling remnant of Okies, in their battered trucks and creaking tin lizzies, might be seen on the east-west highway to the north, or pulled off this highway into the whispering shade of a pepper tree. In Orange County, California, they were like refugees from a foreign country. My country, actually, part of which I had seen from the tilting top of a freight train, but I had not been aroused at the time to ponder consequences. Hard times? When, for me, had it not been hard times? I had not suffered, but I had lived on the rind as well as the bacon. At that very moment, a California writer, John Steinbeck, was giving this problem his full attention, but I would not read *The Grapes of Wrath* until the summer we lived on Cape Cod. I loved most that part about the turtle making his way across the road.

In the summers, as I remember, we sometimes had unexpected visitors. They might come with a friend, or we might have met them at a party, smart Ivy League–type young men and women who liked to sit up half the night and talk, and didn't at all mind sleeping on our car cushions in the front room. The young women might be good at plucking the guitar and singing spirited Russian folk songs. That part I liked. I might even sing along with them, since I had picked up some of the words in my travels. They were all very friendly but committed people, good talkers and eaters, this being the age of the tuna casserole. They preferred to sleep most of the day, and talk and sing most of the night. We had some trouble with our neighbors the Oberholtzers, whose dog might start barking, but after one or two nights our visitors would take off. During the second night I would be asked to join one member of the party in the bathroom for a moment, where I might catch a glimpse, while I was seated on the tub, of the fellow traveler card he was carrying in his wallet. I was usually impressed and a little proud to have had a visit from a real party member. They were smart people. They knew what to say and how to put it on the line. They all saw a great future for me in the party, but I had been born a confirmed nonjoiner—something in my nature told me that the real problem was in the natural order, not in the social. A cardinal rule of my maverick life had been "Don't join anything," and in my ignorance I took comfort in it.

Another one of my wife's English classmates—the first woman I saw wearing blue jeans, with her shirttail hanging out—came to stay with us for two long weeks and taught us songs we sang around the piano. Her family was in the London theater, and she knew everybody I had ever heard of. I greatly admired *The Seven Pillars of Wisdom*, but she had met T. E. Lawrence and didn't like him. Alison was a big handsome girl with broad shoulders that seemed to curve inward, fitting her like a cloak. She was also a writer, and carried along with her a manuscript she worked on when she wasn't sleeping. It was all about her travels and the people she met. She called it *Fellow Travellers*, and read parts of it aloud to us. It astonished me to meet a young woman with that kind of brass and assurance. She had met hundreds of writers and other famous people just by asking around and ringing their doorbells. Some of these people contributed money to her work, and to the party. She wasn't really an official recruiter for the party; she just did it on her own, if the spirit moved her and she thought the person was ready. That's how she felt about me, and half the time I thought she might be right. But the other half I didn't. We had talked for two weeks about political matters and the war that was coming in Europe, and on the last night I sat with her in her car, parked in our front yard. The door at the front was open, and my wife was playing Bach's Partita in E flat major. Alison didn't really feel my wife was party material, but she knew I was. If I hadn't been married, and pretty confirmed about it, that night I might have become a sort of party member. The advantages were that, come the revolution, you would have a lot of friends. In the meantime I could live a sort of carte blanche life with the inside people in what she referred to as the Jewish Alps. It was just a throwaway line, the way she said it, and I didn't know the Catskills from the Smokies, but I could see the players were all smarter than I was accustomed to play with. I was a pinochle player who played for milk bottle caps; these people were using real silver dollars. My child's soul—the one at issue—took flight at the first ominous creak of harness for the high weeds at the far end of the pasture. Running forward as a joiner, I would just run until I was tripped and tied down. More than forty years would pass before the shape of my fears would emerge from the accumulating clouds of numbers, numbers piled on numbers, ciphers on ciphers, in which I saw revealed the faceless mask of the aggregate, the buzzing hive from which we had once escaped and which we now seemed doomed to rejoin. At some point during my lifetime, the simple, separate person, as celebrated by myself, among others, had so increased in number, in status, in self-awareness, that the result had been a loss of the original substance, single, separate and inviolate. Nobody planned it that way. Nobody actually willed it. It had come to us as a gift of sheer numbers. Quantitative changes that we could measure had led to qualitative changes that continued to elude us. We are accountable, but we no longer know for what it is we account.

I knew nothing of this, seated in Alison's Chevy under the bright arc of the street light. My wife, swaying gently, visible through the doorway, continued to play the Bach Partita. I wanted to slip up behind her, as I sometimes managed, to cup her breasts in my hands as she played and inhale the cologne I had given her for Christmas. I was the captive of other forces, however, and sat low in the seat of the Chevy, astonished by the thickness of my friend's denim-clad knees compared with my own. The red and green gems of the dashboard light spotted her hands. A gleaming eight ball capped the shaft of the gearshift. Clipboards with bundles of notes were tilted on the dashboard, dangled from knobs, bulged the flaps of the door compartments. She knew so damn many people. I felt them gathering to block my exit.

"You've got to make up your mind!" she said, slapping her hand on my thigh, but my ears were full of Bach's Partita, my eyes the sight of my wife, a three-quarter view, leaning back from the piano to accept the advances of the violinist who stooped to gather her into his arms. Without benefit of thought, I got out of the car and walked back to the porch.

Some five or six years later, in an apartment on the backside of Bloomingdale's, my wife and I were with a dozen or so young poets gathered to celebrate Alison's first novel. Copies were piled on the floor before us. Her radiant smiling portrait beamed from the jacket. She could have done a lot for me, she said later, as we stood framed in her doorway, if my fear of guilt by association had not cut me off from what was happening. What did I think I was doing? I was still back where she had left me, up a dry creek paddling my bark canoe.

I was powerfully inclined to let my knees buckle while her strong arms were still around me, holding me up. But she had the maddening habit, while she was talking, of fooling with the temple bars of her glasses; into her mouth, her ears and her nostrils they went while she smoked her corn-tipped Virginia Rounds and let the smoke veil her face. It seemed to me that her broad shoulders had got so round they were like the wings of a hawk who could no longer fly.

In the late spring my wife received an offer to teach at the Westover School, in Middlebury, Connecticut, a polar remove from the world of fellow travelers. This teaching position came with a salary somewhat larger than our combined income, but still small. She would be obliged to live in the school, and I would have to find accommodations elsewhere. All of this greatly pleased our friend Schindelin, in Poughkeepsie, eager to have me freshly dipped in the green of New England. But first we would go to Wellfleet, on Cape Cod, where my wife had spent so many summers at Camp Chequessett. After three winters and summers of Southern California, the light burning at the cracks in the green blinds, the summer silent except for the hiss of the sprinklers, I would only come to know how badly I needed the change after it had occurred. We would load up the Ford, make a stop in Cleveland, then go on for the summer in Wellfleet. Along the way we would visit some of the Indian pueblos near Santa Fe, and make a trip to the cliff house of Mesa Verde in southern Colorado.

At a trading post near Table Rock Mesa, north of Gallup, on the road to Mesa Verde, I saw a turquoise ring, in a setting of six silver raindrops, all of it fashioned from the silver melted down from coins. A Hopi Indian had pawned it for $3.25. It looked great on my third finger. My wife bought it for me, although she knew it would cut into our blanket money. The pawn ticket said the ring dated from about 1885.

There were Navajo squaws in the post, in all their splendor, one of them as tall and fierce as a Japanese warrior, swapping blankets for supplies of flour, sugar and bacon. One had a papoose in the harness at her back; her skin had the shine and color of a new penny. The many things I felt it is impossible for me to describe.

We arrived in Cleveland after midnight, the summer night throbbing with the beat of cicadas, my father-in-law, in his B.V.D.s, asleep in his chair on the screened-in porch. Mother was at the door to the kitchen, spreading papers on the floor as she advanced before us. She was still undecided about which electric refrigerator to buy, and to save the melting ice we drank our root beer without it. I was so tired my head and my eyes ached, but the summer night around me seemed enchanted. Once more we were led through the house, room by room—

. . . so that this room had come as a symbolic climax, as if the house had gathered itself together in the lens of the mirror. Beginning with the kitchen, each room seemed to open on a wider vista, a deeper, more ambitious prospect of American life. A sense of summer leisure, of sweetness and bounty, of innocence and promise without melancholy, seemed to pass through the house, blow in and out of the windows, as if he stood within a grove that Inness might have painted, and gazed out at life. (The Deep Sleep, 1953)

I knew that my wife's impression, as she stood at my side, was of a longing both pleasurable and painful, but I was personally grateful to share an emotion that was part of my expectations. A room of one's own, in a home that seemed both serene and time-defiant. Arcs of haloed light surrounded the street lamps, and some lone, home-bound walker dragged his

heels as he whistled tunelessly. Was it possible that any of
this might change? Rather than break this trance, I preferred
to let it ooze away. I went below to the yard to empty the car,
while my father-in-law stood holding a flashlight. In its beam
we could see the big night fliers. Trapped in the car's closed
rumble seat was the smell of the sage and desert shrubs we
had brought back to her mother from Death Valley. Mos-
quitoes were biting. I heard Fin's hand slap his exposed flesh
sharply, scratch at the bite.

"Don't tell Mother," he said, and I was uncertain, at that
moment, as to just what he had reference: him in his B.V.D.s,
within sight of the neighbors, or the sense we shared of a
male conspiracy.

A week later we stopped to see our friend Schindelin, in her
hideaway outside Poughkeepsie. I found it far more lavish
than she had described it, although her own accommodations
were simple enough. On her wall were reproductions of two
Munch paintings, at which I stared with interest but not
much comprehension. In one, the grass proved to be red, the
woman's face yellow, green and purple. I had begun, but did
not know it, another adventure. We had come back to
Dutchess County and I was being shown the colors of green.

From Schindy we drove through Rip Van Winkle country to
the Westover School, the Middlebury village square possess-
ing the chaste perfection of a shrine. The subdued elegance
of Westover—a walled enclave, with a touch of the nunnery
about it, small dormer windows in a great expanse of slate
roof—led my wife to suggest that I might just drop her off,
then go and hide somewhere. That was not a good start, but it
was a good suggestion. Some distance down the road, I sat in
the car sipping air so lush it filmed my face like syrup. No car
disturbed the peace. In the distance I could hear the damp-
ered whine of a grass cutter. In the deep hollow behind the
square, where the air seemed to settle, it had the hue of
straw-colored wine. Where would I live? There seemed to be
no village. A quarter mile to the north, or was it the east, an
old house had been converted to a general store. I saw the

screen door open and close a measurable instant before I heard it.

My wife was soon back, a handkerchief to her face, which I assumed was an attack of hay fever. When she could speak, her eyes filmed with laugh tears, she explained that she had been met at the door by a handsome Creole maid, who inquired who she was, and if she had an appointment with the mistress. My wife said she did. The maid then declared, "I shell endevah to detuhmin if Mistress Dillingham is ah-vail-awbe," which she fortunately proved to be. Both women had greatly enjoyed this performance, for which the maid was locally famous. Mistress Dillingham had also suggested that I might look for a place to live at nearby Quassapaug Pond, where Waterbury people had summer cabins they might rent out for the winter. Never having spent a winter in a summer cabin, I thought that sounded great. We drove by to look at the pond as we left, the shore near the lodge crowded with cabins, but a young man out on the pier, who rented the boats, couldn't get it through his head I wanted to rent a cabin *through* the winter. If I still wanted to, when I got back in the fall, he would rent me one.

At the time, Wellfleet was—it still may be—one of those summer places that the lucky visitor may feel he alone had captured the bloom of. Summer after summer had filled my wife with the life and lore of the Cape, seaside and bayside, dunes and freshwater ponds—a pair called "the spectacles" were our favorites—the yearly run of the buried treasure on the island, beach plums for jelly, air like wine, and a mix of natives and summer idlers that kept things sharp. When I needed some change, which was frequently, I would round up returnable bottles and cash them in at the local market.

In a small lunchroom established with the tourists in mind, I saw a portly balding man, with a high-pitched voice, often dining with a female companion. I might pick up fragments of literary gossip. It astonished me to learn that this was Edmund Wilson, author of books difficult to find in the secondhand market. To him I owed my acquaintance with

Villiers de L'Isle-Adam, who suggested that his servants should do his living for him.

My wife lived at Camp Chequessett, where she served as one of the cabin leaders. I found a room on the bay side of Wellfleet, in one of the old, handsome and mildewed houses. A block away, where the street forked with the main highway, one of the older renovated houses had just been given a fresh coat of white paint, while the shutters were removed. The sea sun blazed on it daily. It took me several weeks to round up the appropriate camera, one on a tripod with a ground glass, and this marvelous house was my first trophy. Many months would pass before I would see it as a print, but I was confident of the image on my mind's eye. I soon found other matchless subjects, in various shades and intensities of white, but my inexperience with my equipment frequently muffed the performance. I did not at the time have a light meter, an elegant device costing more than twenty dollars. I relied on my instincts and a good run of luck, but my exposures were often bad. An unexpected benefit of my enthusiasm is the way it prepared me for the paintings of Edward Hopper.

One day I took a boat and rowed to Devil's Island to look for pirate treasure and big horseshoe crabs. On the island's beach, the suck of the surf might tip the big crabs to stick up on their spikelike tails, like grave markers. I found a crab big as a breastplate, and black as armor, which I carried into the surf to wash off the sand. As I stood there in the lapping sea froth, I could hear an eerie, rhythmical moaning. It raised the hairs on my neck. There were many weird stories about the island, and parts of it were pitted with holes dug by treasure hunters. The moaning grew worse, and back on the dunes, above the blowing tufted grass, I could see this humped, pumping figure. I thought he might be sick or gagging, and walked to where I saw a big bull-necked man, the muscles in his neck and shoulders corded, crouched on his knees in the soft dune sand between the thighs of an enormous creature. She was so big I wasn't sure it was a woman. Her skirts were thrown back like a collapsed tent, exposing her swollen sowlike belly, white as a squid. One of her soft lobbing breasts spilled out of her blouse, the flesh sugared with sand. What the man seemed to be trying to do was lift the woman's huge bottom so he could penetrate her better. He had his hands and arms beneath her, up to the elbows, but she was simply too heavy for him to lift. His penis was like the neck and head of a great Galápagos turtle, the moist tip of it caked with sand. The harder he thrust at her, the deeper she sank into the dune. I thought his bobbing, pumping head would snap off his neck, like a cork. In the last extremity of his passion, he let out a hoarse bellow and fell forward on her, as if on a sword. The woman had not uttered a sound. I took off and ran, as if I had witnessed a crime, to where I could wade and swim back to the mainland and run to the house. Like Hans Castorp, in his dream in the snow, I had been privileged to see through a chink in the armor that protects the inner temple, where the witchlike old hags, with hanging breasts, dismembered and devoured children. It sickened me to recall it, but I knew—oh, yes, I knew—why it had come to mind. That nature to which we all were captive—in particular the biped who believed himself an exception—turned the very seas into a soup of sperm to make certain of one thing only, the persistence of his ravaging species. In my ears, like the hum of a powerhouse, I could hear the engines of sex at their business, the panting and the groaning, the birds and the bees, the pollen-saturated air.

The next day I saw my wife, in her sailor cap and pinafore blouse with the camp insignia, march by in the weeds at the edge of the highway with a company of her "troops," Raggedy Ann nubiles shuffling along for an ice cream fix in the village. In the voice of a sergeant, my wife was calling, "Left-right, left-right!" as they marched from my sight.

A year later, I would spend most of the summer madly painting watercolors, one of which, a freight car on a siding, was bought by a friend for twenty dollars, my first cash sale in the fine arts. A batch of these sketches, later shown to Lewis Mumford on the chance that I might have an unsuspected talent, earned his appreciative tactful comment that I should continue to work at my writing. At that time I had no Cape photographs to show. Months would pass before my summer pictures would emerge in the darkroom as eight-by-ten enlargements, too many of them pitted with iron from the well water I was using. Occasionally, however, the print reaffirmed what I had seen on the ground glass, the weathered chalk whites and the velvety blacks that I had come to feel I wanted, and had now found.

I'm now vague as to how it happened, but I was persuaded, for part of one summer, to teach the kids of painters, musicians and other idlers how to swim. In a week, some of the young ones were swimming like fish. I was hailed as a magician and, raised to the rank of a paid employee, I soon had more than thirty students, at a dollar a head. With that money I bought a bargain Japanese view camera that looked really great, but proved to be a lemon. On a quick trip to New York, while my wife put up some beach plum jelly, I managed to turn it in on a 4 by 5 Graphic View camera and a Schneider Angulon lens. The wide-angle lens was a revelation. The summer proved to be over before I could really use it, but I had seen my future, and clearly, on the ground glass. A few weeks later I focused this lens on a weathered meeting house in Southbury, Connecticut, the gable like an arrow pointed at the sky. I couldn't wait to see what it would look like in the darkroom, but wait I had to, from late September until the first week of March.

That fall reflected my rising spirits, and was wonderful. My cabin on the pond, usually so dark I had to keep a light burning, flamed with the fire and glow of the leaves that piled up on the slopes around it. In my life I had seen nothing like it. I took long wading walks, and sent my father-in-law descriptions of all the birds I had discovered. Then it was suddenly chill. I crawled from the bed to pull on sweat clothes and sit in the kitchen with my feet in the oven, a pad of paper in my lap. I was full of words, but they blurred on the page. The cabin had no ventilation. I would sit for hours in a stupor of oil fumes, waiting to go to bed. I worked hard but badly, burning the crumpled yellow sheets in a coal pail I kept handy. Unable to write, I did manage a bit of reading, and discovered Thoreau. Why not? Was I not in his cabin, marooned on his pond? I freely marked up the copy of the book I was reading, where he so often anticipated my sentiments and my thinking.

What of architectural beauty I now see, I know has gradually grown from within outward, out of the necessities and character of the indweller, who is the only builder . . . it is the life of the inhabitants whose shells they are.

This statement clarified for me my fascination with structures and artifacts. The experience of stumbling on the writer I needed, when he was needed, would prove to be commonplace. The vernacular structures of American life were all, in my opinion, saturated with the character of the indwellers, creating a form that had grown from within outward. From this moment on, the word *Inhabitants* would label and characterize my project. Page after page of Thoreau helped to focus my dispersed enthusiasms. I was also obliged, beginning early in December, to bail my drinking water through a hole in the ice, and adapt myself to lonely weekends. I was often snowed in. My wife sometimes brought me one of the suet puddings that were a Westover specialty, which I would eat while watching her glide about the pond on the skates I had given her for Christmas. A mistake. I saw even less of her than usual. The cabin depressed her, and she seemed to view my accumulating passion with some bafflement. We were dressed for igloos, and on her visits she seldom took off more than her gloves. In her new environment at Westover her needs and challenges had altered; mine had not. I had a great and continuing desire to roll in my mice-infested, hay-filled mattress. Getting out of her clothes—no small task—was something she seemed to have lost the lust for.

To the young woman at the lodge—a Southern girl, from Knoxville, who sometimes cooked me a chitlin breakfast—I referred to this as my Thoreau period, and I believe she got most of the message. This also proved to be the sort of news that traveled. Word of this bachelor bailing water through a hole in the ice reached the ears of Delia Bronson, a Middlebury widow and retired schoolteacher, who offered to take me into her home, with kitchen and bathroom privileges. I made this move late in February, and just in time. I had not had a bath since the Cape, and my long, uncut hair was matted.

When Delia Bronson saw how I looked with my hair trimmed, my winter duds drying on the line in her basement, I was able to persuade her to let me convert her bathroom into a darkroom, in the interests of art. Neither of us knew where this would lead, but we vibrated to the same high challenge. I set up my machinery (lugged out from Brooklyn, in the rumble seat of the Ford), installed my trays in the tub, my enlarger on the washbowl, and during the long second week of March I managed to print thirty or forty eight-by-ten enlargements, including the meeting house in Southbury. This photograph, happily, awed both of us. I thought it miraculous I was able to print it without the usual pitted surface. Most of the water I used to wash the prints was seeded with tiny particles of rust, pitting the prints like pox. That was the bad news, but the good news outweighed it. Watching these prints emerge in the dark, like objects in a séance, I began to recall, as if I had them before me, some of the prose passages that I had written back in California. I now saw that these passages, like shadow to substance, belonged with the photographs I was now taking, not to illustrate or describe, but to complement the visual image with one of words. My growing excitement was carried to my wife, and to Miss Dillingham, mistress of the Westover School. At her suggestion I agreed to a display of about twenty prints in one of the Westover classrooms. Some of these prints suffered from the pox plague, but they had clarity and brilliance. How had I managed? I feared to dwell on it, and break the spell. The frosty bathroom of Delia Bronson, in Middlebury, had proved to be the scene of this visitation. A few who saw the prints felt that I should be encouraged.

While I had this pressure rising in my boiler, I wrote to James Laughlin, of New Directions, at his home in nearby Norfolk, and hurried over, at his suggestion, to show him what I had wrought. There was also a statement, in the form of a manifesto, in which I clarified the direction I had taken. He asked me to leave some of the prints with him, and a few weeks later he called from New York to suggest I pay a visit to

Delmore Schwartz, in Cambridge. After a fairly dismal winter, my expectations were again in full flower. Before leaving for Cambridge, I wrote to Miss Dillingham, who looked with sympathy and favor on my enthusiasm, and told her of my desire to travel the breadth of the country collecting all these marvels before they vanished. This kind and imposing lady, of regal bearing and proportions, agreed to support my proposed enterprise to the extent of five hundred dollars, available through funds contributed by the students. Five hundred dollars! Nothing will measure the effect this expression of confidence had on me.

I was eager to meet Delmore Schwartz, whose essays I had read, and drove to Cambridge at the first opportunity. In an apartment house near Harvard Square, I sounded a buzzer in the hall, and the door opened. Two floors above me, at the railing of the stairwell, a young woman with a broom, a dustcloth about her hair, peered down at me. What was it I wanted? I said I had come from Mr. Laughlin, of New Directions, to see Mr. Schwartz. She considered what I had said, and with some reluctance beckoned me to come up. In a small, sparsely furnished apartment, Mr. Schwartz sat at a desk, smoking a cigar. He turned somewhat abstractedly to look at me, a cloud of smoke hovering between us. I said something or other about what I was doing, as I opened the portfolio and removed the mounted photo-texts. I passed each photo-text to him, and he looked at it without comment. The woman stood at his shoulder, peering at the photographs, lip-reading lines of the texts. I passed along the material, sometimes with humorous comments, since she read it with such solemn intensity. Mr. Schwartz was silent. His cigar went dead. I realized that he was confronted with a text that required a translation. Nothing he saw or read aroused an echo within himself. With an intensity that I felt faintly hostile, the young woman continued to read, chewing one corner of her lip. I thought her darkly handsome, but overserious. Much that she read I thought to be funny. When they had seen what I had to show them, about twenty photo-texts, I gathered up the materials and put them back in the portfolio. Mr. Schwartz was tactfully speechless. Suddenly, emphatically, the young woman declared, "I like it! I like it!" with the assurance of a judgment, then turned back to her sweeping.

Did Delmore Schwartz comment on that? I've no idea. He sat with his dead cigar, and I felt the burden of his silence. The young woman went on with her sweeping. At the foot of the stairs, my hand on the doorknob, I glanced up, for a last, puzzled impression. The young woman—I thought her gaze almost fierce—stood at the rail, holding her broom.

"I like them!" she said. "Tell him we like them." Then she turned away.

I had the long drive back to Middlebury to reflect on what had happened, and in the fullness of time—it may have been several years—I learned that I had met Mr. and Mrs. Schwartz.

*I*n late May we heard from our friend Schindy, in Poughkeepsie, suggesting that we go to Mexico with her, perhaps in July. She would supply the car and the gasoline. We would provide the travel lore, the tire repairs and the entertainment. Although I had attended college just a few miles from Mexico, it had never crossed my mind to *go* there. My dreaming eyes were focused on Europe. Just before we had left California, however, a book by Stuart Chase had opened my eyes. The Mexico he had discovered did not begin at Tia Juana, but lay far to the south, on the high central plateau, where cities with unpronounceable names revealed a culture that was older than Europe. Thousands of churches, numberless fabulous ruins, a native people who wore colorful costumes and lived happily on the slopes of volcanoes, at the heart of jungles, or walked about the streets of great cities left over from a decaying colonial empire: it all might have been on another planet. I was eager to give it a try, but was this the time? It would take the edge, if nothing more, off the trip I was planning in the fall. Our friend Schindy agreed that her offer was sudden, but it seemed to be this summer or never. War was spreading in Europe. She might be called to Germany to visit her family. If we were going to share this adventure together, it would have to be now, and as soon as we could arrange it.

On the twenty-eighth of June, three weeks later, we were in the Blue Ridge Mountains of West Virginia, near the Cumberland Gap, listening on the radio to the nomination of Wendell Willkie as the Republican candidate for President. It all seemed a little remote to a young man whose photographs and texts would soon be published by the avant-garde New Directions. After a long apprenticeship, was he finally on his way?

We were up early and drove long and late in the hot, humid days of July. In New Orleans we melted in the windless swelter, sitting becalmed in the Vieux Carré, eating slices of un-iced watermelon. I would return in cooler weather to take some photographs. I was the one, of course, to consume several paper cups of shaved ice doused with a purple syrup from a hair tonic bottle, and as my wife assured me that it might, this delayed our departure for three days. I had never been so sick with nausea. I lay on wet towels spread on the floor of the room, and on the third morning I was able to sit up, drink several cups of French coffee, and drive the Ford. We slowly crossed Texas, awash with summer floods, and spent a day in the drugstores of Laredo, drinking Cokes. In the tourist bureau where we acquired our visas, one wall featured a map of Mexico that gave us some indication of what we were in for. Now that we were at the border, the country looked huge. Very loosely speaking, appropriate to the occasion, Mexico City looked as far away as California. Accommodations were minimal. Until we reached the high plateau, the heat was terrible. Our friend Schindy, after a few days of New Orleans, had lost her desire for adventure. Her blouses stuck to her back, her hair to her scalp, and she had settled on a diet of tea and bananas. The smell of the bananas had settled on all of us.

44

In Laredo we were in a motel with comfortable, shaded rooms, the sounds of children at play in a wading pool, and Schindelin took the liberty of suggesting that we might go on to Mexico City without her, then pick her up as we headed north. She would just sit here in the shade near the pool and *read* about Mexico. There were many good books.

Had I had either the wits or the experience, I would have welcomed her suggestion. She was well, but hardly robust, and none of us understood or spoke the language. To look across the Rio Grande, as I had done, to shacks and mud huts on the south side, was to peer romantically into a world about which I knew nothing. In the shimmering heat it looked as appealing as the Casbah ghettos of Morocco, about which I knew even less. A stream of black-shrouded women filed their way across the bridge to do their shopping in Laredo. A few of these señoras carried sick children, and thrust their hands toward me for coins as they passed. In the Laredo paper I had read with some interest that Mexico was girding for a new revolution. A revolution? I was totally ignorant of Mexican history. I thought their hats and sarapes were romantic. A group of mariachi singers, in the cool of the evening, walked about the courtyard of the motel, singing. Marvelous! I reminded myself, while in Mexico, to be sure and buy some mariachi records. I assured Schindy (and my wife, who had read a bit more of the country's history than I had) that we had come too far to deprive ourselves, in a moment of timidity, of a great adventure. Cars full of tourists crossed the border—sometimes, as I had observed, crossing it very slowly. What was holding things up? Their cars and trailers baked in the sun while they sat on benches gripping sheafs of paper. Uniformed bullies of the type seen in American movies swaggered about maintaining order. But that, of course, was normal. On the first day we hoped to reach Ciudad Victoria— pronounced Bictoria—and start the long drive into the mountains the following morning. Sometime later that day we would be in Mexico City.

In the afternoon, in the foothills of the mountains, the landscape suddenly took on a tropical lushness. In Ciudad Victoria the tourist boom had led to new motels with unshaded light bulbs and high, cell-like windows. Dressing for bed, Schindelin observed an enormous green-and-yellow insect on her pillow. Even larger ones were found on the ceiling and scratching at the slippery tiles in the room's corners. She sat up most of the night reading, armed with a folded newspaper to scare off attackers. What I saw both startled and pleased me. Although I had been exposed to a few Pueblo Indians, their "strangeness" had not impressed me as "exotic." This *exotic* would always prove to be in the eye of the beholder, but with my first glimpse of it, in the dark alleys of Victoria, where the women prepared food over open fires, the spell of Mexico for me was exotic. The ragged urchin in Mexico City, who seized another, slightly smaller urchin, and carried it, instinctively, to the safety of the curb as an American child would scoop up a kitten, profoundly moved and reassured me about a piece of our nature that we seemed able to shed, like a skin. I loved these gentle, infinitely sad-eyed children in proportion to their swelling numbers.

In the early dawn we were awakened by the rattle of drums. Standing on a chair so I could peer out the high window, I watched a troop of ragged soldiers, as comically disarrayed as those in the streets of Vienna during the Dollfuss period, march up and down a rutted, gutted lane as a bully with a sword cracked out his orders. The revolution was still at its work, and counterwork. In the Hotel Victoria, an Indian waiter, with a Mayan profile, barefooted in his soiled waiter's jacket, took our "orders" while a doomed rooster dangled from a cord at his back. Sometime later, an elderly señora served us a plate of scrambled eggs we did not eat. Little I cared.

The highway over the mountains to San Luis Potosí curled and spiraled endlessly into a cloudland of peaks where wispy rows of corn were planted in tiers. In the clearings we saw thatch-roofed shelters, smoking fires and naked children. At the edge of the highway, sarape-clad Indians plodded along under high piles of fagots, or walked along spinning out strands of wool. If we stopped to recover from car nausea— both Schindelin and my wife were sick—children suddenly appeared with clusters of small, finger-length bananas. A small boy with the bushy eyebrows of a bandit stared at me as if unaware that I was also staring at him. Schindy gave them all coins. Their bare feet slapped along the blacktop beside us. At the summit, where the car started balking, we crawled around a turn that left the tropics behind us, the prospect opening out on a desert mountain landscape. On one side rain fell, abundantly. On the other it did not. Early that evening we entered Mexico City and wandered about the unmarked streets of the suburbs, pursued by large packs of *muchachos*. On the Paseo de la Reforma, which seemed empty of traffic, we found accommodations in a Victorian mansion. My wife and I were bedded down in an arboretum, full of uncaged birds. They had us up early (it proved to be a Sunday) and we lay listening to the popping of what I thought must be fire-crackers. Cars were racing up and down the Reforma. A fiesta, perhaps? No, that would come later. An election was in process, and the votes were still being taken and counted. It was thought that Camacho had been elected, but there were the usual reservations. When I stepped out to look for a news-paper, the gunfire was still active. Peons riding in a truck, like figures in a Rivera mural, fired their pistols in the air and at anything moving. I ran for the shelter of a tree as they roared past me, grinning and hooting. In the lobby of the new Re-forma Hotel, the tourists were huddled out of what was be-lieved to be the line of fire. I purchased a paper and boldly returned to the street. The carnival spirit was so pronounced I waved at the trucks full of peons. They waved back. A pass-erby who had been hit by the random fire hobbled along with the assistance of a woman, his injured leg dragging. "*Buenos días*," he greeted me, and smiled as they passed.

Our landlady, a very gracious and patrician señora, her strings of beads rustling as she moved about, apologized for the behavior of people participating in the "disorder." It would soon pass. But she recommended caution until the election was over. During the day we sat at her high curtained win-dows watching the carriages pass, and hearing occasional dis-tant gunfire. Mexico was not exactly what my companions had expected, but suited me fine. The señora, after a sumptuous tea, showed us photographs of the gardens where she had grown up in Guadalajara. The people of Guadalajara were all like happy children, and loved to sing and dance.

In the summer of 1940, Mexico City was still a frontier metropolis, closer to the turn-of-the-century frontier than it was to Roosevelt, Mussolini and Hitler. The Zócalo was a park in an impressionist painting, the women strolling about with parasols, the empty benches dappled with shadows. Velvety masses of cumulus clouds could be seen above the treetops. In the afternoons it showered. Sometimes we sat in the tiled, sky-flooded rotunda of Sanborns, with a throng of summer students practicing their Spanish. I was eager to see the snow-capped volcano, unpronounceable, visible in the photomural in the lobby.

The coolness of Mexico City in the morning and evening troubled Schindy with fits of chills and sneezes. The señora advised us to go to Cuernavaca, only fifty miles away but with a temperate and sunny climate. It seemed longer than that with the car windows open, to give the ladies plenty of fresh air, and I gave them both my professional opinion that it was quite like Santa Barbara when settled by the Spaniards. A gutted, empty street led us toward the square, past doorways that opened into cool green patios. We were able to park right there on the plaza, in the shade of the trees of India. At the center of the square the sun blazed, the shadows a shimmering purple. A steady stream of men, women, children and burros crossed the plaza in both directions. The men wore loose-fitting trousers and blouses, their faces deep in the shadow of their sombreros. The women were hooded in a black that soaked up the dazzle, the ragged, smiling children were half-naked, but both the men and their burros moved as if in a trance. One man followed along behind a herd of goats, the tip of his long whip trailing behind him. The frieze-like spectacle of this parade of figures simply left me dazzled. To sit there basking in the sun, my eyes resting on the shadows, the frieze unrolling before me like a diorama, seemed to me an earthly consummation of something dreamed. What invisible terror lurked behind it? Hans Castorp's dream in the snow had made me wary of such sun-drenched perfection.

While the women napped, I wandered about in a daze, my camera hanging unused from my neck. Photographs seemed laughable. My thralldom was complete, although I knew nothing of what I was seeing. What had prepared me, in my American experience, for this enchantment with the primitive? I sat on a bench with two small boys, one of whom gripped my hand like the leash of a pet. They seemed to me children of paradise, careless and amoral as puppies.

I was careful to conceal my thralldom from my companions, who found the children dirty and the poverty depressing. We got rooms near the plaza, in a sort of pension run by a black man who had once been a railroad porter. He claimed to have been—and I believed him—the original model for the smiling black man on the Cream of Wheat carton. His smile now had a few gaps, and his curly pelt was white as a barrister's wig. He had worked for Fred Harvey's dining car service, and swore that he had often seen my father loading his day-old leghorn eggs when the train stopped in Central City. What could I say? His memory seemed greener than mine. With the Depression he had come to Cuernavaca, where no one else served American breakfasts and chicken-fried steaks. Was he ever homesick? No, he replied, not much, but he did miss rooting for the White Sox.

On the third or fourth morning, Schindelin did not appear for breakfast, nor did she eat her bananas at lunch. By evening she had the fever and the nausea. The *turista* would soon pass, our host said, but three days later, filmed with perspiration, her face the color of wet bread dough, she wished she would die. Both my wife and I feared that she might. I managed to find a doctor, a sweet, sad man who listened to me with his lips puckered as he fed nuts to a parrot perched on his desk. He gave me a few pills, which she refused to take. On the fourth night, as we sat up with her, her eyes sunken with exhaustion, she fell asleep. By morning the fever had broken and she was able to sip bottled water. I admitted to neither Schindelin nor myself how deathly sick I believed her to be. In a crisis that easily might have killed her, I had proved to be ignorant and helpless, and the nights I had spent putting wet towels on her forehead had also dampened my thralldom. Wasn't it about time we took off for home? I asked. They agreed that it was.

On our way north, at the pyramid of Teotihuacán, we climbed high up the slopes for the view, which included a parking lot where five or six *muchachos* were washing a just washed car. On the long, hot drive to Texas, we were silent, but I knew that my wife was secretly grateful that what she feared had not happened. Having escaped, I was already thinking of my next trip.

We drove from Laredo to Poughkeepsie, with one short stop for sleep. To a close friend Schindelin later confided that she had never—no, never—expected to return alive, and that she would never—no, never—ever again go anywhere in a car. She meant with me. One of those who liked to get started early and seldom stopped.

She kept that vow until almost September, when I offered to drive her to Wellesley, where she planned to teach. I had swapped the Model A roadster for a 1935 Ford V-8 coupe, with a seat wide enough for me to sleep in on my upcoming photo safari. About ninety miles east of Poughkeepsie, it began to heat up, tighten up, smell up, and then it stopped. It had been a swell car for the money—about eighty dollars on the swap—but the pump hadn't pumped any oil. A passing farmer took Schindelin to where she could catch a bus, but I stayed in Easthampton for almost a week while the mechanic installed a rebuilt motor. It ran so well I drove on to Wellesley and took Schindy for a ride as far as Sudbury, where we had lunch. She had loaned me the cash to buy the car and I wanted her to know it was a good investment.

A week later my wife rode with me as far as New York, where we had a parting dinner at Chumley's, in the west Village, a clubby sort of hangout for newspaper people, who liked to sit around and play chess or cards after dining. In frames around the walls were the jackets of the books some of them had written, most of the books already forgotten, a detail lost on me at the time. It was not a festive evening. My wife was nervous and troubled, and I was torn with the Jimmy Durante quandary, eager to be gone but wanting to stay. We

50

tried to cheer things up with our first real cocktails, but the martini I had burned my throat and brought tears to my eyes. I would never prove much of a boozer. My wife liked the maraschino cherries in Manhattans. We had rented a room in one of those dumps that give rates to academic people, the rugs so dirty you dress and undress without getting out of bed.

In the morning, coming out of the Hudson tunnel into New Jersey, I stopped to take the picture of a church as white and pure as Ivory soap. It might have been brought in during the night from a village in Vermont or New Hampshire. I had a long wait for a break in the traffic before I could click the shutter. This beauty lifted my spirits, however, as if I had sighted a hawk in the city. Near Washington, D.C., the narrow highway was lined with used-car lots and fields of wrecked cars, which I was free to pass by since they had been spotted by Walker Evans. Something about it attracted me, but it was not a subject I was eager to salvage.

In the capital, I stopped to see Roy Stryker at the Farm Security Administration. I had seen the photographs taken by members of his staff, and thought I might find a niche in his program. Mr. Stryker looked at my photographs with keen interest, but without enthusiasm. What did I think I was doing? Where, in God's name, were the people? He listened with amusement to my explanation that the absence of the actual people enhanced their presence in the structures, and in the text. He felt this to be a disturbing contradiction, the sort of thing you might get from a young writer. Stryker's compassion for real people, and their enduring hardships, made him suspicious of my word impressions, and he had the plainspoken American's distrust of anything that smacked of arty. I could feel his concern that I might be using this terrible Depression for some trivial, personal artistic ends. He showed me photographs of people—his desk was strewn with them—long-suffering, displaced, disinherited men, women and children, who parked their battered cars and built their lonely campfires along the nation's highways, and I felt the justice of his disapproval. Was I lacking in compassion? I would have time to ponder this question. My sympathies and emotions were profoundly aroused by the socially deprived and defeated person, by the accumulating and irretrievable losses, but the flame that warmed my heart and indeed burned in my soul was not in the government's plans to put an end to hardship. Hardship, indeed, seemed to me indispensable to what I was feeling. There was something in hardship that I valued, and did not want to see the end of. The peace and relative plenty of the house in Cleveland, with its wide shaded lawn and crowded bird feeders, the breeze stirring the curtains at the dormer windows, aroused a deep and sweet sorrow in me because I seemed unable to truly possess them as I was able to savor and possess hardship. Was there then a contradiction in my life, and in the life of my country, that I would not soon, if ever, fathom, between the good and plentiful life we all wanted and the hard times we secretly cherished? Roy Stryker was right in sensing that my inscrutable purpose was not just in social justice. I wanted the *anima* behind both the justice and the abuses, one that would prove to be the same with or without them. Later that afternoon, in the capital's slums, I took pictures of the tilting, box-like houses, so much like a child's crayon drawing, but he would not have approved my reasons. I found them poignantly expressive. For me, they were unmistakable portraits of generations of hard times, of generations of Old Black Joes, and I could look at them with a pleasure that would have distressed Roy Stryker. What could I make of it? One thing I could make was a photograph.

Later that day, across the river in Virginia, I bought leather boots that laced to my knees, and army-style breeches of tough olive corduroy. They would serve me well as I clambered over fences, or waded through fields of weeds and waist-high brush. That night, at the end of a dark dirt road, I curled up in the seat and tried to sleep as car after car, with dimmed lights, appeared out of the darkness, parked, and then departed. Was it always in the dark we would grope for our pleasure? Shortly after sunrise, I sat up to see I was parked there alone, in the company of birds. I took a walk to stretch my legs, and splashed water on my face from my new canteen.

To be free in this manner, free in my mind and on wheels, yet captive of an abiding and pleasurable enthusiasm that demanded realization—this seemed to me one of the best of possible worlds. It would more than fuel the engine of my purpose on this long trek to California and back, and there was no question in my mind that I would find what was there to be found.

*T*he overrich compost of Southern life and history, which I had sampled in the pages of Faulkner, was visible wherever I looked. Southern atmosphere, as dense and pungent as leaf smoke, to be breathed in and savored like pollen, was in such contrast to my previous experience, I found myself in another country. The ready hospitality, the inflection of the speech, the suspicion that there was less just below the surface than on the surface, the provocative sexuality that was a matter of custom, of tradition, not intended to incite more than a flirtation . . . The warm Southern nights, the music and black voices, seemed as exotic to me as Mexico the previous summer.

But the camera, and the camera eye, is justly looked upon with suspicion. Soon enough I was seen as an intruding alien. I tramped about with this machine mounted on its tripod, or set it up to conceal myself beneath the hood, invariably pointed at some house or doorway judged to be of no pictorial interest. Why would I take *that*, except to reveal what was better concealed? I could only have in mind the exposure of whoever lived there, a blot on the peeling Southern escutcheon. Turning from me to note my car, with its out-of-state license, clarified the picture. I was a Northern snooper out to discredit the troubled, dilapidated Southern self-image. Black and white both felt it, the black with less malice but a more profound discomfort. My presence testified to their worst suspicions about their condition. The separate yet commingled cultures of black and white that make of the South a unique and a tormented culture were at once unavoidably visible and subject to instant falsification. The impoverished black, the debased poor white, had been well exposed in books and magazines, and such distinctions as might be made were in the eye of the beholder, not the camera.

At the edge of Culpeper, in Virginia, I found a house and a dead tree, equally husk-like, both appearing to date from Lee's surrender, that seemed to speak directly to my troubled state of mind. Was it a portrait, or a caricature? Did it reveal a state of soul or a state of abuse? I could see now one, now the other, by merely blinking. What was there to be seen was in the eye of the beholder. But in the basking sunshine of a Blue Ridge October, I felt the ripeness and warmth of survival more than I felt the chill of inhuman custom. The meaning this structure had to give out was a many-layered, many-voiced passage of history, too dense and complex to do more than acknowledge, but in this surviving husk more life-enhancing than life-defeating.

But that was not all. What I had made, when the shutter clicked, was a photograph. It would be weeks before I saw the negative, and many months would pass before I made a print of what I had seen on the ground glass. Would that image restore my original impressions, or would they be replaced by others? To what extent would this new image, cut off from its surroundings, constitute a new structure? How much of the "reality" had it captured? How much had it ignored? Whether or not it had been my intent, I would end up with something *other* than what was there. It would be a new likeness, a remarkable approximation, a ponderable resemblance, but not a copy. This new image would testify to the photographer's inscrutable presence. I was not appreciative of these distinctions at the time I took the picture, and believed that what I had seen on the ground glass would surely be what I had captured.

I made my way south along the foothills of the Smokies, the blues of the mountains to the west transparent in the hazy light, deepening to purple as the sun set behind them. The warmth of the season, the golden October light, the harmony that prevailed between man and nature (man and man was another matter), seemed to clarify for me, in an instant, the attachment of the Southerner to the place he came from. A ballad-like sense of peace, if not plenty, seemed as palpable to me as strains of music. I was subject, as my experience had proved, to a lyrical euphoria when exposed to new places. I had felt it repeatedly in Europe, and to the point of dazzlement in Mexico. If something unearthly had occurred, I would have been an eager and a willing witness. This mood was both so tangible and so fragile I was reluctant to dispel it. I stayed away from the larger towns, and avoided photographing what might arouse comment or suspicion. I confined myself to farmhouses and outbuildings, and the look of fields and fences in the slanting light. I noted how frequently a coat of whitewash would accent a weathered wall, gate, door or brick chimney. Most of the natives I saw were black, deferential to the white man, and eager to be helpful. I soon found that their answers to my questions, as to where I was and where I hoped to be going, were concerned less with information than with a desire to be cordial. Was this the right road? Yessuh. Was it a good road? Yessuh. If places were mentioned, I might not understand what was said. This increased my assurance of strangeness. I slept one night in the car—or rather I spent the night awake listening to the movement of cattle, the snuffling of curious dogs. My first night in a hotel, the bed a creaking antique on a floor that tilted toward the window, offered me a curtained view of the street like an illustration of a page of history. A white horse, ghostly in the light of a waning moon, whinnied in a manner I thought to be human. I relished the family-style breakfast in the morning, which I shared with a guest and seven members of the family, having long forgotten what it was like to eat eggs fried in fat and hot slabs of cornbread. The affable garrulousness and easy hospitality charmed me. I liked being huhhh-ney to the woman who served me. I smoked a cigar that crackled like cornflakes when I lit it.

Two days later, a Saturday night in North Carolina, I watched the town fill up with old cars, buggies and wagons that were packed with denim-clad country people and their children, whom I recognized as poor whites. It was new to me to see a real "tribe" of people, the men and women separate, the kids roving about like unleashed pets, the men inclined to hunker down on their hams like Indians, their forearms on their knees, their hands dangling. It amazed me to see that they might crouch like that for an hour or more, silently smoking, or in animated talk. The women were never part of this commingling of the men. I liked the drawling speech, the turns of phrase, and the breeding I saw in the lean faces and work-honed bodies, their postures and gestures acquired from the daily habits of a lifetime. I liked them, but I feared to intrude, spying on them as I would have Gypsies in my home town. They seemed to me more interesting and intense than the people I had known. The women were lean from work and child rearing, the skin of their pale faces tight to the bones as if to emphasize fundamentals, thin-lipped, inclined to uneasy glances that might be quick to take offense. To watch them in the way I cared to, I sat in the car, pretending to read a paper. I wouldn't have dreamed of trying to take a picture. I had always felt the camera eye to be intrusive, but never so profoundly as when I contemplated directing it toward such private people. The barefooted children, in their hand-me-down clothes, ran about beneath the wagons. How was it that I, a native of the plains, should feel that here I was at long last among my own people?

In South Carolina, near the state line, I stopped at the edge of a sun-baked bean field. At its center, raised off the ground so high that a small child might walk beneath it, was a large, one-storied clapboard house with a shingled roof and high windows without glass. They made deep pockets of shadow, and crisp shadows accented the unpainted clapboards. The yard around it was hard and clean as a floor, and between me and the house was a covered well with a pulley to raise and lower the galvanized bucket. Not a soul or a dog in sight. In the high noonday heat I assumed both might be napping.

The patterns of light and shade, the colors of earth and wood, the shimmering flame of light at the edge of the shadows, compelled me to try and get the picture. In all its weathered and man-shaped details it fulfilled my idea of the beautiful. But I would have to intrude on private property. Stealthily, picking my way along the furrows, extending the legs of the tripod as I approached the house, I set up my camera, stooped beneath the cloth, and saw the blurred image on the ground glass. Beads of perspiration burned my eyes. I backed away, shirttailed my face, then once more focused on the ground glass. Just to the left of the house, perhaps ten yards behind it, in colors that appeared designed to conceal him, a black giant stood in a posture of resting, his hands clasping a hoe handle. A narrow-brimmed hat, tilted forward, shaded his eyes. I pretended not to see him. It made my movements more assured and casual. I was deliberate and open in what I was doing. I moved the tripod, I took several pictures. I felt the passing of time would prove to be to my advantage. On the ground glass I watched him approach. Too late to cut and run, I was paralyzed.

"What you see?" he asked me.

Out from under the cloth I peered up, and up, at the ivory smile in his black face. He was curious. "What you see?" he repeated.

"You want to look?" He did. He crouched low, I hooded him with the cloth, and for a long moment he was silent. Backing away, he shook his head, puzzled. "You don't see it?" He did not. I checked to see if the glass was in focus. It was beautiful. Then it occurred to me it was upside down. "It's upside down," I said, apologetic. That was more mystifying. He had another look at it. What he saw led him to stoop, slapping his knees, then straighten up with a bellow of laughter. Why the image was upside down was something I did not want to go into. We moved to the shady side of his well, where we both had a drink from the bucket. He took deep audible swallows, his Adam's apple pumping. When he had finished, he emptied the bucket over his head, the spill of water darkening his shirt. The drops that fell to the ground did not soak in, but rolled into balls of dust. If he had worn a sheet I would have felt in the presence of the Lord in *The Green Pastures*. Near where we stood, a wire-supported pole went up about twenty feet to dangle four or five gourds, the narrow ends chopped off. Small birds, nesting in the gourds, darted in and out. He watched this with such delight and concentration that I walked away, not wanting to disturb him, and when I looked back from the road he was still there, his wet hair gleaming.

A few hours later, in Greenville, I had my dinner in a café, then walked around the streets as the day cooled. There were structures on the main street I planned to take in the morning, when the light would be better. The Southern night was breezeless and humid. It seemed foolish to spend it cooped up in a hotel room. I followed a dusty side road to the edge of town and parked in the shade of a willow. Later I curled up in the seat, and I lay there attentive to the sounds that came from the nearby houses, the voices of children, dogs, radio programs. I had half drowsed off when lights flickered in the rearview mirror and on the windshield. I heard the throb of an idle motor. A moment later, a cop, with a beefy perspiring face, put his head in the window I had opened. He noted my camera, and the boots I had unlaced to cool my feet. Something about that pleased him. He turned to wag a finger at the cop he had left in the car. Even in my own opinion an intruder like myself had aroused very little suspicion.

"Hi," I said, and smiled.

In 1940 the Second World War had begun, but we were not yet in it. A slight war fever was palpable among those who might be drafted, or felt themselves threatened. In Greenville, South Carolina, I was picked up as a vagrant, and charged with being a possible spy. My camera, at the ready, was there beside me in the seat, and I had obviously been taking pictures. Of what? Of critical installations, surely. The excitement of having captured a spy soon gave rise to a sense of

60

exhilaration. The chief of police, a short, fat man with a nervous, hysterical manner, his leather straps, ammunition belts, and pistol in a holster, might have served Mack Sennett as a model for the comical—as opposed to the beefy and brutal—Southern cop.

I was fingerprinted, questioned, all of my gear was inventoried, then I was taken to the second floor of a jail behind the buildings facing the main street. This was a single large room with bars at the windows, cots placed around the walls, a windowless cell, the door heavily barred, in the room's back corner. A local desperado, by the name of Furman, was kept in this cell.

In the room below—as I found out at sunrise—a chain gang of blacks was incarcerated; the racket they made leaving their quarters woke me up. We had a view through the door, and the glassless windows, over the lower roofs of the town. We could see and hear it come alive in the morning, pause during the heat of the day, become active and noisy approaching the dinner hour, then quiet down in the evening. I shared the room with a motley crew of bums, ne'er-do-wells and poor whites. They had been drinking and fighting, or merely loafing. Some were loud and bitter for as long as ten minutes. Most were resigned. During part of the day and the long night they were full of talk, tales and wild humor. Having me as a new and interested listener meant more than having me as a talker. I did a lot of listening and scratching. Once or twice a day I gave somber speeches to the chief of police as he stood at the door. He liked my performance. While I talked he chewed on a toothpick, scratched his private parts and gazed reflectively over the roofs of the city, over his domain.

On the strength of the hope that I was a spy, a plainclothes official, a kindly elderly man, with whom I briefly discussed Stark Young and Faulkner, came over from the capital, Columbia. He looked at my papers, heard my story, recommended that I spend at least a week in Charleston, then advised them to release me. I had a long day and night to brood over whether that advice would ever be taken. On the third or fourth morning, shortly after the chain gang rattled its way down the alley, I had a tin cup of coffee with the chief—who had for me, he said, no hard feelings—was given my camera, the keys to my car, and advised to get the hell out of South Carolina. That advice I took. Along with me went a large colony of bugs, some of whom took up fairly permanent residence. I drove without stopping, but with the greatest caution, the eighty miles or so to the Georgia state line, then another fifty miles to Athens. In the Athens YMCA I took a long, long shower and washed myself repeatedly with Lifebuoy soap, scrubbing my scalp and hair. The profound relief I felt—to be free of incarceration, of a sense of helplessness that is traumatic—had little or nothing to do with the relatively comical incident. I had also known it in Grosseto, Italy, where I was picked up as a threat to Mussolini, but the jail in Greenville, the character of the law and order, the "outside" world that I could see and share through the windows, left on me a ponderable impression.

While in Georgia—I had heard about Georgia, I had read *Tobacco Road*, I had seen the chain gangs in the movies—I was understandably reluctant to take pictures. I kept a low profile. I had recently read *The Heart Is a Lonely Hunter* and heard that the author had lived in Columbus. I could believe that. The basking Southern heat, the soft golden light, the way structures and people appeared to be saturated with the scent of a past as dense as leaf smoke, smoldering and druglike, in which everybody was a willing compliant victim . . . Walking the dusty streets, I envied the writers fortunate enough to come from such places, still sticky with the pollen that clung to them. It seemed to me they need only close their eyes, open their pores and inhale deeply, to possess their subjects. The sorghum-like richness of Southern life was both on the surface and fermenting beneath it. Through the dusty lace curtains at my hotel room window I spied on passersby whom I secretly envied, as Anderson spied on his neighbors in Winesburg. They were dream-drugged, these people, and I envied the depth of their addiction.

In the nearby countryside, as I was driving around, I saw a glow of lights that I thought might be a fire. It proved to be a small carnival, with a rocking, clanking Ferris wheel, one or two dangerous rides, and sideshows of freaks. It had been set up in a field of trampled grass, the air smoking with the savor of barbecued meat. No carnival or chautauqua of my boyhood generated so much excitement and so many expectations. These country folk, with their throngs of small fry, were the "crackers" I had read about in Erskine Caldwell. I was amazed at the visible kinship ties, the cartoon grotesqueries of Li'l Abner, or the figures in Faulkner's "Spotted Horses," to the people I saw around me. In the context a small occasion provided, larger-than-life figures and sentiments materialized. Given a throng of expectant, deprived rural people, a mythic South might emerge from their shared anticipations. Its sensuality aroused me. I felt the surrounding darkness would soon be cluttered with amorous couples. After the engines had coughed and died, the crowd had dispersed, the tents had collapsed, a cloud of dust so thick I could taste it hung over the field where it had all happened. I spent the night in the car, not far from a banjo that repeated, and repeated, the same chords. Now and then the player cried out in the manner of a flamenco singer. My feeling that hardship, and hard times, if not destructively brutal, if not prolonged to the point of negation, are necessary to a density and richness of emotion that seem noticeably absent in happier situations I largely owe to these few weeks of Southern exposure. I did not say to myself that my life had changed, but with the morning light I felt that it had. Missing from my life had been the emotion that finds its fulfillment and release in the ballad. I had discovered the emotion, but how to cultivate it would prove to be the work of a lifetime. A few years later, when I had read James Agee's *Let Us Now Praise Famous Men* and saw Walker Evans's accompanying photographs of sharecroppers, I would fully appreciate the wide range of impressions I had just experienced.

In Pike County, Alabama, I crossed a field of corn stubble for a better view of several barns and a house, weathered to the color of dead branches. I moved in closer to get the shingled roof of the house, shimmering with heat. Under the hood of the camera, focusing on the ground glass, I heard an angry, bellowing voice. I uncovered my head and looked around. I saw no one. The voice spoke again—it seemed closer—and the corn stubble crackled as if trampled by cattle. The blast that followed was that of a shotgun behind the barns. In the morning stillness the air seemed to tremble like my legs and hands. I ran for the car, dragging the tripod, and some moments later I saw the film of perspiration on the face in the rearview mirror, the wide, staring eyes. Could one smell fear? I thought I could detect it. Inside my clothes I was slippery with perspiration.

A Southern friend had told me that the streets of Montgomery were as fragrant with sex as the smell of magnolia, and I drove about slowly, sniffing the air like a coon dog. The basking, windless heat was stirred only by fans, whirring in the shadows of deep porches. I drank a cold Dr Pepper at a drugstore counter, the mirror vibrating with the throb of a ceiling fan. The postcard I had written and put a stamp on I decided not to mail.

My objective was New Orleans, and I persuaded myself that I should get there a day or so early. I drove south to Mobile, then west along the Gulf Coast, the water as smooth as a pond. Men and boys sat along the shore, fishing, with the lines dangling slack from their long poles. I had not experienced heat that drugged the senses, and had about it a lulling, agreeable torpor. To keep from dozing at the wheel, I parked and took a nap. Animals and people were both becalmed. I understood the necessity of the siesta. Much later I would understand the need for the bourbon and the mint julep.

In New Orleans I had been invited to stay with Otis Lee, who had been one of my teachers at Pomona College. That winter he was on leave from his position at Vassar, to continue his own philosophical writing. The week I spent in New Orleans owed more to Otis and Dorothy Lee, and our long nightly discussions, than the prowling with the camera in the Vieux Carré. There I soaked up atmosphere to the point of saturation, but for reasons that are no longer clear to me I overexposed most of the negatives.

Driving north from New Orleans, I stopped to see my friend

Hubert Creekmore, who was then living in Jackson, Mississippi. He took me to meet one of his friends and neighbors, Eudora Welty, and among other things we talked about William Faulkner. Faulkner's town was Oxford, on my route north, but I had no intention of intruding on his privacy. I was encouraged, however, to intrude, if possible, on his old friend Phil Stone. That also seemed unwarranted to me, as a writer who had as yet published nothing, so I spent most of the day in Oxford sitting in the square, waiting for history to strike me. It did not. Late in the afternoon I screwed up enough gall to appear at the door of Stone's law office. He was there. On my admitting my interest in Faulkner, he took me in tow. Phil Stone was a fluent and accomplished talker, and like most talkers craved a fresh and good listener, which I proved to be. I was directed to the house down the street, centered in a large lot, which now looms in my mind like a Faulknerian mansion, but unfortunately the details are blurred. My car was parked in the driveway, approaching the house, where I assumed I would be spending the night. I would meet his wife. I would be modestly feted. I would be gorged with tales beyond the telling, and I would be dimly aware, during the long evening, of the ghostly passage of black figures, and the musical murmur of black voices. Not asked to stay, I inquired if I might spend the night in my car, parked in their drive. I had told them of my adventure in Greenville, South Carolina. I was given permission to sleep in my car.

I lay awake until daylight, seeking a clue to my pleasurable but disordered impressions. In the light of these impressions, Faulkner's fiction seemed both controlled and understated. The soul of the South, as I was privileged to perceive it, seemed to me more complex, and bizarre, than the reports I had read about it. More incredible to me, I found its strangeness wondrous and life-enhancing, rather than merely monstrous and grotesque. I owed these impressions to Phil Stone's remarkable relationship with the Negroes—*his* Negroes, who deliberately chose not to be free. A few were servants in his house, others occupied barns and outbuildings. Something in Phil Stone's nature cultivated and responded to this reversal

65

of historical roles, the master who became the captive of his slaves. I had been greatly impressed by Melville's profound grasp of this dilemma in his novella *Benito Cereno*, which I saw worked out with even greater refinement in the way the blacks dominated the Stone household. A marvelous "mammy," deep and broad as a scow, served the food she had prepared on a schedule of her own making, her eyes rolling, her lips parted in a litany of Yessuhs and Yes ma'ams. With each serving I exchanged knowing glances with the master and the mistress of the house, eager to share their predicament. An old black named Blue, asked to fetch wood for a fire, in an hour's time appeared with a stick, no more than a piece of kindling, on his crossed arms like an offering. Thanked for that, but urged to get more, he almost collapsed with contrition, then appeared, an hour later, with two pieces of the same size. I had been eagerly brought to the Stone house, to share its hospitality, so that I could bear witness to this drama of the slaves who were now the masters, and seemed even more fawning in their service. The role reversal had been so complete, so lovingly achieved, that Stone felt compelled to share it with someone, even a profoundly ignorant youthful Yankee. He had become captivated by his own captivity. I doubt that was true of his young wife, preoccupied with a squalling infant, but Stone took me off to his study for further comments on his condition. A friend of FDR, and other national figures, he had their signed photographs ornamenting the book-lined room. We smoked stogies imported from Pennsylvania, while he brought me up to date on his pleasurable torments. They were many. Periodically he sent the young men to Memphis, with stakes of money, but separated from the money, they returned to his house. The external world did not appeal to them. Besides, they loved the master and the mistress. The top exhibit—for which I was slowly prepared— was of a satin-lined case full of silver goblets, each goblet twisted on its stem by powerful hands. Who had done it? The loving mammy. It just seemed to happen and she couldn't help it. She was just giving each one of them a polish, and lo and behold, it just seemed to happen. Two dozen goblets. It was clear to both of us that Mammy's twist had made them priceless.

Shortly after midnight, he bid me good night, wished me luck as a writer, and showed me to the door. Before I passed through it I asked him again if I could sleep in my car, parked in his driveway. Yes, that I could do. More than that, if I delayed my departure I might have breakfast with them in the morning. As I made myself comfortable in the seat of the car, I wondered if this, too, was a decision that the slaves had made for the masters. A sleeping guest was a bother. There would be a bed to make, and sheets to be changed. By morning it was drizzling, and just after daylight I opened my eyes to see the aging, half-blind Blue at my window, peering in, muttering to himself. Did he see me? I pretended to sleep. When he shuffled off, in a parody of the gait of Stepin Fetchit, I decided to take off rather than weaken or dispel the incredible events of the evening. I had breakfast in Oxford, grits with my eggs, then drove north to where a bank near the road had eroded to leave a raw gully, red as a bleeding wound. I managed to take a few pictures, in spite of the drizzle, then continued toward Memphis. Perhaps an hour later, as it rained much harder, I passed a field where a harness-patched plow horse, white as Moby Dick, stood luminous in a piece of overgrazed pasture, his heavy head bowed. I should have stopped. That I didn't is why I have forever borne it so vividly in mind.

In Arkansas the rain-washed air dried quickly, like a watercolor. I drove a long day, feeling the need of a change. Late at night, near the Missouri line, I parked off the road to sleep. At sunrise I awoke on the rim of the world. The shadow of the car stretched out before me, the light spreading like a surf, splashing on objects. It may have been the first time I saw the plains as a metaphor for the sea, a place to be possessed by the imagination. I no more than saw it, I did not feel inspired at the sight to possess it, but coming out of the woods, literally and figuratively, where I had been wandering for more than six weeks, I experienced the prodigal son's elation at the sight of the homeland. I think it startled me. My view of the plains had always been dim. My sentiments on the occasional cross-country drives were expressed in my early fiction, where Nebraska was the place you drove all night while your companion slept in the seat. That had been the impression of my friends in the East.

As the sun rose I found much to photograph. Anything that stood up so the light would strike it—an almost audible clamor at sunrise—houses and barns, fences and telephone poles, clusters of trees and dwellings, and like a sail at sea, the occasional gleam of a grain elevator. I saw, but I did not fully sense, that these constructions were pathetically temporary on the vast exposed landscape. In this I found their appeal, their life-enhancing poignancy. My instinct was to celebrate the eloquence of structures so plainly dedicated to human use, and to salvage those that were on the edge of dissolution. The plains provided a scenic prop that was free of obstruction, where the sun was sufficient to delineate the object. I took my subjects on the run, as the light fell on them, frequently not at all to their advantage, since I was eager to see what beckoned down the road, and I was concerned about a change in the weather.

The roll and dip of the plains increased as I drove west, reminding me that my boyhood in the flat Platte Valley of Nebraska had given me a mistaken notion of the high plains. They were remarkably sea-like, the towns sunbaked and windblown, riding the crests of the waves. In western Kansas, near the Colorado border—it might have been Goodland—I found a row of stores, with curtained and blind-drawn windows, slightly tilting false fronts, that would provide me with an inexhaustible image of plains character and experience, mute, implacable and yet expectant. Stubbornly and irrationally optimistic.

Going over Raton Pass, south of Trinidad, Colorado, I recovered the excitement I had felt as a youth on my first car trip to California, the winter of 1926. From the mountains I could see the great blue and rose mesas, like camouflaged ships anchored on the high cloud-dappled New Mexico plateau. The emotions I felt would reassert themselves when I arrived in Los Angeles, in January, and found myself nostalgically pondering my early days and wonderful times on the open road.

In the winter of 1940, Santa Fe was still the town of old adobe houses, warm sun, cool shadows, a bandstand in the square, blankets and silver in the shops, and Pueblo Indians under the awning of the governor's building. Most of the artists and writers had moved on to greener pastures or trickled back to Greenwich Village, but the lobby of La Fonda Hotel thronged with trend-seeking tourists and self-proclaimed old-timers. I listened to their stories. Mabel Dodge Luhan was at home near Taos, where the natives were reduced to Sears, Roebuck blankets. The air was like wine, the light shimmered like tinsel, and I marveled at how I had dreamed of living anywhere else.

I found a room, a ten-minute walk from the square, for five dollars a week, a detail that is part of the period's aura. I spent the sun-struck days visiting the pueblos, San Ildefonso, Santo Domingo, etc., or following dirt roads wherever they led me. Gas was cheap. My problem was conserving film. I watched Maria Martínez shape and fire her pottery, and bargained with Fred Kabotie for one of his paintings. In the evening I looked for a seat in La Fonda's lobby, fragrant with piñon fires and the smell of Mexican food. I loved the slap and creak of new and old huaraches and felt myself one of the chosen.

The big event of the season was the world premiere of *Santa Fe Trail*, with Errol Flynn and Olivia De Havilland. This trail did not come to Santa Fe, but Hollywood did. The ceremony took place in the floodlit square, white with the first snow, and ringed with Christmas lights. The red men and their women viewed the white man's fiesta with their customary resignation. Carols were played. Errol Flynn brushed against me as he made his way into La Fonda's lobby.

In a few weeks I had shot more film than I should have, and suffered from a bad case of pueblo-country enchantment. I had bought some old pottery, some new blankets, and before the fever maimed me, or abated, I managed to take off. I drove through a starry night to Needles, California, where I had a fine breakfast in the Harvey House in the railroad station, one of the first and last sanctuaries of great coffee. As I drove west out of Needles, I knew I was coming down with an old infection. California—before I set eyes on it—had been for me the sanctuary of my great expectations, and my years at Pomona College had fired the clay of these impressions. Once I had crossed the Mojave and from Cajon Pass saw the haze of smudge pots over the valley, through which the tan eucalyptus trees thrust up like feathers, I was hooked. Old Baldy gleamed with a snowcap, and the trees were freighted with oranges and lemons. I stopped to drink my fill of orange juice. In Claremont I drove slowly around the streets and thought the students attractive but extremely youthful. How long had it been? It had not quite been five years. In the post office, with its WPA murals painted by Milford Zornes, a classmate, an old friend was so startled to see me I let myself pass for an impostor. I had received the New Directions volume with the selection of my photographs and texts, along with a brief review from *The New Yorker* in which my name was mentioned. A first on all counts. At the Sugar Bowl Café I was recognized, and experienced the sensation of being interviewed. Fame, surely. I was treated to a piece of pecan pie. To prolong this occasion I sought out Hal Davis, one of my English teachers, who was very kindly and favorably impressed. Publication—in that far time—was a singular event. Many were called, but few were chosen. I stayed with Hal for two days, smoking his cigarettes and giving him the lowdown on South Carolina hoosegows. The sight of my words in print had stirred banked fires and started other juices flowing. I was eager to write. What? The writing would flow out of my aroused nostalgia, the boy who had arrived, fifteen years before, with his father in the sidecar of a motorcycle.

In Los Angeles I found a light-housekeeping room near Echo Lake Park. I put aside what I had begun in Santa Fe, an effort to recapture my days and nights in Greenville, and started a book that began:

When it was cold we walked around. When it was morning the pigeons came and looked but when nothing happened they walked away. When it was warm we sat in the sun.

That was the way it had been in 1926, and the passage of time had given it vintage. Would it prove to have the bouquet—on the green side—of my own wine? In two months I would write what would prove to be the first hundred and fifty pages of *My Uncle Dudley*, stopping where the car collapsed in Arkansas the morning the Mississippi broke through the levee. With this stint of writing done, I was both free and eager to turn back to photography. I should have waited several weeks, until a touch of spring had softened the weather east of the Rockies, but I was anxious to rejoin my wife, who would meet me in Cleveland, then to set up a darkroom in New York and make my first prints from the negatives.

I headed east in early March, driving northwest from Las Vegas through the mining and ghost towns to Virginia City. Overcast skies, strong winds and freezing cold discouraged much picture taking. I put up in the Comstock Lode Hotel in Virginia City, however, until a day of brilliant sunlight gave me the half-dozen pictures I was determined to get. One was the pair of weathered houses on an incline, every exterior detail of the facade preserved, another the abandoned church and Hudson-bracketed house stark against a landscape of desert and sky, more in the style of the Baroque than American Gothic. With these trophies hopefully in the bag, I headed northwest for Boise, Idaho, to visit my Aunt Winona, one of my mother's Seventh-Day Adventist sisters. A long day with her, and other members of the clan, helped to restore the ties I had with my Nebraska boyhood.

In the morning my Aunt Winona, the only one not to marry, stood in the sunlit kitchen and watched me eat. Her first love had been the Lord, the second her father, and in this world she had found no replacements. It was her father she saw when she gazed at me. She gave to this farmhouse kitchen, the light flaming her hair, the time-stopped dazzle of Vermeer's paintings. She poured milk from a pitcher, threaded a needle, picked up crumbs from the table with her tip-moistened finger. She was at once serene, vulnerable, and unshakable. The appalling facts of this world all existed to be forgiven. In her presence I was subject to fevers of faith, to fits of stark belief. Like the grandfather, she saw me as a preacher in search of a flock. (Will's Boy, 1981)

*A*t the end of March I met my wife at her parents' home in Cleveland Heights, the driveway still packed with the winter ice but spring in early bloom in the compost heap behind the garage. A few days later we drove to New York, from where she went on to her job at the Westover School in Middlebury and I looked for a room on the Heights in Brooklyn, near the Brooklyn Bridge.

I had been introduced to Brooklyn Heights the year before by a young woman who had met Hart Crane and bought him drinks in the bar at the St. George Hotel. On some of my visits to New York I stayed in her apartment, dark as a sleeping car, but with windows at the back that framed a view of the river and lower Manhattan. I had never seen its equal. To have an apartment of my own, on the same street, with or without the view of the river, would actually exceed my expectations.

My new friend was about my age, but I felt that she looked considerably older. She had once gone to Vassar, joined a Communist cell, married one of its leaders, and took a job doing social work in Brooklyn. She wore her hair in a bun, sweaters under her raincoat, no make-up, and chain-smoked cigarettes she rolled herself. I liked Edith, but I did not understand her. The dream of her life was to publish an article in *The Nation*.

While I was looking for a room I slept on her sofa. She kept the blinds drawn on the view of Manhattan because the sun faded the spines on her books. She highly respected some books and authors. She made her own breakfast, and left the dishes in the sink to be washed on Sunday morning. As I say, I liked her, but I looked forward to moving out.

I soon found a one-room unfurnished apartment just a block down the street, at 196 Columbia Heights. The freshly painted room, four steps down from the street level, had a space at the back I could convert to a darkroom. That spring it was thirty-eight dollars a month; one with a view of the river ran about double that. In a nearby storage warehouse I found a set of bedsprings, a table, two overstuffed chairs, a bookcase and an old trunk I could use for storage. From Middlebury I brought all my darkroom clutter, including my big, beautiful Omega enlarger, and several jars of jam from my ex-landlady. On loan from another friend we had pots, dented pans and the bent-tined forks that had opened the holes in many cans of Carnation milk. The prevailing breeze, strong mornings and evenings, smelled of the coffee being roasted under the bridge. I was usually awakened by the spatter of dirt and gravel kicked up by dogs on the front windows. These dogs were usually walked by men, in their bathrobes and pajamas, their bare feet in shoddy scuffs and slippers. All I ever saw of them were their feet, visible at the bottom of my drawn blind. I could see the strumming wires that anchored the small trees, the dented hubcaps on the parked cars, and sometimes the legs and aprons of the boys who pushed the big two-wheeled carts that made local deliveries. It seemed to me like those affluent parts of Paris where I hadn't lived. One of the tenants in the building was French—I could see the French stamps on her mail—and if we happened to enter the building together I would greet her, "*Fait beau aujourd'hui!*" or

74

something like that. *"Vous parlez français très bien!"* she would reply, and pass on the stamps my wife collected for a friend.

Where else, that spring in my life, might I have lived besides Columbia Heights? From the roof of the building I had the same view of the bridge as the son of the man who had designed it, and whose fate was to complete it, watching its progress through a telescope.

And you that shall cross from shore to shore years hence are more to me, and more in my meditations, than you might suppose.

So I quoted to myself Whitman.

Two or three times a week, a matter of the weather, I walked out on the bridge to sit on the promenade, watching the freighters and barges pass below me, or I would cross to City Hall Park and buy my Bock panatelas from the discount cigar stores. Then, seated on a bench, I would smoke one, noting the vein in the wrapper, likc Hans Castorp.

Was there anything I lacked? My world was so extravagantly what I had ordered, I lacked only the time to ride off in all directions. Like Fitzgerald, in the streets of summer I would try to walk off my heady euphoria by strolling up Broadway to Washington Square, making a fueling stop for an English muffin at the Schrafft's at the corner of Thirteenth Street and Fifth Avenue. As a walker accustomed to the Paris pissoirs, I plotted my walks with the rest stations in mind, like those on the signs along the big freeways: FOOD AND FUEL.

I had met an editor at Harcourt, Brace and Company who introduced me to the gentlemen's facilities just off the elevator lobby, and as my experience with publishers expanded, so did my access to comfort stations. After such a long trek I would take the subway back to the St. George Hotel, rest a moment in its lobby, allow myself to be thought of as a person of interest, then return to my room.

The days were too short for all that had to be done. Photographs to enlarge, texts to ponder, a fresh draft of the novel I had written in California, the opening pages of which had in-

75

terested an editor at Harcourt, Brace. With the arrival of summer, and the first blackouts, I was appointed air raid warden to my building and encouraged to spend more time on its roof, watching the lights blink off in Manhattan. Those that persisted were like planets, stalled in their orbits. I did not feel the nearness of the war, but I resented its hovering presence. Would it soon put an end to my little idyll, or would I slip through the net? It has been fashionable, since Vietnam, and the wholesale rejection of all military service, to assume that the Second World War was one that the young considered worth fighting and dying for. This young man did not, nor did any of the young men he happened to know. My patriotism was intense, but had much of its grounding in Thoreau's Civil Disobedience. I never questioned that what I was doing, and hoped to do, constituted my war effort. The bloody carnage so memorably reported by a generation of gifted writers had left in me nothing but loathing for the war that was emerging. Much of this found its expression in an unpublished manuscript entitled "Journal of the Plague Year."

On alternate weekends, until her summer vacation, my wife came to the city, and we would go to museums, have dinner somewhere, or spend the time with our old and new friends. One of the old ones, Alec Taylor, had worked briefly as a housemother at Scripps College, where she had met my wife. Double-dukes, as I named her, from the way she would double up her small fists and assume a fighter's posture, combined in her tall, willowy person the extravagant promises and ambitions that made her the symbol of the literary hopeful. She had lived a year in France, as part of the Delaware group, and returned to write a long, lyrical report about her early life and times in Wyoming, her polishing at Bryn Mawr, and her creative adventures and anguish. This manuscript had almost won the *Atlantic Monthly* prize of $7,500! It traveled with her, as she enlarged and revised it, and periodically shared segments with us, and those big-time editors who knew the real thing when they saw it (from what they had once read about it) found in Double-dukes what they had been waiting for. Her manuscript clutched to her front, her voice hoarse and throaty, her way of tapping out tobacco from a Bull Durham pouch the envy of the hundreds who had observed it— none of this was soon forgotten, and it could be had for as little as an advance of $250.

Edith was Double-dukes's friend from their college years, but they had had a slight parting of the ways at the fork in the road taken by fellow travelers.

One humid summer evening, Double-dukes escorted me to the apartment of a friend who taught at Columbia, where I would meet James Agee. They were discussing, quietly but intensely, Céline's *Journey to the End of the Night*. Agee admired it extravagantly. His friend's appreciation was qualified. They were so much at ease with this writer and his book, I was reluctant to intrude on their discussion. Agee was very Southern, to my eye and ear, a poet in every vibrant strand of his nature. He was wearing a blue workshirt, khaki pants, and the rough farmwork shoes of a sharecropper. I liked his quiet manner, his fine sad eyes, his well-bred face. *Let Us Now Praise Famous Men* had not as yet been published, but this brief evening with Agee would contribute much to my reading.

Another friend of Double-dukes was Sigmund Bekersky, a giant Russian from the Ukraine who had once been a professional wrestler. He was a master of the basics of communication, but weak on the details. On our first meeting he greeted me by placing his hands on my hips, hoisting me like a child. He liked me. I was one of many people he liked. As a wrestler he had been well known, if not well paid, and in New York he worked as a nightclub bouncer. When Bekersky rumbled, people bounced. I believe that I came to love Bekersky, but my feelings were complex. He visited us often, when he happened to be passing, usually with a loaf of bread and a hunk of ham he sliced with the blade of his jackknife. Our two cats, Sweeney and Agonistes, would crawl into his open shirtfront while he was eating and hungrily lick the perspiration at his armpits. How he would roar! To my knowledge he did not read or speak much English, but his use of fifteen or twenty words was so good he covered all the bases. This gift he had to embrace us all in his fellowship was lavish. I did not question that it was far superior to my limited powers to love a few chosen people. Was this peculiarly Russian? Or was this just Bekersky, an outsized giant of a man doomed to live his life among pygmies? I remember him with both deep affection and the shame that I soon stopped answering his postcards. "How are you? I'm fine," they said, mailed to me from a series of army bases. He had joined the army when it was found he understood all those unspeakable languages. My feeling is that the women he knew found him a cross between Zeus and Ulysses.

Over the summer we had a few hot and humid nights, the door propped open to catch the draft in the hallway, but life on the Heights seemed to us both like a marvelous resort vacation. We often felt we had the city to ourselves, so many people we knew had left it. Even the subway system (soon to be seen as a monster between Dante's Hell and Purgatory) we thought had been designed for our own convenience, with the medieval Cloisters at one end and Coney Island at the other. It had not yet crossed the minds of either of us that this was one of many feelings that were passing.

My wife had met Howard Devree, an art critic for the *New York Times*, and his personal pleasure seemed to be to introduce attractive young women to the art scene and the galleries. Mr. Devree also liked my photographs—he had reviewed the showing I had had at the New School—and one day he came to visit us in Brooklyn with a carton of Atget photographs, printed by Berenice Abbott. These prints were much superior to those I had previously seen, and appropriated some of the ruins of time that I felt to be my peculiar province. Once more I had found that what I felt to be uniquely my own way of seeing was little more than a measure of my ignorance. If I could see all that existed, it would surely take the bloom off many of my enthusiasms. I was spared that revelation, however, since this humbling knowledge would usually come to me in small doses for the rest of my life.

78

By midsummer I had printed several hundred of my new photographs, and made a selection for *The Inhabitants*. I had also set up appointments with Clifton Fadiman, at that time the book editor for *The New Yorker*, and Henry Allen Moe of the John Simon Guggenheim Foundation. Mr. Fadiman proved more of a reader than a looker, but he kindly sent me over to Donald Klopfer, of Random House, who was having his shoes shined on my arrival. This impressed me as the height of sensible advantage, like the gas lighters that came with hotel lobby cigar cases. He was both sympathetic and realistic. Such a book, he said, would cost a lot to produce— and who would buy it? I had not diverted myself with that dilemma. I did take reassurance in the fact that the conception itself, photographs and words in a new nonillustrative relationship, had caught the fancy of an observer who did not share my own enthusiasm. Feeling as I did, I knew there were others, somewhere, who might feel the same.

Henry Allen Moe seemed to be one of them. Just the year before, Edward Weston had been the first photographer to receive a Guggenheim Fellowship. Why shouldn't I be the second? This kind of confidence did not dismay Mr. Moe, who seemed to take kindly to my optimism. Through the veil of cigarette smoke that hovered between us, and the butts that cluttered up his ashtray, I observed that what he saw and read brought a twinkle to his eyes which I could appreciate. I liked his succinct comments, his sensible questions, and his no-nonsense brevity. Did he feel I might try for a fellowship? He did. I would write him a statement describing my intentions (which proved to be a long one) and submit it with examples of my work.

It had not yet crossed my mind, as a city dweller, that to get somewhere I could signal a cab. I walked my heavy portfolio back to the Seventh Avenue subway in what proved to be the rush hour. My luck was running good. After a shower, I told my wife all about it in the coffee-fragrant draft that blew through the window. To celebrate our prospects, we walked down to Fulton Street for a dinner at Child's.

*   *   *

By October I had completed a second draft of my novel, and submitted it to Lambert Davis of Harcourt, Brace. His Southern accent put me in mind of my friend Leon Howard. In Lambert's office I had met Edward Dahlberg, a self-possessed man with the detached manner of a diplomat. He was about to publish *Do These Bones Live*, a book very much to my taste, and I felt that much of it took my measure.

Lambert liked the quality of the material I submitted, but felt that my story petered out, rather than concluded, with the kid's return to Chicago and reunion with his Uncle Dudley. The tale of a carful of picaresque loafers and idlers traveling from Los Angeles to Chicago in the mid-twenties needed a more dramatic windup than the one I had supplied. Perhaps, he said, I could think of something. In my highly charged state of mind, that did not take long. On the subway returning to Brooklyn I recalled my adventure in Greenville, and how appropriate that scene and situation might be to a character like Uncle Dudley. During my stay in Santa Fe the previous winter, I had written up a draft of the Greenville experience and recorded the details that I now needed. Within a few weeks, I had a new, long concluding chapter, with my Uncle Dudley, in the Greenville jail, rehearsing the well-known abuses to Yankees at the hands of the fat-assed, perverse and brutal caricatures I had found to be so true to life. There was also Furman Young, a Southern hillbilly sprout of Yankee independence, who would arouse Uncle Dudley to his defiant gesture of spitting in the eye of the cop, Cupid. These sentiments were appropriate to my own, and I felt pretty good about what I had done, not being at that time a writer of fiction with an overview of what he was up to.

That overview would come several months later, on the day the book was published, and a friend came by to share this special occasion with me. She was dying to read it. I sat and smoked my discount panatelas as she read. My happiness was boundless as I observed the gleeful fits of laughing that frequently interrupted her reading. Marvelous! After all, I thought it a pretty funny book.

She broke off her reading a little after midnight, eager to

get back to it the following evening. My feeling then, as I sat smoking cigars that had lost their savor, was that she read with continued interest but without further interruptions of laughter. The book finished, she took the occasion to praise my Mexican cigarettes. We discussed Mexico briefly. And *My Uncle Dudley*—had she liked it? Oh, yes, she had liked it. Her feeling was, however—it was just a feeling—that she shouldn't have stopped the night before, at the point that she did, then begin again the next evening. It seemed so different in tone she almost thought it a different book. In the first part she had laughed and laughed—that was what she remembered!—but in the second part, good as she found it, it seemed so damn serious. Was she reading it wrong?

So I learned the hard way that an overview is something you should have before a book is published. Some readers seemed to like the change of "tone" in the novel, once Uncle Dudley ends up in the clinker, but other readers, not so serious, regretted that it stopped being funny. I sympathized with both readers, and sometimes would have liked to have it both ways. I have a boy's affection for the man I would have loved to have had as an uncle, a man who was decent enough, kind enough and on occasion funny enough, but hardly ever really smart enough to win at the game he found himself playing. The old fool who turned to spit the cop Cupid in the eye, to the great pleasure of his nephew, was an extension of the sentiment that had shaped Mark Twain's Colonel Sherburn on the occasion of his potential lynching, and in the course of time, as measured by the drip method, it would prove to have a lasting effect on me.

Persons attempting to find a motive in this narrative will be prosecuted; persons attempting to find a moral in it will be banished; persons attempting to find a plot in it will be shot.
BY ORDER OF THE AUTHOR

On a cold day in December, I learned that my father had died in Chicago. This event was so detached from my expectations, it had, at the time, little effect on me. I seemed to lack the faculties necessary to grasp it. From my early boyhood, my jovial, optimistic father had seemed a genial, neighborly relation, seen by me through the agent's window of the depot or as he passed on the sidewalk across the street from me, wagging his hand. He was no good at all at buttoning and unbuttoning rompers, and I did not like the taste of the kisses flavored by his red-capped indelible pencils. On one occasion, he slipped the belt from his pants to slap it halfheartedly at my well-padded bottom, until I was rescued by Anna. The cause? He had caught me with my pudgy hand in the pocket of his pants, fishing for coins. I bought nut Hershey bars with this money, or soda pop that I learned to drink in concealment, shaking the bottle to work up the fizz. He was the man whose wavy brown hair had been shaved from his head, right before my eyes, when he had erysipelas. Harder to account for, and more lasting, he had brought home from Omaha a red-lipped woman described as my "new mother." Later I would be farmed out, for several years, to an Irish family, then be gifted with the second of my new "mothers" (not a moment of all this could I have lived without), but it strained our father-son relations. He was a handsome man with an eye for the ladies, who gave me money on the rare occasions that I saw him. The last time that I saw him, he studied me with amused perplexity. I was his son, now a young man on his way to Europe. He chewed a match—one of the habits I hated—as a woman took a seat on the arm of his chair, and rested her hand on his shoulder. It pleased me that she was attractive. The idea of going to Europe puzzled him. What was there? Two years later I would write him to say that I was married, and living in California, to which he replied on a sheet of the green lined pulpy paper I remembered from popcorn bags, the periods drilled through the paper after the indelible pencil had been moistened at his lips. What did it say? He would like to make me a partner in his new plan to sell fresh eggs to hotels.

He would be dead for several years before I would be diverted from the story I was writing. I had a landscape in mind, and this man in it. There was not much else that I could say about it. The writing took its tone and texture from the opening lines, and in several hundred pages seldom departed from it.

In the dry places, men begin to dream. Where the rivers run sand there is something in man that begins to flow. West of the 98th Meridian—where it sometimes rains and it sometimes doesn't—towns, like weeds, spring up when it rains, dry up when it stops. But in a dry climate the husk of the plant remains. The stranger might find, as if preserved in amber, something of the green life that was once lived there, and the ghosts of men who have gone on to a better place. The withered towns are empty, but not uninhabited. Faces sometimes peer out from the broken windows, or whisper from the sagging balconies, as if this place—now that it is dead—had come to life. As if empty, it is forever occupied. (The Works of Love, 1952)

The narrator of the story, a man named Will Brady, is described as one who neither smoked, drank, gambled, nor swore. Had I ever known such a man? To the extent I knew my father:

A man who headed no cause, fought in no wars, and passed his life unaware of the great public issues . . .

The author of this story, unlikely as it might seem, was unaware both at the time and later of what he was up to. Only when the volume was published, three or four years later, and a few of the sympathetic reviewers spoke of this Will Brady as a man they had known, personally, did it first cross my troubled and haunted imagination that in this way I hoped to get to know my father. It is an old, old story, and not at all unusual that a young man would feel compelled to tell it.

One Sunday, on the crowded train from Grand Central Station to Brooklyn, I stood holding one of the straps. My wife, in the seat before me, wore a small hat with a veil, her gloved hands resting on the purse in her lap. Something about her appearance, her person, attracted the attention of those who could see her. She sat erect but relaxed, compact within herself, proper to the verge of primness, but those who observed her were attracted by her air of good breeeding. It gave the women near her, as it did me, the reassurance we get from something of value. Her own attention was held by the blurred glimpses we got of the local stations. At one moment she extended her hand to finger the pocket of my coat. In my constant self-preoccupation, my wife was one of many things that I took for granted. I asked myself, as the train clattered through the stations, what I had done to justify my having such an exceptional and lovely wife. In truth I had done little, one thing had led to another, and at thirty-two years of age I had this companion who accepted the demands my life placed upon her. I felt toward her at that moment such a surge of affection I found it impossible to speak, but by the time we had reached the St. George station this flood of emotion had drained away, and I was thinking of food. In the neighborhood deli we bought a carton of milk and a can of tuna, both of us having learned to eat and like what we could share with the cats.

The bombing of Pearl Harbor took place on the Sunday I signed the contract with Harcourt, Brace to publish *My Uncle Dudley*. This mix of personal elation with national disaster may have been characteristic. In late March, I was once more back in full flight, with the news that I had received a Guggenheim Fellowship. How often had I fantasized, with my wife, what we might do if we received such a windfall. If not all the money in the world, $2,500 seemed a good piece of it. We agreed that we could live the longest, perhaps for two years, if we were back in California. I needed to make the trip west to take more photographs, and the college town of Claremont was stocked with old friends and suited our needs. On the trip west we would make a few stops in Nebraska.

Early in April, *My Uncle Dudley* was published—an attractive volume, bound in buckram, with a paper label on the spine to appease the author—but the event did not make much news. The resident reviewer of the *Herald Tribune* found the story confused. What was going on? He found it

White House, Cape Cod, 1939

House in Winter, near Lincoln, 1941

Gano Grain Elevator, Western Kansas, 1940

Reflection in Oval Mirror, the Home Place, 1947

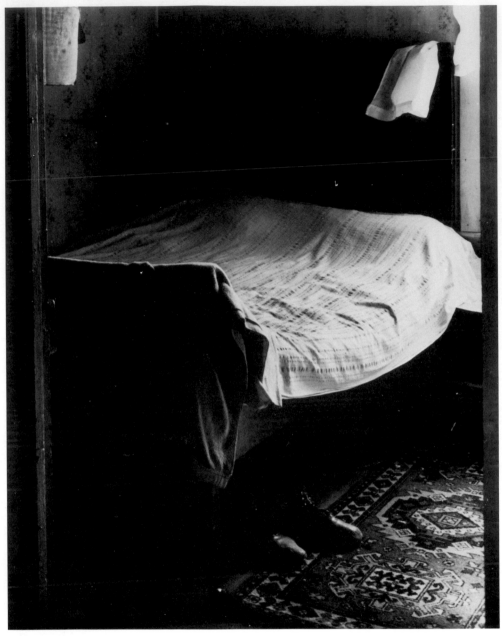

Bed, Ed's Place, 1947

Drawer with Silverware, the Home Place, 1947

Dresser Drawer, Ed's Place, 1947

Model T, Ed's Place, 1947

Straightback Chair, the Home Place, 1947

Uncle Harry, the Home Place, 1947

hard to determine. It was my first exposure to the problems of a writer addicted to compactness, and economy of statement. One reviewer in San Francisco had no such problem, and spoke of the author as one who might bear watching. In a copy of the book on my shelf I have his review. It gives the plot of the story without a hint of confusion, and in closing he wanted to say that Mr. Wright had made his point. That is what he said.

*T*he great pleasure I took in New York, and the feeling I continued to have that my future would be tied up with living on Brooklyn Heights, did not diminish the sense of life-enhancing escape I always experienced traveling west through the Hudson tunnel. The pull of the West, a convenient illusion for any duffer with a yen for flight, had become a magnet for me with the discovery of California. Our friend Schindy was right about the seasons, and the problem of the chap on whom no snow fell, but the lure of California was for me like that of the *Wandervogel* for Capri, or Hans Castorp for Greece. The basking heat, the shimmering light, the matchless tranquillity of the California mornings, would take their monotonous toll in time, but how welcome they loomed from the exit of the tunnel.

One of my real deprivations as a boy had been my inability to shrilly whistle, using either one or two fingers, but one thing I could do was give a blast to the horn and slap my hands on the steering wheel. It had been supplied with a tan suede cover used by the better-class mechanics, and mounted on the dashboard was a compass that would keep me headed westward. Except on those occasions when I insisted on going south.

It pleased my father-in-law, on our stop in Cleveland, to exhibit me to his colleagues as a Guggenheim fellow. It also pleased me to be so exhibited, and I comported myself as a fellow in good standing. This called for my joining my father-in-law on the stoop of the rear porch, where we pulled the husks off fresh Ohio sweet corn. Mrs. Finfrock liked the evening meal to be somewhat formal—the exchange of her bathrobe for a summer print—the four or five of us seated around the table at the rim of the overhead lamp. Fin was supposed to be on a diet, and he took only small portions of food on his plate, but I had often had lunch with him in the city, and observed the bags of snacks he kept handy in the car seat. His great weaknesses were peanuts and banana candy. Since I had last seen him, he had taken to napping on the wicker sofa on the screened-in porch. If the day was humid, he might spend the night there. After a trip to the john in the basement, he might be heard wheezing as he came up the stairs. I accepted this as normal for a man sixty pounds overweight. His great pleasure and relaxation was cards, especially bridge, at which he was a modest master, but since I was unable to grasp bridge, we usually played pinochle or rummy. While his wife pondered her next move, he might go to the icebox for a cold root beer, or step out on the porch and smoke a cigarette. Later in the evening we would take the dog, Sox, for his midnight walk. This usually called for a stop at the drugstore on Euclid, where Fin would be served his double-chocolate Coke, then we would stroll under the oaks and elms that had heaved up the neighborhood sidewalks. This was great for Sox, providing him with many places to sniff and scratch. One of the neighbors had a player piano, with some of the rolls I used to pump in Chicago, and the later it got, the more she liked to play "My Blue Heaven" at a fast tempo, "The Sheik of Araby" at a slow one. A girl like that was giving some boy a pretty bad time.

One evening, as the dog tugged at the leash, Fin spoke to me about his son, Charles. He was worried about Charles, who seemed to be having trouble with his law school teaching. Charles had seemed to me exceptionally smart. I could not understand his having trouble with his teaching. His father explained that his nerves were giving him trouble: he seemed to feel he was being followed by people. At the college where he had been teaching, he had been picked up on the street with a pistol in his pocket. My father-in-law turned his back to me as he said this, and I could see that his broad shoulders were trembling. To see so big a man openly weeping stunned me. The dog had circled his legs with the long leash, so that he had to stand there, unable to move. I've no memory of what I said. Perhaps I said nothing. I made a fuss with the dog, untangling the leash, and we stood in the comforting dark together, smoking cigarettes. Fin's white shirt was dark with sweat where it stuck to his back.

"Son," he said to me, "am I crazy?"

"Of course you're not crazy," I replied. "Good God!"

"Then Charles is crazy!" he said. "You hear me? You've got to help me conceal it from Mother."

"I can't believe it," I said.

"Charles believes that I'm a threat to his mother. The last time he was home, he threatened me with his pistol."

He stopped speaking, and let the dog lead us along the street. I couldn't believe what I had heard. My feeling at the time was that Charles *might* be a bit crazy, but not to the point of shooting his father. And why his father? In so many words, he had hinted to me that in his opinion his mother was mighty peculiar. How crazy could normal-seeming people really get? I had from the first noted the strangeness of Mrs. Finfrock, but she had learned to live with it, as had her family. She was respected and admired by her friends. I had noted in myself a grudging respect for certain qualities in her nature. As we reached the house, my father-in-law spoke to me.

"Not a word of this to Mother," he cautioned me. "Not a word," as if he thought I might actually speak of it. Shortly later, my wife called me upstairs, and I lay sprawled at her side in the airless room. The cicadas sawed away in their ascending lisp. My father-in-law had explained to me how the beat of this sawing accurately registered the temperature, a characteristic piece of his nature lore, which I could never accurately remember. What was I to make of the disclosure about Charles? Was it actually something I should share with my wife, knowing how she felt about her brother? My father-in-law, in his private anguish, had lifted the lid on a loony bin. Dimly I apprehended that Fin, in his eagerness to protect Mother, was concealing from himself the tangle of emotions that had brought on Charles's "nervous breakdown," the label of the time. In this house of leisure and promise, fear had taken root in the water closet in the basement and the compost pit behind the garage, wherever the man of the house went to hide from what he was thinking. Of course, I didn't really believe it. I kept my eyes on the wings of the moths I could see against the street light, as they crawled on the screen. In the morning this touch of nightmare would vanish, and we would all go on with our lives.

I had not returned to my Uncle Harry's farm since my boyhood in Omaha. Why did I now feel that I should? Neither Harry nor Clara had expressed affection for me. My father had "farmed me out" to them part of one summer, as he had farmed me out to the Mulligan family. But my intrusion as a young man, with a city wife, would be far less acceptable to Clara than my visit as a small boy. I knew that, but my father's death had aroused in me a desire to know more about my people. Were they my people? I had no other way of finding out.

My joshing, genial, often blundering father, with a talent for botching his great expectations in butter and eggs, as well as in women, had often spoken with distaste for his dirt-farming brother who didn't seem to have "the brains he was born with." This brother had spoken, if at all, with something like contempt for the ne'er-do-well who ran around with loose women and farmed out his son. I had not warmed to the sullen, scowling, slow-moving man who belched at his meals and sat forever in the privy, the sun on his flour-white knees, while he read the Sears, Roebuck catalogue. I had heard him say frequently to his wife, "That kid ain't worth his feed."

That especially hurt, since I didn't find the "feed" all that good, after the Mulligans. One of my unwelcome chores had been to moisten a rag in vinegar and wipe the mold from the pies in the storm cave.

In Omaha I showed my wife the Mulligan house, on Capitol Avenue, still the color of sun-faded chocolate, the porch clapboards warped and peeling where they were thumped and scraped by the swing. It seemed a lot shabbier than I remembered, and the hill less steep. I was able to see, as I knocked at the screen, that gas jets still lit up the hallway that led back to the kitchen, a curtain at the bottom half of the sink window. Nothing had changed. The lady of the house, her untied apron strings dangling, did not herself remember the Mulligans, but she had heard the name. The draft blowing through the house smelled of the drip pan under the icebox. It had been my chore to see that it was emptied. What else had I forgotten?

Over the half curtain at the window I could see the dead tree trunk in the yard, and the battered sheds that lined the steep alley. The summer it had been paved, piles of sand filled the Mulligan yard for weeks. In that sand I had lost a chameleon. I was eager to stoop and peer under the porch to check on other possible losses. There had been a cigar box containing marbles and a piece of gray, grass-stained flannel, a pocket torn from the seat of Babe Ruth's Yankee baseball pants. There had been a Junior Flexible Flyer sled. Learning that I had once lived in the house, as a boy, she peered around me for a better look at my wife. Had she, too, lived here? No, just myself. I felt the shame of this admission. The other half of the duplex stood empty, with a FOR RENT card propped in the window. In my time it had never been rented. Had this been the curse of the large, shouting, Jewish-speaking family who lived in the house next door, the kids known to have head lice? My friend Davy Goodman, with his spindly legs, would peer down to taunt me with his Jewish curses. The wall was crumbling. What had been the meaning of the word *took-us*?

A used-car lot, with wind-whipped banners, had replaced the redbrick schoolhouse at Twenty-ninth and Farnam. Used cars concealed the cinder-covered playground. The success of this "vanishing act" stunned me. Red bricks into thin air? A part of my life had been spelled out in the high ceilinged rooms, in the nurse's annex, in pom-pom pull-away played in the cinders. I wore holes in my knee pants, pulling up my stockings. My legs were fast but thin. Nothing at all remained. I was able to conceal my shock since I lacked the faculty to grasp it. Was I prepared for what might be next? The Blackstone Hotel, where the tall, gentle Max Cohn had worked at the soda fountain, looked to me largely unchanged. What if Max Cohn still worked there? Before eloping with the daughter of my second new mother, he had loaned me his red bathing suit for the summer. That, too, had vanished. Had it been returned?

My Uncle Harry's farm did not prove to be where I thought I had left it, but to the south of Norfolk, toward Battle Creek. Battle Creek itself seemed to be where it should be, along with the spur of the railroad line on which I had ridden up from Columbus. So, too, the catalpa trees still lined the drive leading from the road to the barn. No dog barked, but I saw a scrawny cat slink into the shade. I parked the car in a yard spongy with mounds scratched up by chickens. On the roof of the house, a blue ball tilted on a rusted lightning rod. A single tattered shade tree, dead at the top, with a clump of green foliage like a hula skirt at its middle, still shaded a bit of the porch, but not the house. I had forgotten until I saw the enamel water pail, the dipper floating, that nobody ever used the front door to the house. It was through the rear door, and the kitchen, that one entered the house and left it. Once green and flat as a billiard table, spaced off with the croquet wickets, the stretch of yard between the house and the barn was like a huge, dowdy mattress, sprouting shoots of straw. I saw a few old hens, with their shabby bottoms, scratching in the moist earth near the porch, where Clara emptied her dishpan. Patches of clumped, matted dead grass concealed the last of the wickets and the half-buried balls. Doors tilted on the sheds, fences were down, a few straggly trees stood in the orchard, and every visible object, implement and structure seemed to be at the end of a losing battle. If my wife had not been with me, I might have sneaked off. The old man, surely, would be gone, and my Aunt Clara should be spared the sad memories I would bring her.

The rusted screen door, poked full of holes at the bottom, was latched. In the early afternoon of a hot, humid day, the draft blowing off the kitchen smelled acridly of pickling beets. Why didn't I leave? Nobody seemed aware that we had arrived. The throaty clucking of an old Plymouth Rock hen, bits of dried dung clinging to a few tail feathers, held me like the sound of chords once struck on Clara's player piano. I called out, but nobody answered. I called again, and after several moments I heard the scrape of a pot moved on the stove. The woman who appeared, thin as a lath, wore a faded frock that hung limp from her shoulders. About its waist, the strings dangling, a freshly beet-stained apron. Over her wide, unblinking left eye she placed the fingers of one hand, as if taking an eye test.

"You don't remember me?" I asked. "I'm Will's boy, Wright," I said, hardly a recommendation, and it took a moment for her to place me. Her tongue moistened her dry lips.

"You've grown," she said flatly, unlatching the screen. "Come in where it's cool."

We passed through the heat of the kitchen into the front room, where the blinds were drawn. Heat and light, for Clara, were of one compact. In the dim, greenish light she felt cooler. As I introduced my wife, I saw the years twirl on the reel of time between us. The child she had known, now married. She gazed at the young woman who stood beside me. "You folks have children?" We shook our heads. "Well, I suppose there's time for that," she said, "isn't there?" but she expected no answer. The rocker in which she sat herself down creaked as it rocked.

Later we sipped well water from the amber-colored glasses kept high in the cupboard for special occasions. She did not need my help to reach them down. She inquired about my wife's people, and heard with relief that they had settled in Ohio. She knew about Ohio, having crossed it in a wagon on her way west. My wife also had a grandmother, aged ninety-four, still fending for herself in the town she was born in, establishing a kinship that supplanted my own deficient background. When the children did come, they would have at least one foot on the ground.

Some moments before he came into the room, my Uncle Harry stopped on the back porch to skim the drowned flies off the pail of drinking water, and toss them through the hole in the rusted screen. We could hear the gulp of his swallows. He came in without a greeting, his overalls hanging slack from his narrow rounded shoulders. His gray watery eyes, as he faced the light, seemed to have no pupils. He gave little sign of interest or recognition. Clara said, "This is Will's boy, Wright. You remember Wright." It was more of a statement than a question, and he let it pass. "Wright's here with his wife," she added. Hearing that, he perked up. His eyes blinked in preparation for looking at her.

"They see Ed yet?"

"They just got here. Now why'd they see Ed?"

"Well, s'I, how come you ain't up? Well, s'ee, it's in my legs. Can't seem to twitch my toes."

"Why you telling them that?" said Clara, smoothing the wrinkles in her apron.

"Who's Ed?" I inquired.

"Well, s'ee, been lyin' here three or four days, can't use my legs."

This time I puzzled out what he had said the first time. The "s'I"/"s'ee" was dialectic shorthand for *says I/says he*, making it quicker to get on with his story.

"Ed's a Cropper," said Clara. "He farms across the road." It was not a subject she was eager to explore.

My wife said, "Would you have a picture of Wright's father?" I had recently regretted not having a picture, no likeness of this father who was now gone.

"Of Will?" Clara replied. "Now why'd we have picture of him? We didn't see him but once or twice in all those years."

"My father died last fall," I said.

"Will dead?" Harry sat up, spreading his knees. "Why, he's one of the young ones, next to Mae. Now why'd he up and die?"

"I've no pictures," I said. "Not a one."

"I can't think why we'd have pictures of *him*." Clara had little liking for my father, dead or alive. On a trip to the farm before I had come for the summer, he had driven up from Columbus with his new wife, Gertrude, a pretty girl with red lips and a fox fur neckpiece. I had been eight years of age, too young for the scandal.

Harry said, "Come to think . . ." and wheeled slowly as if my father might be standing right behind him. On a table near the front door, family pictures were displayed. All appeared to be young females. Without comment, Clara left the room: I heard her opening a drawer in the bedroom off the kitchen. She reappeared with a shoebox of snapshots and clippings. Harry was using a nail taken from his pocket to loosen the caked tobacco in his corncob pipe. Twice he said, "Dadgummit!" out of respect for the ladies present. I realized that my once dour and sullen Uncle Harry had ripened into an amateur performer. This was one of his acts. He found a kitchen match in one of his pockets, flicked the head with his thumbnail, checked the match to see if it was a good one, then stooped slightly to drag the match up his pants leg, with the sound of a sheet tearing. It burst into a smoking flame he cupped his hands around, held to the bowl of his pipe. A billowing cloud of smoke veiled his head.

"If you can find your glasses," Clara said, "suppose you tell us who's in this picture?" She did not hand it to him until he had found his glasses. The bridge low on his nose, he held the photo at arm's length, moving it toward him, then away, adjusting the focus in the manner of a trombone player adjusting the slide.

"You wearing your glasses?" Clara said, and covered her bad eye to check on him. He had pushed them back on his head to rub his knuckles at his eyes.

"Lord, it's fadin'," he said. "Come to think, they never had much as faces."

"Most of them dead and gone, think it would be fadin'," Clara said. "Same as you and me are fadin'."

"Now there," he said, pointing, "that's Mitch." He put a splayed nail on a tall man with a moustache. A row of men and women had gathered in a light snow at the front of a farmhouse. They had either dressed in black for this occasion or it was a Sunday. I counted fourteen of them; five were women. "Mitch was the oldest. Mae was the youngest. That could be Will standin' there with Mae."

Did the last man in the row resemble my father? He had no face, but his wavy hair was parted in the middle.

"If you're not in it, he's not either," said Clara. "The two of you come west to homestead together. You forgotten that?"

"Not him," said Harry. "He never did a day's work in his life."

Even Clara felt that might be going a bit too far, with my wife present. She fidgeted, said, "If it's work that matters, all of you might as well have stayed back in Ohio. What work have you done here?"

He seemed to be wondering. The wet cluck of his pipe was like that of an old hen. "Out in Cozad," he went on, hitching around to face the west, "last time I saw Emerson he was spry as a kid."

"Had pictures on the wall he hand-painted," said Clara.

"One of a dog," said Harry. "Swear he'd come right down and bite you."

"And now he's gone. Same as we'll all soon be gone."

My father had first set eyes on my mother in Chapman, where he had made his start as a Union Pacific station agent. There had been little there at the time, and in the spring of 1942 there was less. She had been born on the bluffs just south of the Platte River, and buried in the cemetery visible from the highway. That was about all I knew about her. My Seventh-Day Adventist grandfather had moved the survivors of his family—the boys had taken off—to the country neighboring Boise, Idaho, where, just twenty years later, I would first see them. My mother's sister, Winona, had tried to keep in touch with me, but I had proved a bad correspondent. My wife had reminded me that I should send her a letter postmarked Chapman.

On a Memorial Day, my father had hitched up the buggy and driven his four- or five-year-old son to put flowers on his mother's grave. I was full of emotion and blankness. Weeds had been scythed from some of the graves, but not others. We sat in the grass and had a picnic. My father worked the handle of the pump, cupping his hand over the nozzle so I could drink. But it proved to be messy. Water spilled on the shiny toes of my Buster Brown shoes. My mother was here, somewhere, and I felt the hollow hallowedness of the occasion. On the long drive back to Central City, the horse's tail flicked on the buckboard, the reins made a lapping sound on his rump.

The town Chapman had planned to be, at the turn of the century, had not materialized. Basements had been dug for stores that were never erected. I saw little evidence that this remarkable windfall had been appreciated by the local small fry. A bicycle lay on its side in front of the general store, blocking the hitch bar. Through the screen at the door I could see a matronly woman wiping the knobs of the syrup dispensers. Harness and lanterns hung on hooks at the back, the horse collars like frames without pictures. A man with heavy web suspenders over oatmeal-colored underwear dipped scoops of creamy flour from a barrel, emptied the scoop into a paper sack. The sleeves of his underwear and the hairy backs of his hands were powdered with the flour.

The building to the left, with a wide, waist-high window, droned with the vibration of a ceiling fan. Over the curtain at the window I could see, as if it were levitated, the horizontal figure of a man being shaved. A mound of lather concealed his face as the barber stropped his razor. A wall mirror reflected the opposite wall of the shop, hung with a display of calendars, but the rear of the shop featured an oak partition with an elaborate grille of wrought iron. Even I knew a bank when I saw one. At the top of the grille a large syrup can held a plant that dangled large shiny leaves and tendrils, well suited to the grille. The barber, Eddie Cahow, a small, gray-haired man, wore the cuffs of his sleeves turned back, and held the long blade of the razor like a bird he had caught in its flight. At that moment he had paused to make a clearing in the lather at the tip of the client's nose. As I opened the screen to his shop, he held up the razor, invoking silence.

"You be quiet a minute," Cahow said, "and I'll tell you who

you are." He turned to look at my side-on reflection in the mirror. "You're Grace and Will's boy," he said. "I'd say mostly Grace."

Finger-painted on the mirror was the notice that shaves were fifteen cents, haircuts a quarter.

"When I saw you," said Cahow, "I said, There goes two, three people I know."

Through a puff in the lather the client said, "Whass the genmun's name?"

"Morris," I replied. "Will Morris was my father. Grace Osborn was my mother." He tilted his head for a look at me.

"Mr. Applegate here," said Cahow, "farms on the bluff. About a hunder sixty acres. John," he said, "you remember the Osborns?" John moved his head. "White house with a cupola. See it on your left. Don't think there's anybody in it right now, is there, John?"

On another occasion I would learn that Mr. Applegate had courted Aunt Winona and, mindful of her, he had kept the house in good repair.

A half mile to the south we crossed the Platte River, a wide spread of sandbars and channels of shallow water, then followed the road up the face of the bluff to the flat tableland. A gleaming white house, like a freshly painted signboard, stood at the side of a field of ripening grain. The cupola gave it the look of a small church, the window blazing with the sun's rays. I thought it a small house for the family that had been born and raised in it. My mother had climbed the ladder through the hole in the ceiling, and my maverick Uncle Dwight, for nineteen summers and winters, had learned to hate his god-fearing, Seventh-Day Adventist father. Far to the back, behind the unpainted sheds, a freshly painted white privy sat on the bluff's rim. I tried to picture the girls making that trip in the winter. How was it made by my ill and pregnant grandmother, dead in her late thirties from child bearing and rearing? In addition to his farming, my grandfather had been a bullish land speculator, in Texas and Canada, for the glory of God.

I set up my camera and took pictures of the house, the

white surfaces gleaming in the slanting light. On the ground glass, seen against the sky and the field of grain, it bore little resemblance to a farmhouse, and looked new and unused. Without a basement or a foundation, it sat flat on the ground, shoots of grain thrusting up through the boards of the porch. On my mind's eye the whiteness was that of winter, a house of worship, set in a field of drifting snow under a darkening sky, my grandfather a bearded shrouded prophet peering at me from the cupola window.

Down the road a quarter mile, set back in a clump of trees, a low, unpainted structure, with late lean-to additions on both ends, as well as the back side, seemed to be held to the ground by the spread of a huge lilac bush. It screened the porch, and clutched at the shingles of the roof. "That's it!" my wife said. "The house with the lilac bush," and we followed the drive back to a yard cluttered with small sheds and rusting farm implements. It relieved me not to see Mr. Applegate's Chevy pickup. The suppressed emotion I had felt in his manner, at the mention of my mother and Winona, would only be aggravated by the presence of my wife. As we walked toward the house, a figure appeared on the dark porch. A billowing summer frock, with a flower pattern, concealed her enormous bulk: the short, fleshy arm she raised was like a vestigial wing. On her wide, rounded shoulders her head looked small. My wife went forward to meet her; seeing me left her confused and speechless. Her name was Esther, a soft fleshy mound of a woman with a perspiring face, and an extravagantly sweet nature. That I was the child of Grace Osborn she could not believe. She was able to move, wheeling slowly, like an engine in a roundhouse, and make her way to the door of the house, where she called out, "Leah! Leah!" There was a shrill murmuring answer, but no one appeared. Esther turned her figure sidewise to enter the door, rubbing it firmly with her backside, and we followed her into a small, dark room. Leah Applegate—the image of her sister, strands of her long dark hair stuck to her forehead—filled a space that was bolstered with pillows to support her flowing figure. Were they twins? They spoke with the same girlish, murmuring voice. Leah made no movement to rise, and I leaned forward to grip her small, damp, plump hand. A tent-like smock exposed flesh that puddled at her throat. On the round center table, set out for us to examine, were clippings, photo albums and mounted studio portraits. In a large family portrait, of four girls and two boys, I recognized the handsome face of Dwight, and Winona with her large, melting eyes. They were assembled in a row, heads inclined together, but the young woman at the end of the row did not resemble her sisters. Sidewise, she gazed directly into the lens of the camera at who or whatever might be lurking behind it.

"That's her, isn't it?" my wife said.

"Isn't she the prettiest thing?" Esther exclaimed. Grace Osborn was a beauty, but a young man, in line with her gaze, might feel in the curve of her lips a mocking challenge. "Well?" it seemed to ask, and waited for an answer. How had my father fared with this glimpse into liberation? Had he read it, in the fashion of the time, as a young woman who needed taming?

There were other studio portraits, most of them made in Grand Island, of elderly men and women, including one of a young man with clearly defined features, his wavy hair parted in the middle. A good head, set a bit high on the pedestal of a stiff collar, he might have looked inviting to a young woman who needed help from the seat of a buggy. What had she had in mind for the child whose birth would cost her her life?

I asked the two sisters if we could borrow these portraits long enough to make copies of them. Esther declared that we could have the pictures—after all, these were my people—but my wife insisted that we would return them. Leah, the somewhat larger of the two, fanned her perspiring face with a folded newspaper. Lace curtains hung at the closed windows. From my boyhood I could hear the high voice of Clara warning Harry against the night air. Back in the shadows, as my eyes adjusted, I saw plates ornamented with flowers, several Kewpie dolls, calendars with kittens, horses, puppies. A large tabby cat, with clear tiger markings, slept on the seat of a chair I could see in the kitchen. Somewhere in the house a caged bird twittered. Esther gave us a small bag of freshly baked oatmeal cookies to snack on while we were traveling.

She had been east to Lincoln, as a girl, and west as far as Kearney, where she attended teachers college. In Central City she had taught in the grade school, but she missed her brother and sister. We last saw her, her fingers wagging, through the lattice of the lilac branches, a gentle, affectionate, sweet-natured woman one might describe as a cow, meaning no offense to either. She had known my mother, perhaps walked in the road holding her hand, and felt the mocking intensity of her gaze.

*I*n Claremont we found an apartment on West Sixth Street, over a garage. The house was occupied by Mrs. Ewing, the college librarian, and her housekeeper. The housekeeper, an energetic, plainspoken woman, who walked about with her broom as a trident, had taken a keen interest in my wife, who she felt deserved a better fate. In a novel I would begin a few months later, she has the name Gussie Newcomb. Concern for my wife's welfare brought her to the foot of our stairs every morning, seeking reassurance that she had survived the night. I would see her, her hands shading her eyes, the broom inclined on her shoulder, profiled against the strong backlight. Seeing me, she would inquire if my wife was in. She usually was. A fan placed at one of the windows stirred the warming air. By midmorning, it was usually so hot I would take a walk to the library and sit in the cool but humid air of the basement. Before noon, the perspiration from my hand would smear the pages I was writing.

We had old friends in Claremont, some of whom lived in larger, cooler houses—swimming pools were not as yet mandated—or we might plan a day-long gambol at the beach or at Lake Arrowhead in the mountains. These options were always available, but we soon found it too much trouble. The drive to the beach was hot. We came home too sun- and windburned to sleep. By fall we were at ease with our preoccupations and looked forward eagerly to the rainy season.

In Whittier, about an hour's drive to the southwest, my wife had relations, two sisters of her mother and one husband, Uncle Pete. Uncle Pete worked as a clerk in a Whittier grocery store, and on holidays, or one of the ladies' birthdays, he would drive his Maxwell sedan, with the two ladies, over to Claremont. They usually brought a cut of meat that Uncle Pete considered a bargain, or one of Aunt Alice's masterly cakes and pies. Solidly trained in these matters by her own mother, a woman who made the best crusts in Maumee County, Ohio, Aunt Alice did not spare butter or the use of a fork in blending the shortening. We ate up the cakes in a day or two, but nursed the fruit pies as long as a week.

I was greatly attracted to Uncle Pete, a tall, gentle man with large-knuckled hands and a great fund of experience in groceries. He was only at his ease behind a counter, his hands rolled up in a wad of his apron. He particularly loved to cut slices of "store" cheese, extending toward me, on the blade of the knife, a sliver of the product I could sample. He hand-sliced his bacon with a stroke that went back to seal and whale blubber. He was the first to reassure me that my blind loyalty to the Monarch label on a can of peaches was soundly based on their flavor. In the dim-lighted, high-ceilinged store where he clerked, he used a yardstick to topple the cans from the high shelves, caught them in his apron, then wiped the top lid with a swipe of the cloth. Those gestures were skillful, but chiefly they were expressive of his respect and affection for the product. I noted in him a chronic reluctance to sell cans of hard-to-get Monarch pears, peaches and cherries, or the big dried bulk prunes from Santa Clara. He may have been the first man to arouse in me the suspicion that the good things had had their day, and were on their way out.

"I'd put that on the back of the shelf," he'd say to me with a wink that creased both of his eyes. Every four or five words, his voice tended to crack, and led him to repeat the word in question, as he furtively exchanged a glance with Aunt Alice. She was in no way a tyrant, like her sister in Cleveland, but she had more than a touch of her will and assurance as to what was right. Uncle Pete did not. He quailed like Tom Sawyer under the gaze of Aunt Polly. In some way that defied my imagination, Uncle Pete and Aunt Alice had fathered a son, James, who lived in New York and kept books for a plumber. We had stayed a night with Pete and Alice several days after we were married, lying awake on the daybed in the living room, constrained and heedful to make no sound that might be considered inappropriate. I could hear the ticking of the clock Uncle Pete had been careful to rewind. This day had been festive and somewhat careless, but the morrow, if nothing else, would start on time.

In the morning I parted the curtains at the window to watch him sharpen the blades of the mower. A straw hat shaded his face, the sun was hot on the back of his neck. Later he pushed the mower around the plot of grass as it gave off a different pitch, according to the stroke, the quick thrusts that he made at the end of each row a pleasurable affirmation and a semicolon. There's a proper way to walk when you push a sharp mower, which calls for a flexible bend at the elbow. Both that morning and others that followed, I was slow to realize that one of the good things on its way out was Uncle Pete.

Aunt Nettie, Alice's older sister, had taught school most of her life in McComb, Ohio, the third grade being her specialty. She didn't like them so much as toddlers, or later when they started to get smart. A small, white-haired woman, with a frosted complexion, she set the table three times a day for meals, and helped wash and put away the dishes. Finding the right get-well cards kept Aunt Nettie busy, and writing them kept her alert and flustered. Nettie's feeling that my wife might have shopped around a little more before succumbing—I had not even completed my college education—had not been eased by my brief brush with fame, not a word of which had been reported in the Whittier papers. Nor had the lending library she sometimes used ever heard of me, or my book. If I was bit too eager at the Sunday dinner, helping myself to a second slice of angel food cake, Aunt Nettie peered over her glasses to register her disapproval. In what way—she had asked my wife—was I not unemployed?

Under stresses of this sort I had begun a story, "The Vision of Private Reagan," concerned with the rituals of burial in Southern California. My view of these events was that of a young man who had been spared the actual experience. Uncle Pete and Aunt Alice *had* attended a funeral, and Uncle Pete's dry report of his impressions did not conceal from me his dismay. As we sat in the yard with our iced tea glasses, watching a squirrel nibble at a piece of Alice's cake, he made several futile efforts to express this dismay without disturbing the ladies. What he said was that I ought to look in on one myself. This seemed to me very much the sort of challenge that a fiction writer should face up to. I had not as yet heard of the "virus of suggestion," or that the fiction writer was a person on whom little or nothing was lost, but I was open to the thought that a writer might come down with a great infection from a remarkably small exposure, as in love.

I wanted to find in Private Reagan—the GI Joe who had attended the funeral—the Great American Sap who persists in his folly in such a fashion that he becomes wise. From where I had this idea, I don't know. It was true to the nature of much of my varied experience, and might have been my own observation. Over the winter, this short story proved to be a long one as it worked its way to a macabre conclusion, the author blithely unaware that he was engaged in what would prove to be black humor.

My story was too long for magazine publication, too short for a book. I sent it off to Diarmuid Russell, of the new agency Russell & Volkening, who replied that he had been much entertained, but the length of the piece would prove to be a problem. While waiting on this decision, I turned to my impressions of the brief stops we had made in Nebraska, first on the farm near Norfolk, then in Chapman. Recalling and expanding on this experience gave me great satisfaction. It aroused me in a similar way, only more so, as digging for treasure in the dunes of Cape Cod. I felt the unquestioned assurance that if I kept digging I would find something.

One day I heard "Gussie Newcomb"—I took the trouble to hear her—gossiping with my wife at the foot of the stairs. A young man she had known, personally, had turned out to be a "missing person." This phrase rang in my head like a chime. What had I been doing, as we crossed Nebraska, but searching for a *missing person*, namely myself? I named this person Agee Ward, a GI who had been reported as missing, with nothing to show for his past existence but a small album of photographs.

I conceived of Agee Ward as one who became more of a presence through his absence, rather than in spite of it: a man who was there. My fresh impressions of the past, acquired on Harry's farm, in Norfolk, and in Cahow's barbershop, in Chapman, would provide me with the background, and Gussie Newcomb, in Claremont, would contribute the foreground. This proved to be more than enough to take my mind off the future of Private Reagan.

As I browsed in the open stacks of the college library, my eye fell on the new books from the Pantheon Press, with their flat spines and European styling. I had not previously read a line of Charles Péguy, and other Catholic writers, outspoken rebels of the beleaguered conscience. Péguy was very much a stylist of my own persuasion, spare, cadenced and uncompromising. I lacked the training and the faith for Léon Bloy, but Georges Bernanos aroused and nourished a deep strain of religious feeling in my own nature. My Aunt Winona would have said I was not my mother's son for nothing.

While I was waiting to be drafted—the dangling man of Saul Bellow's novel—I reached such a stage of impatience that I enlisted in the navy. With my colleagues, about forty of us, I appeared at the induction center in Los Angeles. The examination proved to be a memorable experience for me and is fully and explicitly reported in my novel *The Huge Season*.

I was rejected by the navy for a heart murmur, but a few months later I was back to repeat the performance for the army. My rejection by the navy singled me out as a figure of

107

some interest. I was given a soiled-carpet examination, with special attention from the interns who were curious about heart murmurs. Some heard something (the beat of the heart?), some did not. It took time to reach a consensus. With Uncle Sam's pension system involved, the vote finally went against me. In the early evening I was back on the bus for Claremont, home free.

In our second year in Claremont we made the acquaintance of Morris and Catherine Opler. Morrie was also on a Guggenheim, his specialty being the ethnography of the Plains Indians of the Southwest, but in California he proved to be the resolute champion of the American-Japanese after the panic of Pearl Harbor. This story has been told, and is now familiar, but Opler seemed to be alone at the time in his support of their rights as citizens. In less than a year we established a friendship that survived our mutually provisional, in-transit existences.

My wife had applied for a teaching position at the Baldwin School, in Bryn Mawr, Pennsylvania, and in the late spring she was notified that she had been hired. The pay was good, two thousand dollars a year, and we both liked the idea of living close to New York. Once more we drove across the country, making our usual stop in Cleveland, where we learned that Charles was being treated for his "condition" at a state institution. Since I had last seen him, my father-in-law had changed. A strict diet had enabled him to lose weight, but he looked gaunt. Any exercise resulted in shortness of breath. The dog, Sox, had been given to friends since Fin could no longer walk him in the evening. The lively, clever mutt had filled the house with life, and without him it seemed vacant. Mother moved about in her bathrobe, as usual, indifferent to the mood of dejection. Even playing cards was a strain for Fin, his pale face filmed with perspiration. Mother was heedful of his superficial needs, totally ignorant of the others. In the cool, efficient manner of a nurse, she would dab at his face with a tissue. Even the effort to brush away her hand was too much for him. We left a day early, sparing him as well as ourselves. Fin's mother, ninety-five years of age, and living alone, was having trouble taking care of herself and had finally been persuaded to live with them in Cleveland. Mother did not like her mother-in-law, a woman who had been heedless, for almost a century, of every health rule known to science, as well as being stubborn and stone-deaf to advice. Mother did not look forward to a confrontation she had hoped to be spared, but she would do whatever proved to be necessary.

"She doesn't fool me for a minute," she said to my wife. "Hoping to outlive me has kept her alive." Munching a carrot, she added, "Well, we will see what we will see."

The first week of our arrival in Bryn Mawr, in the high lush humid heat of August, my wife had an attack of hay fever that put her to bed. She had a history of allergies, and had endured all the tests that were then in fashion, but never before had she found it hard to breathe, with fits of continuous sneezing. Was it possible we had moved to a place where she couldn't live? A doctor in Cleveland, who knew my wife's allergic history, sent on a simple drug that brought miraculous relief.

Thanks to the favorable impression my wife made on the people in the banking and real estate business, we were able to lease an apartment in Haverford, not far from the Baldwin School. Just a block to the south, on what was called the Pike, and directly across from the Haverford campus, an antique and secondhand store supplied us with the basics for setting up house. Not very practical, but wonderfully ornamental, was a purple velvet platform rocker that neither time, the sun, nor human bottom appeared to have touched. A full leather-bound set of the Eleventh Edition of the *Encyclopaedia Britannica,* in its own mahogany case, proved to be all ours for forty cents a volume. The owner of the store, a figure I would later recognize in the stories of Isaak Babel, put stock in many things, but not in books. The apartment itself, part of a duplex, with a porch of smooth cement level with the yard, was concealed from the street by rhododendron bushes. At the rear we had the remnants of a victory garden left by the previous occupants, and closing off the yard, on a high embankment, the main line of the Pennsylvania Railroad. In addition to the heavy rail traffic of freight, we had the daily commuter trains to Philadelphia. It persuaded us to do most of our sleeping and working in the room at the front.

After two summers in California, I welcomed both the humidity and the lushness. The Philadelphia Main Line had once been the affluent and elegant enclave for Philadelphia money and breeding, neither in short supply. At the turn of the century, mansions had been built and Japanese trees and flowering shrubs had been planted. The spring would bring the miracle of the flowering dogwood. Most of the money and breeding proved to be north of the tracks and the turnpike, but with quick access to the uncrowded electric car commuter service to Philadelphia. The *toot* of these cars, which I could hear from both directions, after stops had been made in Bryn Mawr and Ardmore, would soon displace in my mind the clang of streetcar bells and the sound of iron wheels spinning. That sound would have much to do with my new attachments, and the writing, ten years later, of the Main Line novel *The Deep Sleep*.

The Baldwin School had once been a posh resort hotel, a short carriage ride from the city. Old resort hotels, in my opinion, make marvelous private schools for girls, since the young female is both less rowdy and more ornamental to the setting. I would never tire of the festive hooting and the cardiac apprehension of Parents' Day. Not being a parent, I was spared the risk, but had all the pleasures of the occasion. The college of Bryn Mawr, the alma mater of our Double-dukes, as well as other distinguished nonconformists, was just a few minutes' stroll to the west, one I sometimes took when the leaves were turning.

We had no more than settled in when a professor and his wife rented the apartment upstairs. The ladies met on the morning of the second day at the trash burner at the back of the yard. The ascending pitch of their conversation, with an occasional shriek of laughter, reached me where I was working at the front of the house. Loren and Mabel Eiseley proved to be from Nebraska, by way of Oberlin, where he had been teaching anthropology. For the time being (the summer), he was on loan to the University of Pennsylvania, where he had done his graduate work. Mabel Eiseley was from Hastings, where I had managed to spend one of my boyhood summers. It seemed unusual to both ladies, and remarkably amusing, that they had both married men from Nebraska, a territory not frequently heard from.

We spent that first and most of our other evenings together on the front porch, screened off from the traffic by the rhododendrons. The large dog of a neighbor, making his daily rounds, would appear about the time we were all getting thirsty and leave about the time we were cleaning up. In my opinion, he loved Eiseley's deep voice, pitched to a subterranean rumble. Some years later, however, dozing off as I rambled, Eiseley accounted for it in this manner: "Morris," he generously said, "when I listen to you go on and on, I can relax, knowing the world is in good hands." Good hands or not, we were both from the plains, and when we dipped into the past the same subsoil came up with the roots, and similar artifacts surfaced in our diggings.

My friend's naturally melancholy temperament led me to nickname him Schmerzie—a shortened form of *Weltschmerz*. I think he found it apt. He had a scholar's and a poet's perspective on human affairs, therefore he did not lack reason for pessimism. In our endless and pleasurable discussions, usually several times a week over a period of years, Loren was inclined to provide the perspective, while I proffered the notions of the eager amateur. That we were both the issue of the plains of Nebraska made for much good talk without friction. We had been turned on the same lathe, and were nourished and motivated by the same expectations.

Loren's wife, an Irish woman of the breed James Joyce had married, and bearing her some resemblance, had little patience with our speculations, but she enjoyed my jokes. Her own opinion of bone hunters and their reconstructions was frequently expressed with Irish directness and sarcasm, especially those fictions of Cro-Magnon and Piltdown man based on the molar of a missing jaw. Mabel put me in mind of one of Willa Cather's lost ladies who had found her escape as a professor's wife. Her taste in fiction ran to Henry James, who would have loved both her hats and her style. Loren took pride in her appearance, her independent spirit, and walked at her side with his hand cupped to her elbow, at ease in the role, the suits and the ties, that would have been appropriate to my father.

When we met in the summer of 1943 I was the more published writer. My example may have encouraged Loren to get on with his own unique nature writing, the essays that expressed the two aspects of his experience and his temperament, the poet and the scientist. On occasion he would read one of the pieces to me, or try out a passage he felt a bit unsure of. His taste at the time was more discriminating than mine, but he welcomed my reassurance. That first summer together we began the long walks through the woods just north of Haverford and Bryn Mawr, escorted by dogs, sometimes a small pack of them, eager for a similar adventure. A big gray-muzzled red setter, with a henna-colored coat, combed the woods on both sides of the road, baying hoarsely when he turned up something. We could hear him thrash off through the brush, the pack howling at his heels. When he eventually returned, winded and slobbering, his coat wet and muddy from the streams he had forded, Eiseley might stoop to take the noble head in his hands, gazing into his eyes for his own dim past. It came easily to him, as it did to D. H. Lawrence, to profoundly empathize with the spirit that animated all living creatures, and might be intuited in the bone fragments of the dead ones. A man of this persuasion, and Eiseley's talents, might come to feel that bones, in an age of raucous babble, spoke clearest for the living. In his silences it was the voices of the dead to which he was attentive.

*M*y wife had not seen her cousin James since they had been kids together back in Ohio. He had come east to New York planning to be an architect, my wife to teach school, and I to be a writer. We were living in suburban Philadelphia at the time, and James and his wife were living in Brooklyn, near Coney Island. I wondered what it was like to be living near the sea, and an amusement park. James's mother had written to my wife that he was now married, and a father, and she thought it was time that we all got together.

We met at the Child's restaurant near Penn Station, where chicken croquettes was the luncheon special. James was a tall, dark, easygoing young man, who kept books—for the time being—for a plumber on East Fifty-third street. When I asked him if he thought it might rain—he carried an umbrella—he said the weather might be different where he lived in Brooklyn than it was in the city. To me, that made it sound interesting. He liked to sit with his hands on the handle of the umbrella, like a diplomat.

James wanted us to come home to Brooklyn with him, and meet his wife and her family. She was the only girl among five adoring brothers, none of them married. I liked the way James could tell a story using the Irish brogue he had picked up from his in-laws. No matter what it was my wife said, he. was able to turn it to her advantage. I can see you haven't changed, my wife said, and he replied that his wife would be sorry to hear that, flicking me a wink as he said it. He had worked out a sort of routine, with his talk, so that it flattered the woman in question. He always seemed to take my side, but in such a way that it pleased my wife. In his marriage, he said, he had got most of Ireland, but all his wife had got was a husband. Her father had himself come from Ireland, after the war, and still talked a brogue strangers found it hard to understand. Nearby, in Brooklyn, he kept a stable with a carriage and two horses there was no longer much use for. What it did, though, was keep him out of mischief.

A few weeks later I was back in New York and called James to say hello. He insisted that I spend the night in Brooklyn with them. I met him at the subway, and we rode about an hour hanging on to the straps, then another twenty minutes to where we got off. I hadn't realized Brooklyn had such depressing neighborhoods. Empty lots were everywhere, some of them strewn with junk, some of them with piles of smoking rubbish. Sidewalks were torn up, fences pushed over and battered, and some of the shabby frame houses were tilted. The three or four blocks I walked along with James made me think of Céline's slums in Paris, where the aged might be living like rabbits in the warrens at the back of the yards.

James told me that his wife had been born here, and her family had lived here most of their lives. One of the things about the Irish that he had noticed was how little they liked to move. Her brothers got around more, since two of them worked in Queens, but Mary herself had only once been to Times Square. It had frightened her more than it pleased her. She couldn't stand to mingle with so many people she didn't know. One thing that James planned to do, when they were settled, was get a car and drive out in the country. Mary had never seen the country, except in the movies. She didn't know how she would like a place that seemed to have so few people in it.

All her family had assembled to meet me, and sat tight around the kitchen table. There seemed to be about nine, including her handsome older brother, Jerry, and his fiancée, Maria. Jerry had the chiseled features you see in some of the Irish, with the build and natty style of a jockey. He wore a checkered suit, a diamond tiepin. Gold flashed when he smiled, and he had an appealing way of flicking a wink as he sucked air between his teeth. His brothers were more like the father, Paddy-type Irish, with their hair cropped short like the pelts of grass on the clay heads in florists' windows. For almost ten years Jerry had been the catch of the neighborhood. There was some resentment among the brothers that it was an Italian girl who had caught him in a neighborhood where Irish girls were not lacking. They took comfort, however, in Jerry's reluctance to get to the altar. He had now been engaged for just going on twenty-one months.

James's wife, Mary, was at her ease with men, having grown up with so many brothers. Her pale blue Irish eyes were almost as colorless as water, her hair, like her brother Jerry's, prematurely white. She had been the one to bring Maria home, after her first communion, and now she was pushing for an early marriage. Not to imply that she was forward, or felt that much at home, Maria sat the whole evening with her raincoat draped about her shoulders, and her hat on. The real problem was not so much that Maria was Italian but that her brothers were in the numbers racket, and drove fast cars. Going for her was the fact that she came from and looked forward to a big family.

All the while we were talking, Mary's father, Patrick, stood in the door to the hall, his lower lip protruding with a pouch of snuff. At his back he held a can, into which he frequently turned to spit. Patrick did not read or write in any language, but he did it all with his bloodshot twinkling eyes, and the appreciative glances he gave the ladies. When food was served he took his plate and sat in the dark on the stairs, because of the way he smelled of the horses and the stable.

A meal was served and cleared away, beer was poured, and

115

at our backs Mary moved around the table, filling and refilling our coffee cups. To do that, she explained, was why the Lord had made her so short. Sometime after midnight I noticed that James was missing, and found him asleep in the trough of the daybed, since there was not space in the room to open it properly. (On the nights Maria stayed over, she slept with Mary.) When I joined him, in an upright position, my eyes were level with the gap between the sill and the blind, through which I glimpsed a landscape of ruin lit up by moonlight. Unmistakably I felt the vibration of the arriving and departing subway. Something in the room jiggled. It proved to be the subway nickels in a saucer on the mantel. One of Mary's younger brothers had stayed on to discuss a personal matter with his sister, their voices muted like those exchanging confessions.

Sometime later, I awoke to see three of the brothers under the street light, talking. Smoke rose from their nodding, huddled heads like buns under a food warmer.

In December, I called Mary to say how I would miss seeing them all at Christmas, and heard from her that the marriage had now been set for April. Would I be there? I was excused when it was understood that I had never been to the Bronx. In the escort of her family, Mary was driven to the wedding in a limousine with black windows, one of which was lowered so she could see out.

On my visit in March, I learned that Maria's new baby was sickly from the Bronx air and water. Whose eyes and hair it had Mary didn't know, since neither mother nor child had paid her a visit. Mary was now expecting again herself. Did Maria think Mary, in her delicate condition, should now be traveling all the way to the Bronx? It sadly distressed her that Maria's sickly infant would be sorely needing, but not getting, the loving comfort and attention of an Irish family. All that Mary had learned would go wasted like food on the back burner without Maria and her baby there to receive it.

In May, a fire burned the barn where Mary's father kept his horses, and he was terribly burned trying to save them. To escape from this sorrow, James moved his wife and child to a small town in Massachusetts, with a priest known to Father Curran. James clerked, like his father, in a grocery store, and worked as a volunteer in the fire department. At Christmas he sent us a snapshot showing him in his fireman's hat, riding on the truck. Mary had difficulty with her second baby, which she had planned to name Jerry if it was a boy, but it proved to be another girl, allergic to eggs and milk.

One winter day, in Grand Central Station, I recognized the tall, dark man coming toward me with a frail white-haired woman who might have been his mother. Her unseeing gaze looked through and beyond me. I raised my hand to wave, but neither of them saw me. Since I had last seen them, they had both learned to live in a world of people they didn't relate to. In a Christmas letter from James's mother, we learned that Mary had not adjusted well to country living, her health was poor, and at thirty-two years of age she had lost her teeth. Her mother added, however, that the two children seemed to be fine.

After a gap of many years, I sometimes wonder about the splinter in the groove that diverted me to Brooklyn. At that time I had been following a groove of my own, returning home along the tracks I had made going out, and I was not prepared to find myself tangled up with somebody else's family. It led me to spend hours just riding the subway. I came to see the subway as an extension of the nervous system, crucial connections maintained, lines of energy flowing, even while the passengers were in transit. I never felt much in the way of family ties myself. One of my classmates in college, who just might have been Irish, every two weeks would send a fiber carton of his laundry home to his family, whether he really needed it or not. He thought only his mother knew how to iron his shirts.

On a map like those on the walls of railroad stations, I once marked in all the places I had lived, and the places I had been, with chicken-like tracks indicating my travels. I meant to go back, one day, and put in the lines I knew to be missing, adding dense patches of crosshatching to those places important to me. Figuring roughly, for example, I must have crossed the railroad tracks in the town I was born in many thousands of times. Like the chicken in the story, it was the other side of the tracks that attracted me.

The streets in Omaha that I walked the most, especially in the summer when I was barefoot, have all been bulldozed away to make a great cloverleaf freeway intersection. I've often driven out of my way to try and capture the way I feel about it, but it escapes me. Am I compelled to resolve these real losses with imaginary gains?

Where Menomonee Street meets Lincoln Park in Chicago, the streetcar trolleys fill the night with their flashes, and once lit up the room where I should have been sleeping. From that corner, walking west on Menomonee Street, to where it ends at Ogden Avenue, then down Ogden to Larabee, I suppose I've walked, in both hot and freezing weather, so many times it's a mystery my legs aren't shorter. Just down Menomonee Street, there used to be a sign that glowed warmly at night, advertising a toothbrush. I loved that sign, but somehow it never led me to buy the brush.

People beyond counting walk the streets of New York, wearing away the tracks of all the other walkers. Somehow, it's the wearing in of the tracks I like, the wearing off I don't. The meaning of this, if it has one, has to do with the maintenance of connections. When I turn and look behind me, I like to see where I have been. One of the jobs I once thought I'd wanted as a boy was to push the line marker on a baseball diamond, restoring what the game had obliterated, making again the insignia I see on the TV when the crowd rises to sing the National Anthem. When they sing "Oh, say can you see," that is what I see.

I took my new manuscript to New York in September, and met my agent, Diarmuid Russell. He had formed a partnership with Henry Volkening at a bad time for fiction, but a very needy time for young writers. Mr. Russell was a handsome, cultivated man, both reserved and direct. I had learned that he was the son of A. E. Russell, the Irish poet and essayist, and I was both impressed and respectful. He had no good news for me about "The Vision of Private Reagan," but he wanted to reassure me that I should not lose heart. I was a good writer. One day, surely, my time would come. I liked Mr. Russell's direct no-nonsense manner, and stretched my legs to stay abreast of him after our lunch.

While waiting on what he might think of the new book— and beginning a habit that would spare me much torment— in my imagination I returned to the plains, where one of its native sons seemed to obstruct my field of vision. I did not see him as clearly as I *felt* him. Better access to him, if and when it came, would come through my feeling that we shared a mutual language. That what he felt, I felt. Through these feelings I would find the words.

What little I saw was like a dark, featureless figure who stood before a sod house, set into a barren hillside. The horns of cattle were strewn about on the sod roof. I had never seen such a thing myself, but I had glimpsed, from time to time, a few early photographs. I found these bleak images captivating. In a way I did not understand, the very lack of detail seemed to my purpose. The tilted windmill, with a few of the blades missing; the hazy, shadowless blur of the glare that led me to think of the landscape of China: that I had written down. A strange conjunction, it seemed to me, the sandhills of Nebraska and the plains of China. Searching for the voice appropriate to my feelings, I had written:

In the dry places, men begin to dream. Where the rivers run sand there is something in man that begins to flow.

Not all of it was so compactly stated the first time, but that was the *voice*. From the voice, like a seed, the rest of it would grow. On another page:

Will Brady was born on a river without water, in a sod house, near the town of Indian Bow. In time he grew to be a man who neither smoked, drank, gambled nor swore. What is there left to say of a man with so much of his life left out?

What indeed! And what was that but to my purpose? The one man I knew who neither smoked, drank, nor gambled, and rarely swore, was my father. This fact somewhat bemused me, but I gave it little attention. The past was still the past until I unearthed it. My concern at the time was to establish the *tone* that would make possible all that followed. My preoccupation with *The Works of Love* would continue for some years, and it would not be published until 1952.

I put these pages aside when I heard from Diarmuid Russell that Harcourt, Brace had rejected my new book. Lambert Davis had liked it, personally, but he did not see it as a successful commercial venture. My first novel had done very poorly, and a second book, with a similar response from the

120

public, would seriously diminish my future prospects. I should think hard about this second novel, he said, since for many writers it was their last.

Lambert Davis was right, on every count, but I was not a *smart* writer. How did the writer think of *anything* but writing? The *voice*, for example, that mystifying clue to what was as yet unspoken. How think of anything else? And if that eased off, and you had found this voice, and spoke in it as naturally as your own, there were the words and the characters, and the details to think about, and what, as you sat there, you found yourself reading. For the writer—the true fiction writer—does not write to say what he thinks or feels, but to discover what it is. What I discover I am thinking and feeling takes all the time and thought I am able to muster, and it is seldom enough.

In his accompanying letter, Diarmuid cautioned me not to take this advice too much to heart. That was the way of editors and publishers. Their problem was that they had no way of telling the margarine from the butter. Could I supply him with a copy of *My Uncle Dudley*? He had an editor, Maxwell Perkins, who might like to read it. I did have a copy and sent it on to him, painfully conscious of its shortcomings. What would the editor who had read and published *The Sun Also Rises* and *The Great Gatsby* think of this piece of homespun? I had never seen my writing in this perspective, and it gave me pause.

About this time, my wife brought the principal of her school, Rosamund Cross, to our place for tea. A graduate of Bryn Mawr, self-possessed, attractive, liberated, with a cordial but professional manner, she had a story to tell of her brother's involvement in the naming of a new navy destroyer. Her brother had been lost at sea, and the boat had been named in his memory. The ceremony, which took place at a pier in Brooklyn, had been attended by Miss Cross and her mother. She dramatized the comical aspects of the ceremony so well we were still laughing hours later. And again it was the subject of *missing persons*, and the effort to accommodate these losses.

This incident so intrigued me I applied myself to it. I chose a man and his wife: the man gentle, somewhat passive—on my mind's eye I saw my father-in-law, and felt again his loss and his sorrow—the wife a woman he referred to as Mother. Their son would prove to be missing in a naval engagement, and would be honored with his name on a destroyer. The tone appropriate to this story seemed to be on my tongue, waiting for me to tell it, just as the characters were there in the wings, waiting to play their roles.

The tone of the book wavered between pathos and farce, a mix that seemed appropriate to the subject. Mrs. Ormsby is the object of the author's ridicule, but her role as Mother also gives it substance. I made a good start on the opening Ormsby chapter, before I was distracted by a letter from Diarmuid. Maxwell Perkins had read *My Uncle Dudley*, and expressed an interest in meeting the author. This heady news suspended all work.

Through Schindy we had met Peter and Nanny Sollinger, who lived in a large house in Brooklyn. The Sollingers were Swiss, from near Zurich. Nanny taught German at Brooklyn College, while Peter researched and wrote his book on Sutter, the Swiss explorer of the American West. The son of a peasant, Peter had taught himself to paint, to play the cello, to clean and wax all the floors, to make an apartment in the attic, to add a garage to the house, to hang storm windows, which saved the money to purchase a car, and in the early morning to research and write his scholarly book. I marveled at Peter's self-discipline, his quirky independence, his large gnarled hands that were like the roots of grapevines, but I found it hard to keep abreast of him when we took walks, his instinct to be in front was so persistent. In every detail, his knobby head—the stiff brush of his hair, the roughly hewn, craggy, masculine features—was that of the Swiss wine bottle caps popular at Christmas. It pleased both Nanny and Peter to have American friends who liked Schubert and Mozart, Thomas Mann and Jakob Burckhardt, as well as camomile tea

122

and Jewish Danish. They lived not far from the Avenue J stop of the subway, which was a bit of a ride for us, but we enjoyed their friendship. The great love of Nanny's life was her violin, which she played with some moaning and great intensity. I could listen to Nanny, but I could not both listen and watch her. If Peter and I began a conversation while the ladies were playing a sonata, Nanny would pause in her playing and come to stand between the folding doors she did not like closed, until we had given her our full attention.

"You understand it is not for me," she would say, and then return to Mozart.

Peter had been the romance of Nanny's life, and she had literally pulled him up by the roots and transplanted him in Brooklyn. In most respects he thrived. I loaned Peter a collapsible, newfangled camp cot the summer he and Nanny visited Yellowstone Park, which he returned to me, a year later, with the comment that it didn't seem to work. The heavy steel supports had been twisted in a manner nobody I knew could straighten out.

The Scribner building and bookstore on Fifth Avenue was directly across the street from a Child's restaurant. I often sat there with a cup of coffee, gazing up to the high windows of Maxwell Perkins's office. He would be the first literary legend I both met and appreciated. The oak-paneled offices on the fifth floor had not been altered since the days of Henry James, whose books were there in the library.

Mr. Perkins had the curtained corner office at the front, with a view of the skyline and Fifth Avenue. He rose from his desk to offer me his hand, then returned it to grip the lapel of his coat. One of the large Western hats given to him by Hemingway was tilted back on his head, framing his shyly smiling face. I liked him on the instant, and began to tell him all, a predictable and regrettable response. Hearing the code word *money*, Max took out his wallet. How much did I need? With some shame, I backed off. He was not given to "loose" talk himself, and he did not expect it from others. We talked about the book I was rewriting, *The Man Who Was There*, and then we talked about writers, *his* writers, Hemingway, Fitzgerald and Thomas Wolfe—on whose unpublished manuscript he was then working—and there I sat in the chair those writers had sat in, discussing them with Max Perkins, a legend. He had read and liked *My Uncle Dudley* but thought it slight. He would feel the same about *Man and Boy*. His complaint about the brevity of my fiction would be the one I heard the most. He liked heft. I would seldom be a writer of heft.

Back in Haverford, I looked again at *The Man Who Was There*, pondering how I might give it more weight. I read again the story of Private Reagan, and it occurred to me that his bizarre vision might be appropriate to the world of Agee Ward. I made some changes, and a few months later heard from Diarmuid Russell that Scribner's planned to publish it.

This occurred in the spring of 1945, and one of my first readers, a teacher at the Baldwin School, a Swiss woman with a profound dislike for speed reading, called me to ask if there was not something peculiar with a line of text on page 219. This line read: "To get her mind off Boulder Dam I took the road up Baldy wanted to know about Boulder Dam." I allowed as how the line did sound a bit strange. A word or phrase had been dropped. I would hasten to check on it. On checking this out—which took some time, since I lacked the original copy of the manuscript—I found that eight or ten pages were missing. I called Max Perkins, who surprised me by saying that the error would be corrected in later printings. How did one get later printings of a book with so many pages missing? It was not a topic in which Max had much interest. Some months later, conducting my own inscrutable investigation, I discovered that the editor in charge of the galleys had been suffering a mid-career crisis, complicated romantically, that had finally revealed itself in pages missing from assorted galleys. They had simply vanished. The prime exhibit, designed to calm small losers like myself, was a mystery novel, written by Marjorie Bonner, the wife of Malcolm Lowry, which was published without its concluding chapter. No question that this book was a mystery that remained unresolved. Only a handful of readers, besides the author, took the pains to point this out.

Vanished also, during that season, had been the prospect for a second printing of *The Man Who Was There*, nor did it again, to my knowledge, receive the close, nonspeed reading that hinted at missing pages.

Thirty-two years later, when the book was reissued by the University of Nebraska, the line that had troubled my Swiss friend had been deleted, the gap skillfully closed. The writer of the novel pondered the gap but he did not recall what he might have written, nor have the missing pages ever surfaced. A truly missing passage from the tale of a missing man.

Diarmuid Russell had thought it ill-advised—in light of what happened to my second novel—to trouble Max Perkins with a book as strange, as expensive and as innovative as *The Inhabitants*. But I was so confident I ignored his advice. On an early fall day, I appeared at the Scribner offices with my portfolio of mounted photographs, and I vividly remember sitting at Max's side as he looked at them one by one, and read the texts. His Hemingway hat was tilted back. He was pleased, but reluctant to say so. What might he be getting into *this* time? I was equally certain that whatever he had seen, and read, had given him no more than the bloom of it. How was the book to speak louder for itself?

The wall of his office was at his back, the high windows on Fifth Avenue to his left. I took several of the prints, a handful of his paper clips, and clipped them to the drapes that concealed the neighboring office. He was amused. I was delighted to see how good they looked. Did he mind? He seemed more pleased than provoked. I took an armful of the mounts and expanded the exhibition to two walls of his office. The light was marvelous. We both agreed it made quite a show. Just for the hell of it, would he let them hang for two weeks? He fussed a bit. What might his visitors think? It would be a good way of finding out, I said, how the public might respond to the book.

The photographs and texts were on his walls when I left, and they were still there two weeks later, when I appeared to take them away. What did he think? He let me wait while he tilted back his chair and took a grip on the lapels of his coat. A few pigeons were pacing the sill of his window. His secretary, as important to Max as his hands, came in with her pad and pencil to tell me how much she had liked looking at the photographs. The Perkins glow gave his smile a cherubic cast. Still faced away from me—he *was* a shy man—he said he felt obliged to publish the book, although it made no sense as a commercial venture. Pete Dymock, from the production department, came in to tell me how much *he* liked it, and he wanted to know which of the photographs had been taken in Georgia, his home state. That was how it came to pass that *The Inhabitants* found a home.

In 1938, before we left California, I had at last found a copy of *The Sleepwalkers*, by Hermann Broch. The author's range had dazzled me, but more to my purpose, I was profoundly moved by his portraits of Mother Hentjen and her lover, Esch. Such people as these, such discards, in a sense, were compacted of the elements that aroused my imagination. Memories of Esch had been at work in my portrait of Private Reagan and his bizarre vision. In my enthusiasm, I had written a letter to Broch in care of his American publisher, Little, Brown. It delighted me to eventually receive his cordial response, with an address in Princeton I might write to.

When we settled in Haverford, I wrote to Broch again, and he suggested we might visit him in Princeton. We managed to do this in the spring of 1945, when I had my just published novel *The Man Who Was There* to show him. Broch was a guest of Erich Kahler, an Austrian writer and scholar, who, like Broch, had recently escaped the Nazis. They lived just a short walk from Albert Einstein, in a large, comfortable house on Evelyn Place. On that first trip to Princeton I also took along my portfolio of photographs and texts, which proved to be of great interest to the émigrés who had gathered for a Sunday dinner. Kahler's very old mother, dressed in black, her eyes sunk deep in their sockets, sat near the fire on our arrival, reading Greek with Broch. I felt she perceived me, if at all, through the veil of another century. Her concern for Broch was that of a grandmother left in charge of a much-

126

loved but somewhat wayward child. At one of the meals, I sat near Broch across from two Viennese women, the refinement of their awareness of each other spun out of the air itself by Rilke's *Malte Laurids Brigge*. Did people of this quality manage to persist in a show of signs that spared them discussion of the unspeakable?

*I*n 1946 I applied for a second Guggenheim Fellowship, and I was fortunate enough to receive it. I exchanged my 3¼ by 4¼ view camera for a 4 by 5. In early May of the following spring, I drove back to the farm near Norfolk. The Depression-ravaged dirt farm of my previous visit was partially concealed and softened by the growth of spring; weeds concealed implements; a gone-to-seed over-ripeness seemed appropriate. I found my Uncle Harry at his ease, smoking a cob pipe, tinkering with an inner tube. Clara was more resigned than bitter. I found her seated in her rocker, her lap full of eggs, chipping at the dung spots with her thumbnail. To my suggestion that I take pictures they expressed no objection. Did they know what I had in mind? They had seen *The Inhabitants*. Feeling the need to justify, rather than explain, I said I wanted to capture what it was like to have lived on a dirt farm for fifty years, to have lived on this farm for half a century. There was no comment. I recall Clara moving her head from one side to the other, to see and appraise the room she sat in. Her shoes were unlaced. The ties of her apron dangled on the floor. I could hear mice stirring in the kitchen's basket of cobs. "I don't know why," she said, "but if it's what you want to do, you're free to."

It had never crossed my mind that she would give me access to the *inside* of her house. I was about to reassure her: You can trust me, Clara. . . . Trust me to do what? Wasn't I too greedy to be trusted? Didn't I privately feel I had earned this privilege? Just a few weeks before, I had come on a statement that gave me, I felt, unlimited access.

. . . is to be subject to the superstition that objects and places, coherently grouped, disposed for human use and addressed to it, must have a sense of their own, a mystic meaning proper to themselves to give out: to give out, that is, to the participant at once so interested and so detached as to be moved to a report of the matter. (Henry James, The American Scene)

I was hardly detached, but otherwise I was qualified. These objects and places spoke to me profoundly, and I was moved to a report of the matter. My Uncle Harry was indifferent to the nuances of exposure. The young man with his camera had come at a time the usual reservations were in abeyance. For Clara, the whole farm was a ruin, an accumulation of losses, a disaster that her Protestant soul must accept, and here comes this youth, a prodigal relation, who saw in these sorry remains something of value. She could not imagine what, but she could believe it was what he saw. The reservations of a lifetime would struggle in her soul with the dim, unlikely hope that the youth might be right.

At the end of the first day, one of a steady drizzle, I had brought my camera on its tripod in from the porch to make sure it was out of the rain. I stood it up in a dark corner of the kitchen, the lens reflecting the lampglow. Clara gazed at it for a moment with her good eye.

"It's not taking pictures now?" she asked me. I assured her it wasn't. "Just so I'm not in them," she said, and glanced down her flat, faded frock. Would anything convince her there was something of value in what she saw?

I was put in the upstairs bedroom I had had as a boy, almost thirty years before. The window frame was just a few inches off the floor, due to some miscalculation, the folds of the gathered lace curtain as dry and crisp as paper. The storm window, put up several years before, had not been taken down. On the doily of the bureau, a satin-lined box that had once contained an ivory-handled comb, mirror and brush set now held several corroded rifle cartridges and the partial handle of the missing mirror. Why had she preserved it? We were alike in that we perceived these objects in the light of our emotions, and judged this the mystic meaning they had to give out.

At the start, my Uncle Harry ignored me. I saw him pass with a hoe, with a pail of water, with another inner tube that needed repairing, indifferent to my presence. I drew him in with questions. Would it rain again? He replied that it usually did. Soon he trailed me around, offered dry suggestions, tested me with his deadpan humor. He still smoked Union Leader, if and when he could find his pipe. When I suggested a picture of himself—the greatest ruin of all—he was compliant. Actually, he had been waiting. In the museum of relics the farm had become, he was one of the few that still almost worked. He pointed that out himself.

I had him walk before me, through the door of the barn he had entered and exited for half a century. He had become, like the denims he wore, an implement of labor, one of the discarded farm tools. A personal pride, however, dormant since the Depression, reasserted itself in the way he accepted my appreciative comments. Why not? Had he not endured and survived it all, like the farm itself? Over several days I had remarked that he changed his hats according to the time of the day and the occasion. A sporty nautical number in the early morning; at high noon and afternoon, one of his wide-brimmed straws. In the dusk of evening, he preferred an old felt, with a narrow brim, the color and texture of tar paper. All hats suited him fine. The only piece of apparel we both found out of fashion was new overalls, blue stripes on white, that in no way adapted to his figure or movements and gave off the rasp of a file. He was quick to sense my disapproval and stopped wearing them.

It was Clara's suggestion that I might look in on Ed's place.

Ed was a bachelor, related by marriage, who had died several weeks before my arrival. His small farmhouse was directly across the road. I found the house as a bachelor would have left it. The bric-a-brac of a lifetime—pillboxes, pincushions, shotgun shells, flashlights, a watch and chain, a few snap-shots. Although the bed had been made, the imprint of his body remained in the mattress, his feet were visible in the shoes beneath it. What I saw on the ground glass evoked in me a commingling of tenderness, pity and sorrow, to the exclusion of more searing emotions. Was there another American emotion to match pathos? Were not tragic sentiments alien to a free people who were free to choose, and chose more earthly adornments? "Ed passed on last month," Harry had said, as if he had glanced up just a bit too late to catch him. What he seemed to see was a movement of the bushes edging the drive.

One evening, Clara had again shown me a photograph of the Morris family back in Ohio in the late eighties, showing all members except my father and Harry, forming a line in front of a clapboard house in a fresh fall of snow. Their names had been read aloud to me by Harry—Mitchell and Emerson, Ivy and Mae, Martha and Francena—on and on through a dozen. A crack in time had been made by the click of a shutter, through which I could peer into a world that had vanished. This fact exceeded my grasp, but it excited my emotions. The following day I took the photograph into the open air and pinned it to the clapboards on one side of the house. I saw it clearly on the ground glass before the shutter clicked. Was it in this wise I hoped to postpone what was vanishing? A simpler ritual of survival would be hard to imagine. By stopping time, I hoped to suspend mortality.

Since I had taken all of the interior shots without artificial lighting, I was anxious to get the negatives developed, and see what I had done. While they were being processed in Lincoln, I drove around through the neighboring towns, and found many structures of interest. In Central City I woke up the barber, dozing in his chair after lunch. He remembered my father—a railroad man who had turned to raising chickens—but he had no memory of the boy who had sat on the board placed on the chair arms, heard the chirp of the shears, and smelled the tonic water doused on his hair. There had been a lot of boys. Looking at me, front and side, brought none of them to mind.

I stayed on for several days in Lincoln, photographing what I found on the roads around it. Some twenty miles to the south, in beautiful rolling country, lush and green with the spring rains, I came on a house set back from the road in a clump of evergreens. Through the broken windows of the first floor I could see the fields behind it. The tilted, creaking windmill had a mournful look. I carted my camera and tripod up the rain-gutted driveway past a trench piled high with empty cans and trash. Most of the cans looked new, with colorful paper labels. As I approached the house, and set up my tripod, the mournful groaning of the windmill held my attention. The wind wheel itself soared high above the trees into the slanting light. I noted the low fenced-in porch that occupied one corner of the second floor. Farther back I could see a partially opened screen. Tatters of curtains hung at a window. I was focusing on the ground glass, my hands cupped to my face, when I saw this hand, or rather this claw, curl slowly over the fence rail, then grip it. The chill of terror I felt tingled my scalp. I controlled my impulse to run, fooled a bit with my camera, then made my way down the drive to the road. From the seat of the car I dared to peer back, to see the tuft of white hair above a dark forehead. The wind wheel screeched and grated. After two false starts, I managed to make a clammy-handed getaway. The sense that I was pursued led me to crouch over the wheel, press the gas pedal to the floor. I felt I had seen enough to know that this creature might have been one of my abandoned relations, preferring to crumble with the ruins rather than to leave them. Topping a rise, I saw, with relief, the tower of the new capitol building. "You be sure you see it, Wright," my Aunt Clara had told me. "It's one of the wonders of the world."

On the ground glass of the negative viewer in the Eastman photographic store, I had my first clear and reassuring impression of several weeks' work. I also wanted a simple, direct narrative that would read, if possible, like a novel, giving uninhibited expression to the sentiments and conflicts of a late-returning native. I had grown to feel such affection for the home place, and its inhabitants, that I was at ease with the sentimental appeal it would have for this urban man and wife, and their snotty kids. That was how I saw it. A young man not unlike myself, a long-departed native son, who had thought he had put all this behind him, caught up in the appeal it proved to have for his city wife and kids, and for himself. At the point he was prepared to "settle down," however, perhaps in the house just vacated by Ed, his wife would bring him to his senses and they would continue down the road, his home town the next in my series of photo-text volumes.

I had these scenarios in mind while I was driving back to Philadelphia, trying out the voice I felt to be appropriate, that of a man who had been born and bred in this landscape, had once, briefly, lived on this farm, and had fortunately never lost his faculty of dramatizing his reflections in the vernacular of his experience. What would better suit my sentiments, and my intentions, than the first-person-singular "I" of the very involved author. What reason did I have for concealment? The story of a native's return was an old one, and I would give it a Nebraska accent. As for the dangers of this voice—sentimental, self-indulgent, so appealingly "natural" yet so open to counterfeit and make-believe—I knew about such things in the abstract and I would try to keep the writer under control. There were many precedents, most of them good ones. "I should not talk so much about myself," Thoreau had advised me, "if there were anybody else I knew as well."

How sensible that sounded! And how much to the point of what I had in mind. In my enthusiasm, I was aware of everything about this voice but the pitfalls, the first being the author's evangelical fervor for what he intended to do. How could I miss, since all I had to do was clearly express what I was feeling! These feelings were running so high that I sat down, on arriving in Bryn Mawr, to capture snatches of the dialogue I had been having with the characters, most of them anxious to make this city boy and his family feel right at home.

In mid-July, I stopped writing and went into the darkroom, which also happened to be the coolest part of our new accommodations. On the sale of the property in which we had been living, we had moved over a garage in suburban Bryn Mawr, with "access," as it was called, to the kitchen. We had come by this windfall, in very elegant surroundings, including a museum of antiques, because my wife proved to be the teacher of one of the resident girls. Her older sister had also attended Baldwin, but was currently at Bennington, in Vermont. Our move was actually illegal, in such a restricted area, but the ample and hoarsely baying landlady (I liked her, and arranged an appearance in one of my novels) appreciated both our company and the rent. We had the run of the house, when it was empty, and of the patio most of the summer, the long-gone-to-seed and weedy garden ornamented with concrete statuary. I used the pantry off the kitchen as my darkroom. Over the summer, my friend Eiseley continued his nature studies in the surrounding acreage. After a long day in the darkroom I would show my wife and the Eiseleys the new enlargements I had made. Washing these prints in the tub, then squeegeeing them dry on the ferrotype plates, was back-breaking work. I had to have the glossy prints for the book, however, and I frequently misjudged in the darkroom what I saw later in the full light of day. I wanted both the crisp detail and the bold pattern of light and shadow, velvety blacks and luminous whites. Mabel Eiseley, in particular, was appreciative of the Home Place interiors. With a hundred or more of these prints to choose from, I turned back to the narrative, samples of which I read to the Eiseleys. Early in September, I had a complete, readable draft.

I felt so confident about what I had done—I was so open to my own persuasion—that I again went directly to Max Perkins. He liked it, but he had his reservations about the prospective sales. Charles Scribner, Jr., had just joined the firm, and Max gave him the book for his opinion. To my astonishment (Charles was just out of Princeton), he was enthusiastic about it, and took charge of its production. My idea was, after *The Inhabitants*, to publish the book in the format of a novel, with a photograph facing each page of text. Cropping would mutilate the carefully framed eight-by-ten images, but would focus on a few of the essentials. It seemed imperative to me, at the expense of the photographs, that the text should read like a novel. Young Scribner shared this opinion. Once more Pete Dymock would supervise the press run, and no sensible expense would be spared in the book's production. The jacket would feature the photograph of a piece of burlap, on which, in red, the words THE HOME PLACE would appear to be stenciled.

The first-person voice of *The Home Place* seemed equally effective for the next book, *The World in the Attic*, where Muncy's city-bred boy will prophetically comment, "Is this God's country, Mummy, or is it still Daddy's?"—a question this book would try to answer.

What was I feeling? Something I might call Home Town nausea. I can get it in a lunch room, or at the bend in a road where a telephone pole tips out of a clutter of weeds. Or a track crossing where you lean out to peer into nowhere in both directions. At such times it's hard to tell where the nostalgia stops, the nausea begins. While you're in the grip of one, the other sets in.

After a few weeks of work, it seemed to me that the writing had less of the sentimental "grit" that I could taste in *The Home Place*, but retained the bounce and expectancy crucial to Muncy's experience. But as the plot thickened I was made aware of the hazards of the first-person voice. The ease and flow of the story either concealed, or made light of, the double role of Muncy as a character and as a stand-in for the author. I found it an authorial privilege to exploit this ambivalence. At any moment, just by clearing my throat, I could speak from the wings on matters of morals and taste where I happened to feel strongly. This agreeable afflatus buoyed up the author, and I would soon come to recognize its presence in numerous works of Mark Twain. The ambivalence that is part of the voice itself is subject to both deliberate and unconscious manipulation. The voice that I am now using to describe this occasion, and to comment on it with some detachment, is relatively free of the "self" deception that comes so easily to the "I" as narrator but is inherent in the "I" itself, usually concealed. The impersonal narration that the reader wants, and that is crucial to the craft of fiction, is to some extent qualified or confuted the moment the writer says "I." The nuances of ambiguity in this practice are endless. Years after *The World in the Attic* was published, I would read *The Fall*, by Albert Camus, and have full exposure to the complexities of the voice I had ingenuously adopted. *The Attic* was part of my own emerging world of fiction—not a place on the map, like *The Home Place*—and I was licensed to accommodate or reject as much of the past or the present as I found to my purpose.

The characters of Mr. Purdy and Caddy Hibbard, for example, were imported from my wife's home in Cleveland—Purdy Mother's neighborly handyman, Caddy Hibbard her grandmother—but the unexpected appearance of Tom Scanlon, peripheral to the interests of the novel, would prove to be crucial to much of the fiction I wrote in the fifties, including *Ceremony in Lone Tree*. As I walked along a spur of tracks, in *The World in the Attic*, that proved to lead me nowhere, I was putting down the rails and ties necessary to the novels shaping in my imagination. Joyce's "commodius vicus of recirculation," part of my nature before it was part of my reading, an up-and-downward spiraling of my preoccupations, would prove to lead me away and upward even as it led me back and downward. The role of recurrence is so central to my nature that I sense, in what appears to be new, the other side, the far side, of what appears to be old, and contradicts our sense of time as linear. We plainly lack the faculty to grasp time, in its essence, but the spiral accommodates my own impressions and lends itself to the purposes of fiction. Tom Scanlon, in *Ceremony*, is preparing to sit at the window with no obstruction but the sky:

Come to the window. The one at the rear of the Lone Tree Hotel. The view is to the west. There is no obstruction but the sky. *Although there is no one outside to look in, the yellow blind is drawn at the window, and between it and the pane a fly is trapped. He has stopped buzzing. Only the crawling shadow can be seen. Before the whistle of the train is heard the loose pane rattles like a simmering pot, then stops, as if pressed by a hand, as the train goes past. The blind sucks inward and the dangling cord drags in the dust on the sill.*

*I*n February, after a long and humiliating decline, my father-in-law died. My wife's mother called from Cleveland, and we took the night train from Philadelphia. Flares were burning to keep the track switches from freezing, as I had so often seen them in my boyhood. We were met at the station by the family doctor, the first to tell us that he thought it all for the best. In her kimono with the faded dragons, a recent gift from her daughter, Mother came to the door carrying the clothes she would put on in the bathroom. The house was cold, the heat having been turned off to save fuel. Mother approached me, to pluck a few hairs from the collar of my topcoat. Did I detect in her appraisal of my tie a flicker of approval?

"Do you suppose," she said to my wife, "that one of your father's shirts might fit him?"

"We've already gone into that, Mother. Daddy's shirts are all too long in the sleeves."

In the cold winter light at the bird box window, the Grandmother clattered her cane on the radiator. I could see only the tight topknot of her gray hair, the claw of the hand that gripped the cane. Had anyone troubled to tell her that her son lay dead in the upstairs bedroom? Flecks of light glittered on her steel-rimmed glasses. Her suppressed rage seemed to actually shrink her to a grizzled, wizened fury. On me and my wife, on her daughter-in-law, and on the house itself, she passed a verdict of eternal hellfire.

"We are all going to have to be on our good behavior," said Mother, "and that includes Mrs. You-know-who." Once more the Grandmother raised her cane and brought it down with a whack on the radiator.

"She wants her oatmeal," said Mother, "but I am no longer so sure that Mrs. You-know-who is always going to get just what she wants."

Nevertheless, during the week we were in Cleveland, we were all on our good behavior, including the Grandmother. One of my father-in-law's white shirts (the cuffs doubled back) looked quite acceptable under my coat. One of Charles's black ties pleased both ladies. A steady flow of friends, and a few dignitaries—snow had been cleared so they could use the front entrance—stopped to pay their respects to the dead, but lingered to marvel at the Grandmother, just one year short of her centennial celebration. The front room glowed with their admiration. Where had Mother been *keeping* her? they asked. A grizzled and bearded ninety-nine-year-old lady who told her stories like the comedians on the phonograph records, and who had also, among other things, set her sharp eyes on Abe Lincoln. (Who was to say that she hadn't?) A tall beanstalk of a man, solemn and silent, gripping the lapels of his coat as he rambled. What he had said had not much interested an eight-year-old girl, but she would have voted for him if she could have. She had always voted Republican.

Seldom as low as it had looked that morning, the Grandmother's self-esteem was restored by the praise and attention of the guests. One story followed another, all of them good, many I had not previously heard, their climax followed by a period of silence that some felt to be ominous. Was she, perhaps, a bit overexcited? For a long countdown of twenty or

140

thirty seconds she was silent, her head bowed, as if she had put it all behind her, then her right foot would lift from the floor until her right hand pegged it down, with a slap on the knee. These yarns were told without a pause, through half-clenched false teeth, her mouth spread wide in what might have been a complicitous smile or a painful grimace. At these moments I saw how closely she resembled her son. He, too, forced his words between half-clenched teeth, and suppressed all but the snort of his laughter. A box of chocolates placed in her lap was found to be half empty before taken from her.

All of these days of mourning, the Grandmother flowered, mumbling to some, croaking hoarsely to others, and sometimes uttering little barks in her sleep, as if playing with children. All the bad birds had the run of the bird box now that her attention was elsewhere, the big fierce jays hammering on the window until Mother came at them with a broom. The social life tired the Grandmother; she might sleep through the early breakfast or fail to appear at lunch, obliging my wife to go to the basement to see if she might be down there ironing. There was no way to tell, except by looking, if she was squatted on the stool, under the dripping water closet.

Wearing blue pumps, with bows, carrying a small blue purse, the veil of her blue straw hat shrouding her remarkable eyes, my mother-in-law, with her sober, dignified manner, would have been highly approved of by her husband. The service attracted a large number of his former students, assorted academic people and numerous local merchants, with their families, all who knew Professor Finfrock as "Fin." The family shopping having been left to him, Mother knew none of these people personally. Mr. Garbanzo, owner of the delicatessen where Fin got his liver sausage and his cheesecake, gripped my hand firmly between his own and looked hard into my eyes. His own were bloodshot from weeping. His wife, too (who helped him on weekends), searched my face for the loss that made it difficult for her to speak. She stared at my wife and me with sorrow and compassion. To have had such a man as a father! Even her children, hovering behind her, knew and loved him. In the men's washroom, bluff and hearty merchants stood about blowing their noses, puffing on cigarettes. Sidelong, I caught their glances. Had I known him well enough to measure my loss?

My wife excused herself, and I later found her seated in the car, red-eyed and tearful. Why was it necessary for us to experience our losses through others? In my measurably less loving sorrow, I remembered I had not wept for my father. Had my too-great self-sufficiency deprived me of the ties that were common to so many? "They really loved him," cried my wife, "they really did!"

I was at once sorrowful, saddened and shamefaced. My family ties had been on the fringe of other families, from where I spied on them from pantries, or concealed by the cloak that draped the dining room table. Later I would be consoled to share this hideaway with Isaak Babel. The losses I had experienced were real enough, but not of the sort that diminished my nature. No man was an island, but I was far from being washed into the sea. I had not felt the shock nor the grief of Miss Lyle, the dead man's secretary, who had been put to bed and sedated to make this loss bearable. What I felt the most intensely was that I had been cut, but proved to be a poor bleeder. I lacked the close, the confining, the indispensable ties that when cut left lacerations. I was a Band-Aid victim, and it was my full knowledge of this deflated loss that filmed my eyes.

We took the train to Covington, in central Ohio, for the burial. Real grass still covered these graves, some of it new, the dark, wet earth piled like coal to one side. A few relations, with their families, stood behind us, and at the edge of the graveyard I could see a few others, reluctant to be counted among the serious mourners. At my side, however, a lean, dapper-looking man, a topcoat over his barber's smock, had found a place for himself. Tufts of white hair grew out of his large ears. He felt it important to explain to me that he had left his shop full of clients, to pay his respects. Fin had been his friend for fifty-three years. Two or three times a year, with the exception of these last years, Professor Finfrock had driven all the way to Covington for a shave, a haircut, a massage, and to be brought up to date on all that had happened, in case anything had. For all of Fin's fame—that had been the barber's word—he had remained a small-town man at heart. Local Covington people were those he really cared about. As a fairly young man, the barber had recognized that his friend Fin would be an exceptional man. And how was that? His hat size. A full quarter size larger than the average. And this was after his hair had been trimmed at the sides, not when it was full.

It was to him, the barber advised me, that the dean of the law school unburdened himself in both professional and personal matters. It would surprise me to learn, he said, what they had discussed. Speaking frankly to the man who was now head of the family (the barber had been the first to declare it!), he suggested that I should pay him a visit and have a little talk while having my hair cut, since he could see that I shaved myself.

We rode back into town together, the barber seated at the front with the cabdriver, who happened to be one of his clients. His shop proved to be a flight of steps up from the street, overlooking the roofed bench of the shoeshine stand. Through the wide front window, like Eddie Cahow's, I could see that one of the barber chairs was occupied, the client stretched out horizontal, but the second chair sat empty, the cloth folded across the chair arm, facing the street. Did this provide me with the missing context to my own dormant emotions? My eyes filmed over. I put the tip of my tongue to dry lips. I could hear the voice of Eddie Cahow greet me as he tapped his comb on the starched cuff of his sleeve. The barber was aware of my swollen emotions.

"I could tell you some things that would surprise you," he said. "Now you come and see me!"

For the moment we stood there, I was certain that I might. What secret life did my father-in-law share with his barber?

Speaking directly to me (was it as head of the family?), my mother-in-law said, "Do you think that was called for?" It was to me she had spoken, not my wife. I could feel both her concern and her assurance. "Tell him," she said to her daughter, "that if he wants to be surprised, he needn't come all the way to Covington for it."

This would prove to be a simple statement of fact. No one would surprise me, again and again, and again, like my mother-in-law.

Clarence Millard Finfrock, much loved and sorely missed by those who were not members of his intimate family, was the only paterfamilias I had experienced. I had grown accustomed to his solid, reassuring, expansive presence, his easily given affection. "My son-in-law," he would say, introducing me, a statement in which we both took pride. One day a van would arrive from Cleveland with Mother's Oriental rug, the Chippendale secretary, the Webster's dictionary on the tripod stand, the signed volumes from famous bird lovers, the two framed Audubon prints, and three barrels of unsorted worlds from several attics: Charles's samurai sword, his tennis racquet, and the catcher's glove and mask of "Fin" Finfrock, along with two Louisville Slugger bats.

Max Perkins unexpectedly died before *The Home Place* was published, a shock no one who knew him was prepared for, but it pleased me to think that he would have liked the book's critical reception. Privately I was alerted to my own accumulating losses. It put me back to work on *The World in the Attic*, which I delivered to Scribner's in the fall, at which time I had a long and frank discussion with my new editor, Wally Meyer. Once more, the reception of a book of mine had been good, but not the sales. There was no indication, Wally pointed out to me, that the buying public shared my enthusiasm for the new photo-text format. There was growing indication—which he showed me—that even reviewers were confused as to the purposes of the author. Was he a writer who liked to take photographs, or a photographer who liked to do a little writing? In either case, it played hell with the publisher's intent to establish a new author. The public had never taken well to the ambidextrous talent. Wally Meyer had read, and liked, *The World in the Attic* as a *novel*, without any reference to the photographs. If I would excuse him for speaking frankly, the photographs *distracted* him from the writing. That had also proved to be true of other readers. If I was to hold on to the readers I had (*had?*), I needed their undivided attention. To put it plainly, Scribner's would be glad to publish *The World in the Attic* as a novel, without pictures, but not as another photo-text volume. Why didn't I think about it over the weekend?

I thought long and hard about it even before the weekend, as I rode on a double-decker bus toward the Village, from where I called Wally to reassure him that I, too, was tired of confused readers, and looked forward to my novel being published without photographs.

*A*t summer camp on Cape Cod, at school in England and in her years at Scripps College, my wife had written her "Dear Daddy and Mother" letters to her father, and he had written to her. Now, weekly, she heard from Mother, on stationery she had received for Christmas. They were unmistakably the letters of the woman we knew, leader of bird club hikes and salvager of paper towels, but they were also legible and of interest. Like my Aunt Winona, Mother wrote a fine, slanting Spencerian hand.

After the festive excitement of the period of mourning, the Grandmother had suffered a relapse and been put to bed. There she stayed, refusing food, ignoring all calls to the bathroom. She was taken to a rest home, where the attendants gave her, among other things, the first bath she had had in years. The shock had been too much. A few weeks short of her hundredth birthday, she died.

That left Mother alone with the birds at the feed box, most of them bad. They hammered on the windows, in the clogged gutters, and drilled holes in the curling shingles. Her neighbor Mr. Parsons, as he had for years, cut the grass, forked up the compost, took down the storm windows, put up the screens, and shopped for items that were not delivered. Three to four months too late, by Parsons' calculations, she had made up her mind about the new refrigerator. Before a sale was offered in this model, she had been advised to sell the house. Until that was done, the old ice chest would do very well.

In the fall she surprised us with an unexpected visit, calling from the bus depot in Philadelphia. Two of the friends she made on this excursion would prove to be loyal correspondents. The one from Ann Arbor she visited over Christmas. Seeing for herself how we personally lived—two small rooms over a double garage—although frequently described and well illustrated, came to Mother as a great surprise. Why didn't we build a house? We were huddled together at a table without room for our legs. I sat silent while my wife explained that building a house required a large sum of money, even with a mortgage. Mother sat—not to be idle while talking— with a bowl of unshelled almonds. Now and then she ate one. "Your father was the one to do this," she said to us both, having reference to the almonds, not the house. One of the many things her husband had mastered in more than forty years of marriage was the seamless way his wife began and terminated discussions.

"You still can't build a house without a lot," she said. "Have you thought of that?"

Back home in Cleveland, having had several weeks to think it over, she wrote to her daughter suggesting a loan of money, without interest, if that would help. My wife wrote back to say that would help. Several weeks later, Mother wrote to say that her loan was contingent on our having a lot. More time was necessary to clarify this problem, and agree on a sum of five thousand dollars. Five or six weeks of clippings, cut from magazines and newspapers, concerned the pitfalls of building a house. Why didn't we just buy one? She called after midnight to ask this question. Several months later—we had shelved the idea—a cashier's check for five thousand dollars was found among a fresh collection of clippings, on the subject of prefab housing.

We never learned, but the way to deal with Mother was to forget that any deal was pending. One day she would surprise you. Sometimes even favorably. Property was expensive in Bryn Mawr, but a few miles farther west, in Wayne, we found a fine half-acre corner lot, with several great tulip trees and no pressing neighbors. The local real estate agent put us in touch with a young architect from Princeton who had been nurtured on Scott Fitzgerald. The first detail he showed us of our prospective house was a carriage lamp. He would build us a house of his own design, on a concrete slab, for $12,500. One of these houses had actually been built, and we liked it. They were California-style ranch houses, a bit of Hansel and Gretel for the Main Line, with an airy open carport joining the house to a garage. To swing this deal we needed five thousand dollars in cash, and a ten-thousand-dollar mortgage. The cost to us, plus taxes, would be sixty-eight dollars a month.

Pictures were sent to Mother of the architect's drawing, showing the shrubs, the redwood fencing, the children and pets at play, and the surround of park-like woods. That much was true. From Cuyahoga Falls, Ohio, where she had gone bird-watching, Mother sent us more clippings of prefabs, and articles warning us about loan sharks. The lot paid for, we still ended up short. With our dream house and much of our future at stake—as I put it in my letter to Charles Scribner, Sr., I was taking the liberty of asking him for an advance of one thousand dollars on my next two books. I was a productive and up-and-coming writer. He had said so himself, on our visit to the Scribner home in Far Hills, New Jersey, the heart of fox-hunting country. I also thought my appeal was in the tradition much honored by Scribner's in dealing with young and needy writers. With some confidence, I sent the letter off. Very quickly I had Mr. Scribner's reply. Charles Scribner's Sons was a commercial publisher, not a bank. Each year they were obliged to borrow the money from a bank to finance the next year's operation. Of the four books of mine that Scribner's had published, not one had been commercially successful. If they had many authors with this record, no bank would be advised to lend them money. He sent his regards to my wife.

I cite this incident not to reveal the greedy self-interest of the publisher who is insensitive to the plight of the author, but the hold that a few self-serving myths continue to exert on "creative" writers, young and old. Charles Scribner's response to my letter was a bit on the blunt side, but sensible. In the last twenty years, the myth-making has shifted from the charitable, far-seeing editor, to the plush contract for paperback, movie and other subsidiary sources of revenue. A half dozen of these "big" deals, usually headlined in the newspapers, will sustain the largely baseless dreams of the jackpot for several hundred thousand writers.

What do you have, a sensible moneylender asked me, in the way of collateral? The word had for me an historic ring! How often my father had called upon it to gild the towers of his Zenith. "Kid," he would say, chewing up a match, "let's see what we got in the way of collateral." It was never much. To my knowledge, it was never enough.

The only collateral we had was two camera lenses, an enlarger and a quantity of books. Having read and appreciated the O. Henry story, my wife would not hear of my selling my watch to buy a comb for the hair she planned to cut. Over a period of fifteen years, I had assembled with much diligence and some sacrifice an unusual collection of American first editions. A few appreciative dealers had fondled them with lust and admiration. We did a thriving business in creative swapping. But I had to have cash.

In the weeks that buyers pawed over our lovelies, and sprawled on the floor discussing the fine points, I learned the irrelevance of "value" in a market of buying and selling. The value of the books was not questioned. But what I mistakenly wanted was money. I managed to sell them, not to a dealer, whose top offer was fifteen cents on the dollar, but to the library of Haverford College, which recognized them as a windfall. My friend Eiseley bought a few titles—one a fine English edition of Doughty's *Arabia Deserta*—and I had the questionable gratification of knowing that I had taken a step

150

he could not himself have taken. So he told me. We were like Huck Finn and Tom Sawyer pondering, in a cave, our blood ties and steadfast loyalties. I shared his feelings, but I didn't want to be beholden to something that could be bought and sold.

Late in the fall, the house construction began, and two or three times a week we drove by to see what had been done. Three of the big tulip trees had to be uprooted to make room for the foundation. The day the concrete slab was poured, I thought it must be for the garage, not the house. How small it looked! The winter rains soaked the exposed studs and beams, and local hoodlums poked holes in the sheets of insulation. Every night it rained, I lay awake thinking about the house. Why hadn't somebody told us not to start building in the winter? On stormy days it looked vandalized; with the melting of the snow it looked fire-gutted. Small fry built fires in the fireplace. Sometimes I feared to drive by, certain that nothing would be there. Then in March the redwood shakes arrived from California, and on weekends I helped nail them to the exterior. It almost looked like it might prove to be a real *house*. With the bedrooms freshly plastered and papered, I spent the nights in the living room, sleeping on a mattress. The casement windows were in place, but not glazed. They were so low to the yard that passing dogs stopped by to peer in at me. The night noises scared me to death. I kept a battery radio playing. The day the windows were glazed, the asphalt tile, in a black and white mix, was laid on the concrete slab. Looking about me in the early dawn light, I was struck by how the surface gleamed like ice. I thought it beautiful! How explain it? The gloss proved to be a film of water. It splashed when I walked about on it. Broken plumbing? Had the builder struck water? No, it was merely the May humidity, in conjunction with the cold concrete slab. Had we built a house only fish could live in? A half dozen of our friends came to ponder the problem while we picnicked in the carport. The solution proved to be newspapers spread to cover every inch of the floor. My wife's mother would have loved it. Later that same day, we actually moved in.

That night, when we turned out the lights, the Japanese

screens at the windows were seductively transparent. People passing in cars honked their horns and hooted. We undressed in the dark. It wasn't just what we had had in mind, but we both agreed, sipping coffee out of a thermos, that if it's what you really want, there's nothing like being in your own place.

In July, to help us with the landscaping, Mother paid us a second visit. She brought packets of seeds from the basement, along with seedlings of ice plant and ivy wrapped in damp paper towels by Mr. Parsons. On this trip she had taken the train to Paoli, a stop a few miles to the west, where I found her on the platform in a deep discussion she was reluctant to interrupt. The gentleman lived in Villanova, where both he and his wife made a specialty of ice plants, and plans were made for us to visit them, before they visited us.

The great view of our place was to be had from the west, and I drove an extra mile to enjoy it. The house did seem to have popped right out of the ground, and looked as natural as a mushroom. There was even smoke in the chimney from the trash burning in the fireplace. I stopped the car to give Mother time to absorb the details. The gravel in the driveway shimmered in the sunlight. Two of the fallen trees had been dragged to make a rustic fence at the rear. My mix of pleasure, pride and relief made it difficult for me to speak. Mother had always surprised us. This time had we surprised Mother?

"Am I to believe you have lilies of the valley?" she said. I had no idea. Everything and nothing seemed to be in profusion at the weedy top of the lot. Mother got out of the car— she wore her low-heeled, sensible pumps for traveling—to zig-zag about in our upper lot, collecting herself a nosegay. Time after time she displayed her backside. Now and then she stood erect to wag her hand at the gnats buzzing her face. She had forgotten about me, and the house, and she was inattentive, in her absorption, to the approach of her daughter. There was no greeting, but a discussion once dropped, somewhere in the past, about nosegays or lilies of the valley, was resumed without comment. They stood together, mother and daughter, in the dapple of morning shadow and sunlight, and I could hear the Latin names of the flowers fall from their lips like liturgical chanting. My wife had been well schooled in these matters, and I noted the eagerness of her collaboration. Her eyes were sharp. She found, in the weeds, specimens that Mother had overlooked. From where I sat in the car, the motor still idling, I loved them both. In being themselves, they were all women who turn from pride-filled young husbands, and idling motors, to consider the lilies of the field, this being one on which we had taken a lease.

I don't recall Mother ever saying what her impressions were of the house. In the tiny kitchen, a dazzle of sunlight off the stainless-steel sink, she removed her attractive bonnet to cool her face with a few dabs of water. Her large eyes were shining as she turned to gaze at me, blankly.

"Where am I to put this?" she said, smoothing out the paper towel she had just dampened. During her three-day visit, mother, daughter and son-in-law worked in the field like peasants.

My study was the bedroom at the back of the house. In the humid heat of summer, I was up and in it early, wearing the swimming trunks I had brought from California. Mother did not approve. She suggested a boady screen at the door to my room. I usually worked till lunch, then picked up again in the midafternoon. If it was going well, I averaged eight to ten hours of work a day.

As I sit here writing, it occurs to me that with the new house I finally had a *desk*. Over the years, in and out of cramped quarters, I had used coffee tables, the seats of chairs, packing boxes, anything that proved to be reasonably solid. I sat on car seats, on cushions, or, if I proved to be lucky, in the low-slung comforts of a Morris chair. All of these accommodations cramped my back, and led to many fruitless discussions.

My first real desk, one with drawers, legs and an actual compartment for the typewriter, had to be dismantled to get it into the study. This proved to be impossible. No way was discovered to get at the screws that cunningly held it together. The solution was to saw off the legs, four inches above the floor, then reattach them once the desk was in the study. It worked well, and I recommend it. I have sometimes wondered if the desk is still there.

This one had a top of dark-green cork-like material in which many names and dates had already been carved, along with three side drawers with adjustable dividers, and a slide shelf at the top on which I could rest my feet. But what good is a desk like that without the appropriate chair?

The secret heart of my long torment was the missing chair. With the purchase of the one on which I am now seated, I brought to an end so many discomforts I prefer not to recall them. But one can see them in the chair's survival. The leather back is split, the cushioned arms are peeling, the padding held in place by strips of black and green adhesive, a cushion now protects me from the springs of the seat, but the great comforts of this chair have not diminished. They are part of my survival; they are the woof of my productive life. The secret of this chair is the back which tilts separately from the seat. That is the touch of genius. That is what I swapped my royalties for, the advance I had received on *Man and Boy*. I went into a store on Chestnut Street in Philadelphia, sat and tilted in the chair, and paid cash for it. It was more money than we had spent for the refrigerator. For weeks I felt both great and guilty. For more than thirty years I have simply felt great.

When Saul Bellow came to see me in my new study, I made him sit in the chair and sang its praises. He had to have one in his house near Bard College. But masterpiece chairs are not so easily come by. Nobody in Poughkeepsie had anything like it. We talked about it a lot, but the last time I saw him in *his* study, he was on one of those things they give to typists. I brought the matter up again, about twenty years later, but I could see it was a sore subject. I thought of it when he won the Nobel Prize. Did he finally get the good chair?

This may seem much ado about not enough, but a great chair is worth whatever it takes, and that is bottom advice.

I still remember the delivery. The rather elegant truck, with the firm's coat of arms, pulled into the driveway and just sat there. The driver checked the address; I understood his problem. Before he went away, I hurried out to reassure him. This was the address. This was where the chair belonged.

Seated in that chair, at my new desk, at my old but reliable typewriter, I was able to release what had been accumulating in me through the distractions and frustrations of house building.

The liquid note of the thrush entered the house through the flowering privet, through the clumps of rhododendron, from where he whistled in the bed of pachysandra, but the Grandmother, eavesdropping on the stairs, wished he would shut up.

The Deep Sleep flowed from this opening line as if I were recording it all as it happened. We had a home of our own, work of our own, I had a desk, a chair and a novel of my own, a ream of rag-content paper, and a lust for work. To save paper, all of my first drafts were single-spaced.

$\mathcal{W}$hen my mother-in-law stepped from the car to pluck a nosegay of wildflowers from the weeds of our lot, I had been brought face to face with my subject. For years I had pondered her remarkable nature, or her lack of it, since I had entered her home and found her crouched to spread newspapers on the kitchen linoleum. The bizarre side of this subject I had written about in a story, "The Ram in the Thicket," but my caricature lacked all of the elusive essentials. What, indeed, were they? What made Mother tick? Why did her husband, a man of considerable distinction, admired and loved by many people, find in her a source of comfort and strength that justified his many deprivations? I was not merely curious; I felt compelled to try to fathom this woman as a matter of a writer's self-respect. Mother was a mystery only a novelist might solve.

The occasion was at hand in her husband's death and the ceremony of mourning. I would see Mother through the eyes of those who believed they knew her, as well as one pair of eyes that suspended judgment. Each of these separate witnesses would have a voice. If there were many sides to her inscrutable nature, this might be one way to reveal them. I felt a compelling interest to know, but no assurance whatsoever as to what I would find. I also felt a kinship with the Grandmother and the handyman, Parsons, both outsiders. So, too, was I.

The novel *Man and Boy*, rejected by Scribner's, when published by Knopf was so well received, critically, that they were persuaded, largely through the zeal of my friend Harry Ford, to publish *The Works of Love*, the saga of Will Brady's downward path from the Western plains to his end in Chicago. I had reduced the bulk of a long and often incoherent manuscript to the solo recital of a single, monotonous voice, unvarying in its tone, but true to Brady's muted nature. It was, in fact, my first plains song, plucked out on one string and mournfully repeated. The brighter touches—and there had surely been a few—were downpedaled or eliminated: adagio, moderato, lento, all the way. One strong, vibrant plucking of the plains chord sustained to the end.

As Brady drifted eastward, and grew older—a slight change in tempo, but not in key—the author increasingly identified with his nature to the extent of becoming a double agent, speaking in one voice for both of them. These passages, and there are too many of them, make an explicit and painful appeal to the reader's sympathies and emotions. Confused as to whose emotions were involved, and the voice appropriate to their control, the writer often lost the distance necessary to distinguish between sentiment and the sentimental. A clear vein of sentiment is crucial to Brady, and constitutes the reedy, windblown music of his nature, but in moments of stress, as he grows older, it frays into the mawkish and pathetic. A more sophisticated writer than I was at the time would have permitted the character some indulgence, but spared both the author and the reader. As a fully committed double agent, I was unaware of this distinction.

My friend Eiseley had read and liked the manuscript—he, too, would identify with the subject—and on the day I signed the contract, in New York, I met Alfred A. Knopf himself, the

Grand Panjandrum, an image that well suited his person. In the comparative dimness of his inner sanctum, lit up by his taste in color, we had a brief discussion about Willa Cather, the original plains exile. I gathered he had sampled enough of my novel to know we were both from the same region. I considered it a great honor, I told him, to have the Borzoi insignia on my books. In moments of indecision I had bought Borzoi books on the strength of their design, their colorful boards, their endpapers, their sensible size, their this, their that; it hardly mattered who wrote them. (I am speaking of *secondhand* books; firsthand books were for buyers, not authors.) One of the books I had not sold to Haverford College had been the Knopf edition of Kafka's *The Trial*, with its marvelous jacket, stamped cloth and limp binding. I stop writing at this point to take it from the shelf and admire it.

In the perspective of survival, these were good years. My wife lived in her work, as I did in mine, and these years we lived our lives together. Old friends and new friends came to visit us in our new home, and in these settings I admired and took pride in my wife. Her friends from England and Holland might pay us a visit, an occasion for much tooting on the recorders, and fortissimo playing on the piano, some of it for four hands. The Eiseleys were often part of these occasions, and became friends of our friends. If I went to New York I often stayed with Harry and Elizabeth Ford, and many times a year they came down to see us with good wine and Southern bourbon in their luggage. Wine had not been part of our lives in the past, but it would figure highly in my future. I soon knew the taste and virtues of good bourbon, but a little of it always proved to be enough. Built into me below the level of consideration was the Protestant ethic of moderation, the least sharable of fraternal virtues. Not to have another one, and still another, and the final one for the road is to cast a palpable blight on the good fellowship fermented spirits exist to encourage. Unless tempted with the heavy Italian vermouth Punt e Mes, for which I have a moderate passion (is that a protesting contradiction?), I am drier than usual when solo, and might forget to order what I really enjoy.

In the late forties and early fifties, I was able to sell the magazine section of the *New York Times* a few of my photo-text articles, similar in tone and style to my books. I might take off for Michigan, to visit my friend Robert Horton, or on the suggestion of a young woman at Scribner's, who liked *The World in the Attic*, I would head for her home place in southern Indiana. Her mother lived in a forest of great towering trees and flaming leaves. The house had been built during the Civil War, a small frame structure, black with age, but glowing with the light that blazed at its windows. The impression it made on me could not be photographed. In the forest gloom, and the dazzle of light at its fringe, I sensed a mythic, pastoral perfection that no actual person may have experienced but that was there for the taking, a landscape of sweet and intolerable longing. I waded about in the leaves, or sat in a trance, listening to the birds. I saw through the screen of trees, as in a painting by Brueghel, the silvery gleam of the Ohio River as it must have appeared to Daniel Boone and Audubon, the first to intrude into Eden. I took a few pictures. They did not capture my state of soul. When I think of a palpable pastoral bliss, one that is there at the window but subtly eludes us, it is that moment I think of. Quite beyond my actual grasp, but wonderfully present to my sensations. An experience that was surely common to Cézanne. In a nearby motel, where I spent the nights, I found a jukebox that matched this setting in terms of what is luminous, palpable and ineffable. A suitably ineluctable icon.

My wife had made the acquaintance of Catherine Drinker Bowen, who lived in nearby Merion, and in the research for the books she was writing she had the need of an assistant with my wife's talents. They knew each other as friends before I was asked over to tea and a piece of the celebrated Otha pound cake. Otha, more than anyone I would know, had brought to perfection the ceremony of service possible only to a few black men in this century. I do not know what he thought, only the way he entered, answered if spoken to, and departed, every gesture an enhancement of the occasion, and a compliment to those present. In Kitty Bowen he found the

160

mistress he should have found, and I was able to share, briefly, in a vanishing ceremony.

Kitty Bowen herself was equally displaced in time, making it possible for those who knew her to share in the ambience of a better age, and the character of a woman who might well have ruled England. If the first Elizabeth had ever had a second, Kitty Bowen would have been that recurrence. I liked her immensely, and would soon regret seeing less and less of her. She was a jealous ruler, true to her breeding, and she would soon take offense at my reluctance to share what I considered my private life. An Elizabethan in every pore, she loved few things as much as good live gossip.

I have forgotten the name of her aging, marble-eyed Pekingese companion, a creature so fond of me, my smell, my vibrations, she would go into a trance at my feet, free of wheezing and snortling, her unblinking, adoring marble eyes fastened on my face until I left. Changed my feelings about female Pekes, it did, I will say that.

Early one fall evening, on a visit to New York, I stepped into a shop near Thirteenth and Fifth, across from Dauber & Pine, to look at a large table of book remainders. Another browser stood across the table from me. We edged slowly around it, clockwise, then glanced up at the same moment, to smile at each other. I had seen his face before—but where? "You're Wright Morris?" he asked me. How flattering I found that. "I'm Saul Bellow," he said, and offered me his hand. He took from the table a copy of George Borrow's *Lavengro*, and asked if I had read it. I had not. He liked the writer, and I the one I had just met. A splendid nose, to my taste (I'm a believer in noses), the pupils of his large eyes dilating as they took my measure. "Doing anything?" he asked. I was not. "Come along," he said, and we walked south on Fifth to the apartment of his girl friend Sandra. She shared the apartment with a young woman who was about to leave for Mexico. We had all been to Mexico, except Saul's girl, and talked about it. She was thinking of Oaxaca. I suggested Guanajuato, celebrated for its air-dried corpses. Surviving

161

members of a family could go there and talk things over with their relations.

They were all headed uptown, to somebody's party, and Saul asked me to join them, but I said I had to catch a train back to Philadelphia. As they drove off in a cab, I felt like a fool. I did not have to catch a train to Philadelphia, or anywhere else. It was nothing more than my long-ingrained habit of going solo, even at moments when I would have enjoyed the company. This had deprived me of good (and bad) times in the past, and it would do so in the future. I had nothing to do that beautiful fall evening but wander about the streets of the Village, and browse for books I was no longer buying. One thing I could do, however, I did. I saw the George Borrow book in another store, bought it, and as I read it I wondered what my new friend liked about it.

With his *Augie March* money, Bellow had bought property up the Hudson River near Bard College, where he sometimes did some teaching. He suggested I pay him a visit, and give a reading at Bard. The house had once been a Hudson-bracketed mansion, a model for those I had seen in Virginia City. It needed a lot of renovation, but did not lack for room. We took walks in the plowed fields edging the river, or loafed at our ease, a very appropriate posture for the new-model hammock that Saul had installed. There was a small garden that looked forward to carrots, and a few vines that looked forward to tomatoes. An experienced veteran with the new hammock, Saul would sprawl at his bracketed ease while I sagged in one of the sling chairs. At that time Saul favored a long-beaked summer cap that enhanced his resemblance to Buster Keaton. Like all hammocks, new and old models, this one was subject to eccentric behavior. Saul and I happened to find it remarkably amusing. Other guests, hearing our hooting, found it puzzling. We proved to have many things in common, including our early years in Chicago, but the binding mucilage in our friendship was that the same things struck us as funny. Not merely amusing, but matchlessly zany. Once started, we found it hard to stop laughing. A

162

shared glance would set us off, and fraternal vibrations would keep it going.

Friends of Saul's were in and out, over the summer, and I remember with affection a lawyer, with the build of a court jester and a great passion for novels, who would appear with cartons of books stored in the back of his Cadillac Coupe de Ville. He was the first to turn up with some of my own. I later met him at a party in the Village, from where he drove me, timing the lights, the full length of Fifth Avenue seemingly without visible contact with the pedals. He lived with his mother, and it was one of the things he did for kicks.

It flattered me, on some of my visits to Saul, that he would read to me from whatever he was writing. I was mistaken in thinking it favored me—he shrewdly used many friends in this manner—but I would guess only the two of us laughed so hard we would have to break off the reading and wipe the tears from our eyes. *Henderson the Rain King* left us both in stitches. I loved the way Saul enjoyed his own talent, and his sensible acceptance of criticism. Many years later, when he wrote me to say that in the past we had had the best of each other, it was the liberating laughter he had in mind, and he was right. When we were out of our minds with laughter, the ties that bound us were at their strongest, the latest in hammocks creaking and tilting as we guffawed and hooted. Halcyon days!

I had written a story, "A Safe Place," about a colonel and his wife living on the Heights, in Brooklyn, that provided the basis for a macabre novel that would eventually be published as *War Games*. Harry Ford had read it, and it worried him. What was a publisher to think of a writer (one losing him money) who followed *Man and Boy* with *The Works of Love*, and followed that with the tale of a man who turns himself into a woman? This amusing and chilling story was a premature example of what would soon be known as black humor. Was the public ready for it? Not the public of Wright Morris. Harry Ford recommended that I put it aside until my status as a writer had clarified. I liked this book—seeded with so much of my future fiction—but I accepted Ford's suggestion to put it on hold. That would prove to be for more than twenty years, when it would be published by Black Sparrow Press.

In the summer of 1954 I attended a writers' conference in Salt Lake City, directed by the poet Brewster Ghiselin. John Ciardi and Elizabeth Enright were also on hand, with a fine assortment of Utah residents. The sun blazed, we took hikes, went on picnics, ate some Chinese food, and talked books and writing. I attracted some fans from Ogden, who labeled me an interesting but vain person. In the sun on the steps, we discussed my novels.

Ray B. West, who would later be my friend and colleague at San Francisco State, stopped by with his wife, Lu, and recommended a Swiss cheese made by the Mormons. I took a few pounds of it back home to Wayne with me. At the close of the conference I drove north to Missoula, Montana, for a visit with Leslie Fiedler and his family. Fiedler had been appreciative of *Man and Boy*, and I thought him a brilliantly gifted critic, one of the few I read with excitement. He had established his own Western outpost, and gone far to people it with new pioneers. I would have liked to kidnap the youngest Fiedler child. She hugged me madly, however, and I was able to saddle up and gallop off.

I had left Pomona College in 1933, and the span of twenty years seemed to be about right for a period of reflection and reappraisal. Those years had also been umbilically attached to Chicago, so I found I had two infections of nostalgia to deal with. Could I do them up in one package?

I had been rereading, with keen interest, that summer the early novels of Fitzgerald and Hemingway, and I welcomed, more than I feared, the challenge to deal with similar emotions in a different setting. My enthusiasm had once been fired by Lindbergh, and I now wanted to bring the same emotions to focus on a tennis player named Charles Lawrence—a very Gatsby-like romantic. I had no model in mind for Lawrence, but I had played some tennis in college and knew the tension that the game could inspire. At some point in my reading of T. E. Lawrence, which I would have a go at periodically, I had come across a photograph of Lawrence, perhaps in England, standing poised as if to my purpose, at his ease and yet taut, his fingers lightly placed on his trim hips. The photo and the poise embodied, for me, the character and the charm of my tennis player. It spoke of intangibles, and extravagant commitments. I began writing with the name Lawrence, and it stayed. The narrator of the novel would be a classmate, Peter Foley, who had come to California from Chicago, and found that Lawrence was one of his dormitory companions. With the first paragraph, I knew I was off and running.

They tell me that my father, a Latin teacher, would place his silver watch, with the Phi Beta Kappa key dangling, on the right-hand corner of the desk in his Virgil class. When he was not lecturing, the students would hear the loud tick. The watch had been given to him by his father when he became a Cum Laude Latin scholar, and the inscription Incipit Vita Nova *had been engraved on the back. A very punctual man, my father wound the watch when he heard the first bell ring in the morning, then he would place it, with the fob dangling, on the corner of his desk. Time, for my father, seemed to be contained in the watch. It did not skip a beat, fly away, or merely vanish, as it does for me. So long as he remembered to wind the watch, Time would not run out. There was no indication that he found his subject a dead or dying language, or the times, for a man of his temperament, out of joint. He died the winter of the flu epidemic during the First World War.* (The Huge Season, 1954)

The Huge Season related one story in the present, the life of Peter Foley, a teacher of English, who commuted between Haverford and New York, and an alternate narration concerned with his college years and Charles Lawrence, the tennis player. Our friend Double-dukes appeared as Montana Lou Baker, a portrait intended as a tribute. I felt very good about this novel, but within a few weeks it was rejected by Scribner's. They had made every effort to promote *The Deep Sleep*, but the sales response had been negligible. My confidence was such that I was more angered than disappointed.

I wrote immediately to Granville Hicks, who had long spoken up for my novels, and he quickly replied that I should pay them a visit, in Grafton, New York, and bring along the manuscript.

With my arrival in Grafton, on a fall day of drizzle, I seemed to pick up with a friendship that had been waiting on this occasion. As at the Home Place, I circled the gabled farmhouse, looking for the appropriate entrance. The house and its furnishings—tables, chairs, pillows—its porches, pets and inhabitants, slipped onto me like a glove. The animation and sparkle of Dorothy Hicks not only charmed me, but concealed, on my first visit, the polio affliction she had suffered as a child. She so skillfully accommodated to this handicap, I was unaware of it. Granville was lean, with the build of a jockey, at his ease in the faded shirts and denims of a farmhand. He had the manner and reserve natural to a scholar (he had been a magna cum laude at Harvard), combined with a voice, and an ease of expression, that I found his most distinctive characteristic. I liked to hear him talk—on those occasions when he was offered a chance. I had met few true New Englanders before, and found it uplifting. Some years later, he would tell his own story in a book titled *Part of the Truth*, and the part that I found the truest was the opening line, "I was a good boy." No one who knew him would have questioned that, or have remarked, over the years, any change in his nature. The grain of his mind extended and sustained the American conscience that had its beginnings a few miles to the east, to which he had contributed his own example that the unexamined life is not worth living.

I soon learned that the voices in the kitchen were those of Dorothy and her young neighbors, gossiping. One of these boys, Calvin by name, who fixed me on sight with an unblinking stare, proved to be a man of two words, yes and no. His liking for me was a matter of vibrations, as it was with the cat and the aging beagle. No better environment was possible for a writer seeking both advice and comfort.

Granville spent most of the second day reading my manuscript, as I sat in the kitchen talking with Dorothy. Calvin's younger, and blondly pretty, brother proved to be a budding backwoods aesthete. It startled me to see this flowering in Grafton, and it was no handicap in Dorothy's kitchen. They both loved and elaborated on the latest scuttlebutt. Calvin had other brothers, as well as a sister, whom I might see helping her mother hang out the laundry, but I gathered that she was not pleased to compete with her brother for Dorothy's attention. Calvin liked to hunt, and on arriving might park his gun at the door, or bring it in to dismantle, clean and polish while he listened to others talk. The intactness of his nature was like that of the rural people I had seen in the South, a self-sufficiency that was free of the nagging torments of self-awareness. By another name would I have liked him less?

By late afternoon, Granville confided that he had read my manuscript and thought reasonably well of it. We discussed it briefly, and went over the pages where he had made helpful suggestions. It pleased me greatly to find that we were both reading the same book, and sharing similar responses. The work done, we relaxed with Granville's martinis, a ritual of many years' standing. Just before midnight, with a nightcap of sherry, we toddled off to bed.

This proved to be merely the first of my many pilgrimages to Grafton. On other occasions we might meet in New York, or in the halls of some college, or as far from Grafton as Venice, where, years later, we would have two wonderful weeks together. Both Dorothy and Granville smoked like chimneys, and needed to be near a supply of American cigarettes. A picture cherished is one I snapped of the two of them, huddled in the great door of Santa Maria della Salute, directly beneath a billowing scarlet banner. A holy place, surely, to get out of the wind and light two cigarettes on one flickering match.

Granville had called Marshall Best, of The Viking Press, to recommend that he have a look at *The Huge Season*, and Best had asked me to drop it off at the Viking offices on my way through New York. Not more than two or three days later, in Wayne, I had a call from Mr. Best. He liked the book. I would soon receive their contract. Was I urgently in need of money? I said a little money would be much appreciated. The sum he suggested, fifteen hundred dollars, would be my largest advance up to that time.

I soon went back to the city to meet Mr. Best, Malcolm Cowley, and other editors at Viking. Mr. Cowley, like Max Perkins, had the benefit of the greatest aid ever devised for the publisher's luncheon, a hearing aid that often malfunctioned. On the occasion of our luncheon, I was never long free of the sense that he had the crucial advantage.

Mr. Best made his home near Danbury, Connecticut, but kept an apartment near the Viking offices. As we sat sipping bourbon, he startled me by saying that I didn't look too well. How old was I? Forty-four. I had never given thought to my age, but not to be looking so good disturbed me. Did he not, Marshall asked me, detect in the character of Peter Foley a man in a bit of a mid-life crisis? Was he right or wrong in feeling that Foley sometimes spoke up for the author? I thought that was certainly possible, but I was not sure where. If *The Huge Season* should happen to be a success, Marshall would like to take the liberty of suggesting that I take a break from work, and go somewhere. Had I been to Spain? Italy? Mexico? It should be somewhere a bit exotic, in his opinion. A real change of scene.

As we talked, I recalled Hemingway's suggestion, in *Death in the Afternoon*, that the place to go if you ever bolted with somebody was Ronda, in Spain. I was not about to bolt—at that moment—but his advice did cross my mind. What I lacked was the appropriate somebody. Nor did I confess—and compromise my luck—that I had just applied for another Guggenheim Fellowship, and if that lightning should once more strike, I was ready for flight to those places pictured in the windows of travel agencies. Before I left the city I picked up a packet of maps from the Mexican Tourist Bureau in Rockefeller Center. I was still landlocked, in my habits of flight, and liked the freedom and convenience of a car. I was one of those who waited, futilely, for the Pan American Highway to Machu Picchu.

The Paseo de la Reforma, the great trees and the throng of Indians in Chapultepec Park, the stream of figures in and out of the dazzle of sunlight in Cuernavaca, the slap of hands and bare feet under my window in Oaxaca, the basking shimmer of heat and light, of *sol* and *sombra*, of the tranquil Mexican morning where the smiling assassin waits in the shadows with his gleaming white teeth: these and other images were still bright as pennies at the back of my mind. They had been newly buffed to brightness by my reading of Malcolm Lowry's *Under the Volcano*, and Lawrence's *Mornings in Mexico*. Was I as ripe and ready as Marshall Best had suggested?

When in March I heard the good news from the Guggenheim Foundation, my sense of release, of buoyancy, was so keen it led me to wonder what I would have done if I had not been one of the chosen. For several years I had been doing most of my living in my writing, and I was feeling the strain on these resources. My experience, as I came up for air, was that of a man who had pushed off the bottom—as Gordon Boyd would soon be doing in *The Field of Vision*. As I recall this moment, I feel again the surge and swell of the emotion I felt at the time, so life-enhancing that I rise from my desk and pace around the room. Was I so much a captive? Or had I, in *The Huge Season*, aroused the fires of old expectations? I felt a compelling need to take off, to hit the road, to be up, up and away, as if I had been reprogrammed by the sentiments of the twenties.

Just west of Wayne, the Pennsylvania Turnpike began to wind and rise into the Alleghenies, and as I passed through the toll gate, early in July, I experienced the sought-for winged sense of liberation, and I was on my way.

One of the gifts of life of this period was my discovery of Henry James's *The American Scene*. It was my practice to find and buy the book I wanted to read, and to find this rare out-of-print volume took me five or six years. I was not a reader of the Master's fiction, where the refinement of his style was a contradiction of what was vital and unique in the American vernacular. As R. P. Blackmur perceived, correctly, in my opinion, James was a *fabulist* with realistic pretensions, but this went gratingly against the grain of my mind and nature. Curiously, and not easily explained, I was able to read *The American Scene* as if its uniquely Jamesian texture was one of the virtues I loved about it. There is no question in my mind that the mind of Henry James is matchless in the many forms in which it is revealed. His effortless power of association, in which one aperçu leads to another, then another, then another—an open-ended series of parenthetical relations—makes it both annoying and exhausting to follow the darts and flashes of his mind, but this experience is simply not to be found elsewhere. I'm sure that readers of his fiction feel the same, but my long apprenticeship to other voices makes it difficult for me to hear his music. In *The American Scene*, mirabile dictu, I am persuaded to give him all that it takes.

I found him both a challenge and an aggravation. Forty years before my time, James had staked out his claim on much I thought to be my property. The keen, sharp edge of my appreciation—like the mind of Thoreau confronting a fact—was that this writer had not merely scooped me, but saw it all more comprehensively than I did.

Here it is then that the world he lives in [the businessman] accepts its doom and becomes, by his default, subject and plastic to his mate; his default having made, all around him, the unexampled opportunity of the woman. . . . She has meanwhile probably her hours of amazement at the size of her windfall; she cannot quite live without wonder at the oddity of her so "sleeping" partner, the strange creature, by her side, with his values and his voids, but who is best known to her as having yielded what she would have clutched to the death.

For the author of *Man and Boy* and *The Deep Sleep*, this was the ultimate stamp of approval, even as it deprived me of my patent. Henry James had been there. My preferred feeling was that I had been prematurely plagiarized. A more sobering reflection, one that I would learn to live with, was that the truth exposed would have as little to do with the manners of the culture as the truth buried: man and woman, mutually deprived, would continue along the way to which they were accustomed.

It also depressed me to realize that the number and complexity of these perceptions, in their effect on the reader, weakened rather than strengthened their impact. There was that stakeout of mine known as the hotel lobby.

. . . It lies there waiting, pleading from all its pores, to be occupied—the lonely waste, the boundless, gaping void of "society"; which is but a name for all the other so numerous relations with the world he lives in that are imputable to a civilized human being.

. . . one is verily tempted to ask if the hotel spirit may not just be the American spirit most seeking and finding itself. . . .

. . . One was in the presence, as never before, of a realized ideal of that childish rush and surrender to it and clutch at it which one was so repeatedly to recognize, in America, as the note of the supremely gregarious state. It made the whole vision unforgettable, and I am now carried back to it, I confess, in musing hours, as to one of my few glimpses of perfect human felicity.

Can it be said that we have finally come abreast of these comments, or have we safely receded from their application, no longer intimately bearing on the affairs of an already altered species?

*A*fter a decade of insistent and intense application, circling and recircling the still points of my fiction, the spirals and helixes of departures and withdrawals, of overlapping associations, of intriguing glimpses of the future, yet seldom if ever issuing in moments of rest, or of satisfactory resolutions, the *open road*—Jack Kerouac would soon publish his book *On the Road*—provided me with a measurable sense of progression, of predictable starts, stops and destinations.

The relief I felt was quite beyond description, and yet it was a sensation to which I was long accustomed. *Taking off* had been one of my father's strategies, and we had often flown the coop together. My emotions were those of an overdue diver who surfaced for air.

I was so eager to get to Mexico, I was up and off early and drove late, sometimes sleeping in the car just out of the glare of the street lights, and this would prove to be the origin of my inflexible mind-set for dawn starts and a minimum number of stops: more than a sufficient cause for friction with my occasional travel companions. The sunrise starts were invariably the high point of the long days. If I was headed east it had its torments, the morning sun burning like a comet on the windshield, but if I headed west, the slow spread of light was like the moment of creation. First the tide of light would splash on objects, or touch with fire the summits of far hills or mountains, then slowly as a tease, or that moment in the darkroom when the first image emerges, preceding the splendor of the visible spectrum. On the occasional farm, splinters of light would be thrown off by the blades of the windmill. Ideally, from my point of view, this magical moment would be capped by the far glimmer of an all-night truck stop, the windows glowing like a train diner. In my experience, the predawn diner breakfast is the one great infallible American meal. Best when you get it in a diner, the bacon sizzling before you, the eggs sunny side up or over easy, the hash browns just to one side, with a crust like a shingle. Proof of the glory of this food is that it survives the predictably ghastly coffee, which brings to mind such things as Postum. The refills seem better, the second or third cigarette having numbed the taste buds.

Back in Pennsylvania, to make sure I would not be caught without them, I had bought two boxes of Marsh-Wheeling stogies, long, slender, black-wrapper cigars of memorable sweetness and mildness, soon to be as essential to Western bad men as their hot shooting irons and evil looks. I would later be accused and with some justice, of having spread this weed and its craving to all points west of the Missouri and not a few south of the border. Some years later, about to leave for Europe, I tried to find the precious stogie in New York, and I remember the look of outrage on the face of a "tobacconist" when he finally grasped what I was describing. Where one could find them, in those halcyon days, they were usually six cents.

Predictably, after the sunrise breakfast, I would be half starved by nine o'clock. My second breakfast was usually several rashers of bacon on a field of golden-brown hotcakes. This was not so easily consummated. Tough and leathery flapjacks, with the texture of tire patches, were not unusual on the wide open road. The disaster could be forestalled if I had a seat at the counter, where I could watch them being poured and see their bottom sides pucker before they were flipped, but it is much harder to spot the leathery flapjack than the false meringue on the pie in the pie case. The higher it is piled—to echo an old saw—the worse it will prove to be.

In Indiana, I think it was, the man seated at my side, who had been rolling himself a fresh Bull Durham, when asked if he would like a half cup of coffee, replied, "Bottom half, please, miss," and got it. Nowhere that I have been is there a language so responsive to what is as yet unheard and unspoken as the one I speak.

For my evening meal, I troubled to pick a town that was big enough to offer me a choice. One with a residential area, if possible, with a view through the front screen down the hall into the light of the kitchen. Such a town would usually shut down about six or seven o'clock, except for the gas stations and the drugstore, but if it had been settled before the turn of the century, there would be an old café, perhaps with a ceiling fan, and a smaller new one. The older one would have its menu posted on the window, and while reading the menu I would size the place up. I looked for the big, old-fashioned coffee urns, the steam hissing at the top, rather than the Silex vacuum on the electric hot plate. I looked for pie, still in the pan on the counter, and one of the handsome aluminum milk dispensers, and in Missouri I troubled to look for, and often found, the big trays of fresh berry cobbler or shortcake. On the menu I might look for the chicken-fried steak that had been one of the staples of my boyhood, along with fresh rhubarb pie and tapioca pudding. Most of the small towns along the rural roads of Ohio were so great for homemade pie I hated to leave the state, but they were uniformly terrible for coffee. After eating, I would stroll, with my stogie, around the street doing a little window shopping, check out the movie, and try the rockers in the lobby of the hotel, if they had one. If the lobby was clean, and had a bit of class, I might take a room for the night. These rooms, with the cracked blinds drawn at the windows, and the sound they always made when the clerk let them up, the light bulb dangling on a cord over the chipped iron bed frame, the bent wire hangers in the open door to the closet, were for me time capsules of pathos reduced to an essence. With the window open I could hear the slam of car doors, the town mutts barking, the goon gunning his motor at the street light, and in the silence the far *yoooo-hooo* of an approaching train before it rattled through without stopping. A commingling of the sordid, the lonely, the despondent, scented the stale air, saturated the objects, and distilled a fragrance to which I was incurably subject. On the nightstand I could see, just barely, the faded red stain on the leaves of the Gideon Bible. On the post of the bed I could discern my father's pants, on the chair at the side he had draped his coat, and I would sense the weight of his body in the dipper-like sag of the mattress. One night it occurred to me that as much as we had shared the same bed, I had no idea if he slept well or not, since I was asleep myself.

Other times, I might prefer to find a residential street where a parked car might not arouse much suspicion, and curl up in the seat with sentiments I could sleep with. One night in New York, while staying with a friend, I had been awakened by a cry for *Help!*—as one might get from a person drowning. No other sound. Just that word, with a big balloon around it that left it suspended in the air above me, like the cry Camus would hear on the bridge crossing the Seine. Had my father ever heard it, or cried out himself? It pleased me to believe he had been blessed with the gift of sleep.

On this trip I had left the freeway to go south to Gambier, Ohio, and pay a visit to John Crowe Ransom. He had accepted a story of mine, "A Safe Place," for the *Kenyon Review*, and had suggested I might stop and see him. As with my first meeting with Granville Hicks, we seemed to easily resume a former conversation that had been briefly interrupted. I filled my pipe from his humidor, and we smoked and talked books until it was time for me to leave. What I, and countless other young writers, had missed in not having him as a friend and a neighbor, this brief stop brought home to me.

A flood had washed out the bridge over the Rio Grande at Laredo, and it had been replaced by army pontoons. The movement of people and cars in both directions went at a snail's pace. The long file of Indians, the women shrouded in black, passed so close to my car they brushed against the sides and the fenders. Some of the older men and the children gave it a friendly pat, as if they thought it alive. For a brief moment, as they drew alongside, each face was framed in the open window of my car: the very old, with their great reserve, their lined, somber and dignified faces; the young and frequently striking women, their hair blue-black in the sun's dazzle; the sculpture-like, sad-eyed children, peering at me like the cupidons in the paintings of madonnas. The frieze seemed endless; the dust raised by their feet filled the car and filmed the windshield. It seemed to me that I had become Mexican before entering Mexico. I would never be wholly free of the impression—even when I saw it contradicted—that these people were *the* people tirelessly evoked, on numberless occasions, to reassure all those who were losing their faith in the species. Here they all were—shy, vulnerable, obviously helpless, and profoundly appealing. If I had been stopped while crossing the river, and escorted back to Laredo, I would have felt that Mexico had come to me, and my adventure had not been aborted. But I was not stopped, and just before sundown I was in Monterrey.

The Pan American Highway over the mountains seemed as incredible as I remembered, but there were fewer Indian women walking the road, and their garments were less colorful. Neither did flocks of *muchachos* follow the car and try to sell me melons or midget bananas.

South of Ciudad Victoria, a whitewashed boulder, no larger than a bucket, was all that indicated the road I would take west to Guadalajara. This narrow road followed the contours of a high plateau, with marvelous expansive vistas of the wooded slope to the south and the west. Here and there, I could see the butter-yellow domes of the churches, gleaming like coins. In veral hours I passed no other cars in either direction. The matchless serenity of the villages, with a few Indian women on the steps of the churches, or one sweeping the entrance with a broom of fagots, I knew to be a gift of the drug-likeinertia and poverty, but I could not resist its appeal.

The cries of a few caged birds, a fountain splashing or dripping, the far braying of a burro, gave it a biblical tranquillity.

In the early afternoon, dazed with the heat and the shimmering light, I entered what once had been a substantial city, with a large towering cathedral, but it now appeared to be abandoned. The shadow of the church darkened the steps at its entrance like the shadows in a de Chirico painting. I had to drive in low gear in the broken and gutted street. A Carta Blanca beer sign at a corner indicated a café. I sat for some time in the drone of flies before a small, shrunken figure, hardly higher than the counter, appeared from the back. One of the eyes she turned to me was like an agate. I used the word *comida*, and after a long delay she brought me a plate of food. A dark sauce of beans, thick as caramel, had been spooned onto an enchilada. I reassured myself that it had been long cooked, and ate a few bites of it, washed down with the warm beer.

Several hours later, approaching Guadalajara through a stream of pedestrian and burro traffic, I stopped at a crowded café with tables along the street. I had some chicken with rice that I thought delicious, and a bottle of ice-cold beer. I smoked a fresh Delicado as I chatted with the waitress, who was pleased with my tip. Just at sunset, I entered Guadalajara and made my way to a motel crowded with Americans. A sallow and sour young woman was not sure if she had a place for me or not. As I leaned on the counter, I had my first flush of nausea and queasiness. Perhaps she saw it in my face. I followed a barefoot boy to a mercifully dark and cool room. Before I could get my shoes off, I had an attack of nausea.

Some time later, the room dark, a clattering roll of thunder approaching, I crawled from the bed into the shower, where I turned on the water and crouched over the drain. The celebrated *turista* is a commonplace but unforgettable experience. I had never before been so sick, for so long a time. The shower rained on me, I whooped and retched, with brief periods of chills and quivers. A dramatic and thundering electric storm, with blinding, incandescent flashes at the windows, penetrating the room like X rays, provided the appropriate backdrop for my inner turmoil. Just at dawn (I could see it at the window), I was able to crawl from the shower back to the bed. Later in the morning, one of the maids, recognizing the symptoms, drew the blinds at the windows and withdrew. I thought surely it would bring me either help or burial, but nothing occurred. In the evening, I was able to lift the phone's receiver and mutter the word *enfermedad*, with many *muy*s. This eventually brought me a pot of tea, served up with advice I did not comprehend. The good woman wet a towel and wiped off my face, washed and wrung out my shorts. The musical flow and rising pitch of her comments I took as assurance that I would live. She appeared again in the morning with tea, but I was leery of the toast. In the cool of the evening, my pins shaky, my flesh the color of the light seen in washrooms, I made my way into the courtyard. A young man was there who spoke English, and he was familiar with the problem. I took the capsules he provided, and his advice not to eat. Back in my room, I sprawled on the bed and slept until the maid woke me up. Sunlight blazed at the window, and after I had showered and shaved, I stopped at the lunchroom for two soft-boiled eggs, bacon and four slices of toast. It didn't seem possible, but that's how it was.

I stayed on for several days in Guadalajara, thinking it might be the place for me to settle. Its size and setting, its freedom from urban blight, put me in mind of Santa Barbara, and I spent most of my time in the sun-baked plaza, people-watching. I had heard the *muchachas* were particularly fetching, and so they were. But what I missed—and seemed to feel I wanted—was the bustle and complexity of Mexico City, with its parks, avenues, *futbol*, bullfights and, from my urgent point of view, the Sanborn restaurants, marvelous places to relax, to watch people and to dine. What I wanted was a city, not the leisure world that was already shaped to the lives of the gringos, most of them from California. I had a look at Ajijic, where Lawrence and Frieda had stayed, the luster of the sky and the mountains just as he had described them, but I was critical of the arty atmosphere and the exiles from the colony in Santa Fe, sandaled, bobbed, bored, and cannibalistic. I liked women. I needed a woman. So why was I so reluctant? In the confusion of my motives and my practice, I was not unlike Lawrence: the will to act was not lacking, but I wanted the Protestant props of commitment.

A very attractive young Mexican woman cleaned my room every morning, and I used the occasion to sharpen up my Spanish. She liked me, but I could see she had her scruples. I liked her, and I had my scruples. It would appear, however, that our scruples were more a matter of context than of morals. If the scene could appropriately arrange itself, I sensed that my scruples might vanish—but not hers. The grain of my reluctant nature, on a push-pull arrangement, made a salvaging of morals a question of mutual commitment. If I was committed, if the lady was committed, the morals would be negotiable. I loathed intrigues and art colony affairs, but on the right occasion I would bolt for Ronda. I liked these brown *muchachas*, the crackle of their gossip, and their easy, flirtatious manner, but divined—being one of their kind—that they were scrupulous with their favors. They, too, had listened to a voice that said, "Now there are some things that are right, and some things that are wrong, and *that's* wrong." And *that*, as Stendhal said of sherbet, was all that it lacked.

I made a stop at Uruapan, near the volcano Pátzcuaro. A once bustling colonial city, it had become a decaying theatrical ruin, like something one might find, I imagined, in Malaysia. The folly of capturing my complex impressions kept me from using the camera I had brought along. Coming out of the mountains, east of Morelia, I caught glimpses of the setting that the valley of Mexico had provided for its long bloody history, and just after midnight I was looking for a place to park along the crowded Paseo de la Reforma. A stream of honking traffic flowed in both directions; Indians were curled up like rugs in shop doorways. In the new open-all-night Sanborns, I had my long-awaited *enchiladas de crema*, and sat smoking Delicados and sipping strong coffee until it was time for an early breakfast. The morning was not as sparkling as I remembered, more like the deep summer haze of Paris, but I liked the throb of the waking city. At the stand where I bought more cigarettes and the waxy matches, a young man with a valise, dressed like a mannequin on Olvera Street, said to the cashier as he hurried off, *"Tiempo es dinero!"* For an instant I failed to grasp what he had said. Here in the land time had once forgotten, money had caught up with time. The Indian woman who squatted, less than a block away, Buddha-like as she sliced up papaya for her tribe of little Indians, had not as yet received that message, but it would soon be heard by her offspring. Into the broad palm of her extended hand I dropped a small clinking piece of time's new substance. I would report this in my first letter to my wife, finding it both amusing and exotic, that as slogans were worn out where they began, they could be exported for a new life elsewhere.

I spent several days looking for an apartment. As huge and sprawling as the city had become, there were few accommodations for a not so affluent tourist. I wanted to be near the Paseo de la Reforma, and the Sanborns where I would sometimes have my meals. I found what I needed off Avenida Gutenberg, in a small residential shopping area. There was a bakery on the corner, a delicatessen with freshly barbecued chickens, a *farmacia*, a dry cleaner—his establishment open to the street, his wife doing her mending on a chair on the sidewalk—and just a block away, a new *supermercado* with a meat market. My rooms were large but dark, on the well of a court where water was ceaselessly dripping and splashing. For the first few weeks I thought this was charming. Later I tried plugging my ears. I never clearly understood why my apartment was so quiet. I had the privilege of sunbathing on the roof, but this proved to have its risks. The Mexican system of heating water is a surefire fail-safe arrangement of letting the steam blow through the roof if the tenants happened to forget about it. I forgot on occasion. A familiar practice. I could see geysers shooting off all around me. At one time the view would have been marvelous, but the increasing smog had veiled it off. Of interest, however, were the señoritas who came to the neighboring roofs to wash and dry their hair. They usually did this in pairs, a social arrangement, and sat about in the sun combing and brushing, gossip a welcome music. Each wall of my apartment was painted a different color, but in the dim light this went unnoticed. I had a three-burner gas stove, an electric refrigerator, and the usual infestation of bugs and fleas in the overstuffed furniture. My landlord, a tall young man with an interest in literature and the arts, liked to sit and discuss with me Mexican painting as he smoked my Delicados. He had picked up his English, as well as his French, from his clients, not a few of them writers. I had often heard of the names he mentioned, but I had not read their books. With understandable pride, he insisted that I would find fewer bugs in his accommodations, but it would be unwise for me to think that I might eliminate them. The key word was control. Frequent spraying would keep them under control. I made the mistake of spreading my Indian blankets on the chairs, so that I took a crop of Mexican bedbugs and fleas home with me, still powerfully active months later in the plush ambience of Mother's Oriental rug.

I was one of the early birds for fresh sweet rolls at the bakery, so inexpensive I recognized my affluent status. By eight o'clock I was at work in the back-aching style to which I was once accustomed, the portable typewriter on the coffee table, the writer squatted on two chair cushions. No time was lost in doodling. I had come to work, and with my second cup of coffee I was at work.

I was intrigued by the appearance of a character that I seemed to have brought along with me, like a hitchhiker, one to whom I was already accustomed to listening. He pretended to be a native of my own "country," and on speaking terms with some of my people. His home town, like mine, had a grain elevator with the name HORD painted at the top of it, visible for miles in both directions. The same name could be seen on the loose boards that fenced in the lumberyard—a few were missing where the small fry made their entrances and exits—and reappeared in black-and-gold lettering on the window of the bank. He knew all this, reminded me of it, and sarcastically mocked my interest in it. Whose side was he on? I listened to him on the chance that I might find out. We had shared the experience, as boys, of walking past the Hord residence, taking up most of a city block, where a chocolate-colored Franklin with a scooped hood, like a fireman's hat, was often parked in the driveway. An electric car with hard rubber tires was kept in the carriage house at the rear. My friend had experienced, as I had not, the incident that took place at the local bottomless sandpit, where he had attempted to walk on water. I scoffed at that, of course, but I listened to what he said. One of the boys I had known, who couldn't swim, would certainly have tried if I had dared him to do it. It was almost more than he could bear, not to take a dare.

This character was in my mind when I sat down to write. I was troubled by the feeling that I was not really clear just where he began and I ended, and just who, at any moment, might prove to be talking. That ambivalence had surfaced in *The Huge Season*, but I felt I had turned it to the book's advantage. So I was provoked to see where this would lead me, but at the same time I was uneasy. I liked the talk I was having with the character, but I lacked confidence in the voice. It was too much my own. Overhearing what I was saying often led me to wince.

The name Boyd seemed to suit his first appearance on the page. His first name would long be a source of annoyance. He would come from a small plains town, as I had, with shaded streets, comfortable homes, a yearly Hagenbeck-Wallace circus, unseasonable spring blizzards, and early fall Chautauquas. Two or three well-to-do families would set the tone and provide examples of the good life, such as a Pierce-Arrow with lights in the fenders. A small boy in such a town, with his older companions, would walk down a weedy spur of tracks to the sandpit, where the moment of truth would take place. On its glassy surface I would see my own reflection, and wait on events. With his boyhood chum, McKee, Boyd would take that walk, and McKee would forever be his witness.

My feeling was, at the time I began to write, that if the scenes and characters were appropriate to the writer's emotions, as aroused by these scenes and characters, memory and imagination would so commingle in the writing as to produce gratifying fiction. That seemed true of what little I had written, but it astonished me to find that the very clichés I had so often ridiculed were essential to my materials—on occasion they proved to *be* my materials.

Not that McKee didn't sort of like Mexico. In the four days they had been in Mexico City ten or twelve people had asked him for the time, then thanked him kindly no matter what he said. He liked that. He paid a little more attention to the time himself. Having it there in his pocket meant more down here than it did in the States.

It was not possible, it occurred to me, to make such an observation about McKee except in the clichés to which he was accustomed. In his nature, which I found appealing, they acquired the luster of a finer metal. His character, indeed, took the clichés of his life and fleshed them out in a way that made them appealing. Slowly I came to realize that these clichés were my subject, and my problem was how to use them, rather than abuse them. As I sometimes felt ambivalent about the character of Boyd—where he overlapped and where he departed from the character of the writer—so I was sometimes troubled by the ambiguous nature of many clichés. How was it possible, I wondered, that they could be at once the truth of the matter and its parody? But so it was I often found them. Later I would ponder the astonishing fact that the truth of clichés contradicted the truths of more sophisticated language, and that the character of a people had its source in their speech more than in their customs. As so often, I would find this impression confirmed in the comments of writers who were there before me, and in the wondrous, mind-boggling perception of Yeats that "in changing my syntax, I changed my intellect."

In my own experience, the written and spoken "cliché" would often embody the history of the American language and, unavoidably, the history of our people, and speak in one breath from many sources. Gertrude Stein testifies to this in *The Making of Americans*, and I believe my own practice, at its best, confronts this truth in its deep reliance on what is heard and felt when the language is spoken. I speak it to myself, as I write it, in order to better estimate its heft and rightness. In the vernacular it is the cliché that testifies to the burden of meaning that words and phrases from the past bear to us at the moment we speak in the present, where we hear, wherever the language is well spoken, the echoes of the writers who first shaped it. In the vernacular they speak with a familiar accent.

184

*   *   *

My car was parked in a fenced lot just a block away. There were two others in the lot, one with a California license and two flat tires. At the rear of the lot, in a lean-to open shelter, an Indian woman with the face of the Maya lived with her tribe of children. Not all of them were so authentic. Two were as dark as Arabs, their fingers tipped with nails the color of pearls. Were they hers? The question seemed foolish. The movement of her arms, as she slapped out tortillas, revealed the fullness and firmness of her breasts after years of child-bearing and rearing. This gave her, surrounded by her tribe, the appearance of a sculptured fertility figure rather than one of flesh and blood. Hemmed in by her little Indians, in the light of the fire and the smoke of the oil that cooked the torti-llas, her appeal was to the Ur-mensch that we now feel may be up ahead of us, rather than behind.

The building "superintendent," a dark, powerful young man with long arms, short bowed legs, had recently come to the city from the mountains near Morelia. His black, bristling hair grew directly from his brows: his face had one implacable expression. It amazed him that I could read and speak his language. On the first occasion I tipped him, he dropped to his knees as if at the foot of an idol. Where had he learned *that*? To my questions he merely looked puzzled. When I opened the door to his wife, her huge head seemed to be part of her narrow shoulders, her short, thin, calfless legs those of a beast of burden. She was able to understand and reply to my questions, and spoke of their pleasure in being in Mexico City. Where they had come from there was nothing—*nada*. *Nada*, she repeated.

Because of my routine, most of my days were like the one that had just preceded, or the one that would follow, but this well suited my state of mind. One morning, as I sat hunched on my cushions, a tiny spider, no larger than a period to which a filigree of hairs had been added, lowered itself from one of the upper floors on an invisible strand of its own mak-ing, sometimes drifting in drafts, sometimes jerkily descend-ing, to where a leaf on the plant at the window provided a platform, a space station. There it landed, spent a long moment considering its options, then took off as if it had arrived with maps and directions, crossing the leaf's prominent striations to the woody jungle of the stalk, where I lost it.

Such observations, encouraged by my friend Eiseley, often led me into reflections that had no resolution. I sensed that I shared with the spider a degree of mindless application that went beyond, in my opinion, the call of duty; and as well, we both spun out of our innards the lifelines on which we precariously dangled. So much seemed obvious, but what increasingly held me was the optional perspective in which we were both seen as I saw the spider—one in which the element of scale was of interest—not the two worlds we shared, but the one world where scale was not determined by observation. In this perspective both the spider and I and the vast sprawling city receded as I caught glimpses of it from the tail of a rocket. I nurtured this fantasy, in moments of daydreaming, and when the first photographs were taken from the moon, the blue-and-white marble of the earth seemed to me a product of my own imagination.

In my boyhood I would sometimes sit through the movie to see the rerun of the Pathé news, where I was able to see the planet itself revolving. In this way, I and others were being prepared for space travel and star wars.

When we think of the world, do we not think of a photograph? Through the rents in the cloud cover, I see the great rolling plains, the pattern of fields and highways, the dry bed of a river as it snakes its way eastward, and where flecks of green and shadow indicate a village I strain to see who it is that returns my gaze. A child clothed in rompers sits in the talcum-like dust beneath the porch of a house. Wide-eyed and entranced, he dreamily gazes through the lattice of side-slats at the world before him, including myself. Between us there is a cloud of shimmering dust motes in which time itself is suspended. If I could peer at this child from far enough in space, where earthly time is in abeyance, would not the child who sat there, recognizably myself, return my gaze? ("The Camera Eye," 1981)

On my afternoon walks I sometimes passed the courts of the Mexican Tennis Club, with their covered bleachers, and heard the slap of the drives and the sound of the good net rallies. From a banner hung at its entrance I learned that the U.S.A. and Mexico were playing a Davis Cup match. I could hear the applause as I bought my ticket.

Balls travel both a little faster, and a little farther, at the elevation of Mexico City, and this was giving the American players some trouble. I yelled encouragement. Not too many months before, in my fiction, I had identified with the dreams of Charles Lawrence in *The Huge Season*.

A few seats away from me, in moments of tension or excitement, one of the spectators audibly cracked his knuckles. In time this led to an exchange of glances. He was a moderately dark, stocky fellow, with the large, melancholy eyes I had noticed in many of the young men. Double faults, in particular, deeply pained him, eliciting grimaces and woeful groans. On a bad shot he might clap both hands to his face. I grew somewhat reluctant to applaud the winning shots of the American player. Between the sets, I sidled over to console him with a cigarette. He did not smoke. To be so unresponsive to my kind offer also pained him. It seemed to me that the pupils of his eyes dilated. The whites were bloodshot. He had a very early five o'clock shadow. A further source of anguish to him was that he did not speak a word of English. Well, he did speak a word. Twice to me he said "Okay." Accents were a problem for both of us. Take the word *olé*, for example. I used it often, in my cheering, but usually had it wrong. We sat and practiced it together. By the time the American, Tony Trabert, had squeezed out a win, we had made plans to see the next match. After the final match of doubles, on a Sunday, we walked down the Reforma together to drink some Dos Equis at Sanborns.

Jaime García, with his sorrowing bloodshot eyes, an expression that often seemed on the verge of tears, was a man of leisure, in his fashion, and assistant to his brother Eduardo, who worked for the light and power company. Both lived with the widow of an older brother, and her four, five, six or more pale children, all of them *muchachas*. Other members of the family were businessmen, sportsmen and taxi drivers. The important detail was the kinship. As one of Jaime's friends, I also shared it, and might be hailed by a stranger in a passing taxi, or embraced in the crowd at the bullring. With his American friend Jaime practiced an infinite maternal patience. My improvement in the language overwhelmed him. Other members of the family were not so impressed, but they were schooled in charity. My effort to teach Jaime English, however, was ill-advised. He intuited, and rightly, that it might interfere with the delicate imbalance that bound us together. We were *camaradas*. He did not want that disturbed.

We saw some bad baseball, a lot of pretty good soccer under clouds of circling *golondrinas*, and for me, and only for me, he sat through one bullfight and walked out on another. That I found this spectacle of interest measurably altered the way he saw me. We went to movies, attended several plays, watched parades, and went to Cuernavaca to buy phonograph records from a member of the family. Two or three times a week we dined together, went to a burlesque, where the jokes were lost on me, then walked for hours around the streets until the only sounds were those we made ourselves.

On those occasions when I tried to speak what was on my mind, or explain to him what I was writing, I might glance up to see, through the muddle of language, the pained and affectionate concern Jaime felt for my handicap. His characteristic melancholy would deepen, his large eyes would grow moist, and his mouth would form an oval as if the breath of life was being forced from him. The profound reluctance of his lips to smile left his cheeks as smooth and wrinkle-free as a child's. A wry pucker was as close as he got to laughter. But when we were together, there was something amusing in most things we set our eyes on. Getting me to laugh was one of his triumphs, one of the things he felt was "good" for me.

On the faces of the children who begged around the bullring I would see the same resigned, irrevocable sadness, a condition to which they seemed born accustomed. How many years of revolution, of discredited expectations, of dreams that proved to be baseless, had Mexicans endured? Already grass was growing and the masonry crumbling between the flagstones of the new University City, the symbol of the Mexican future. It would not prove easy to convert the energy that ground the maize and slapped the tortillas into what burned the lights in Mexico City. And what else was there? There was *nada*. Jaime and others like him had perceived that *tiempo* in Mexico was not *dinero*, and that more than ruins and little Indians would have to come out of the stony fields and mountains. Those sculptured masks that so amazingly resembled the waifs sleeping in the doorway to my apartment seemed to rest their eyeless gaze on neither the past nor the future. Did they dream? Did they intuit one energy replacing another? Jaime García's most characteristic gesture was the shrug.

*S*ince my friend Jaime did not like bullfights, I went to them alone. I went because they were there, and the bullring itself fascinated me. From where I preferred to sit, high in the *sol*, the bowl itself seemed to converge on the sandy oval at its center like a bull's eye. This impressed me as a model for my idea of a field of vision. I had been to many of the spectacles before I sat close enough to observe the details. I wrote my wife to the effect that I could take it or leave it—she planned to pay me a visit over the Christmas holidays—but before I mailed that letter I came down with the virus. I saw a great *mano a mano*, I put my tongue to dry lips, and after the hooting I sat around the bonfires of newspapers in the *sombra*. I was hooked. I wrote my wife to prepare herself for a long day at the bull-ring.

He watched the matador, the young magician Da Silva, step from the wings of his imagination, erect but abstract in his pearl gray suit of light. On the column of his spine, like a capital in mourning, the funereal hat. He did not look up to see, nor seem to care about, the bull. The beast stood, a little winded and perplexed, with his rear end to the fence, in his nonexistent corner. Like so many brushes in the palette on his hump were the ribboned darts. Two of them sticking up. But Da Silva? He stood alone with himself. He came to face them, doffing his hat, bending back from his hips like a diver, and with a fine carelessness tossed the hat over his shoulder, like a pinch of salt. (The Field of Vision, *1956*)

Perhaps I was most attracted to the stark ambience of the ring itself, all *sol y sombra*, without intervening stages, a Goya-like spectacle of hooting hucksters, peddlers, and food purveyors with their meat and sliced melons under clouds of flies. Music came from the café, open to the street, with a platform at the front or off to one side, featuring all the members of a large family plucking and strumming guitars and violins, with the zithers placed in the laps of the children. A woman costumed like a Gypsy, her face painted, strings of beads swaying as they dangled, rings of glittering gems on all her fingers, would hoarsely shriek above the strumming clamor. One or two of the smaller children would circulate among the tables, their dirty palms or the crown of a straw hat extended. Never before had I sought out, Sunday after Sunday, such touching, racking, pitiless heartbreak. They looked fed, some of them even too fed; the maestro of the assembly would have high leather boots, a velvet jacket, and a sombrero that dangled at his back on a noose. But the air of sorrowing supplication was more penetrating than the music. The children had the smooth faces of the clay figurines found in the ruins, but the wide sad eyes of my friend Jaime. Were they all born knowing? So it seemed.

Music—if that was what it was—led McKee to wheel around and look behind him. A whirring sound. At the front of a café called La Casa de Usted. *On a raised platform near the entrance there were ten or twelve people, maybe more,*

some of them sitting, some standing, but all of them making
this whirring noise. Mostly violins.

In mid-December my wife flew down from Philadelphia. A few days later, with a supply of Kaopectate, we drove south to Oaxaca. The American motel was full of the guests who made the Christmas pilgrimage yearly, but we were able to find a room in the suburbs overlooking a very lovelorn burro. In the dawn light his hoarse braying had us in fits of fury and laughing. Midmorning—they came at a loping trot—we heard the slap-slap of the bare feet of the Indian women with their baskets of fresh tortillas, wrapped in towels, balanced on their heads. The central plaza of Oaxaca, a dappling of shadows and dazzling sunlight, featured a bustling market of the Indians who had come from the surrounding villages. Nothing could have been more native and festive. My wife bought pottery and baskets for her friends, and I bought blankets and baskets for the house. The silver jewelry she loved we would buy later in Mexico City and Taxco. Until far into the morning, the mariachi singers serenaded the houses that were near us, the clear hooting of the tenor like the cry of a coyote.

Several times a day we assured each other that Oaxaca would figure in our future. This sentiment was dampened for me, however, by a visit we made to Mitla—the chill of the tombs and the scale of the ruins, low, horizontal masses enclosing a vast empty plaza that seemed to be waiting out the centuries for the appropriate conquering army. These dark-souled people, as Lawrence had intuited, shared the gift of self-fulfilling prophecies of doom. Their expectations were terminal. The lines that defined and delimited Mitla would have profoundly appealed to a modern dictator. The gentle-seeming Indians in the market of Oaxaca, weavers of blankets and baskets, makers of tortillas, were hard to visualize as the descendants of these fate-driven tomb builders. What had turned them on? More puzzling, what had turned them off? The lines of order at Mitla were those of the hive, evoking submission and silence. Were these lines, dormant for centuries, making a comeback in new disguises? The Zapotecs were the creators of Quetzalcoatl, the painted serpent that cast its spell on Lawrence, but what impressed me more was that seven centuries of pitiless sunshine had not penetrated the chill of the tombs. Back in the sun's merciless glare, I was slow to warm up.

On the long drive back to Mexico City we made a stop at a motel in Puebla. At breakfast I thought I recognized the young American giant at a nearby table. His small, pretty blond wife, tight-lipped and harried, spent most of her time sampling the food before she spoon-fed it to her two small children. In her pinched, worried face I confronted the Mexico stripped of the adornments of my imagination, a stony, harsh, forbidding landscape of dark alien people, dismaying customs, indigestible food and polluted water. Her out-of-scale husband, who seemed to love what he was eating, had been hailed as the superstar of the future when shipped from Texas to join the Yankees. He could run, occasionally he could hit, but he could seldom judge a flyball in the sun. They had sent him back to Texas, and from there he had gone to Puebla. He was a young man who, if asked, would say that all he wanted to do was play baseball, he didn't care where. The young woman he married, her stringy hair no longer as glossy as pulled taffy, had once smiled when she heard that, and peered up at her giant with a sense of wonder. No more. In her longing for all that she had left behind, she glanced at my wife with envy, and at me with something like loathing, sensing, and correctly, that I had spotted her fallen idol. I spoke to him, briefly, as he packed his car. He still liked baseball, but not the travel. As soon as he learned to hit the curve ball a little better—well, maybe more than a little—he'd be back in the States. That was what he said.

Returning from Cuernavaca, back in November, I had made a wrong turn on a one-way street in Mexico City. Never mind that the street had not been marked where I made my turn. Coming toward me was a battered car packed with what I took to be soldiers. The driver of the car swerved to block the street, got out from behind the wheel, and swaggered toward me, cinema fashion. While his friends hooted, he sized me up. If I would move over in the seat, he told me, he would drive me to the nearest police station. I had heard many stories of this sort, but little advice as to what one should do. I had a loose wad of pesos in my pocket, and I thrust them toward him, a fistful, some of which he dropped in the street. As he stooped to retrieve them, I got the car in reverse, wildly backed away, and made the turn at the nearest corner. From there I raced for the Paseo de la Reforma, which was not far. There I illegally parked, waiting anxiously to be arrested, but the morning traffic flowed smoothly by me. This incident unnerved me for several days. My eyes had taken sharp impressions of the fellow and his companions, the animal that has cunningly learned to survive with a blend of servility, fawning and gratuitous cruelty toward anything that is helpless, and I realized that the aura of infatuation I had maintained for Mexico had lifted. Behind the altar, the old idols gnashed their teeth. I felt something of Jaime's distaste for the exotic contrast. The Indian at his siesta in the midst of the traffic, the tribe of little Indians camped in a clearing, each of them cared for by the one who preceded, a network of links in the long chain of being—for all this my own uncritical ardor had cooled. Where I parked my car, one of the little Indians had learned to lift the hood by crawling through the floorboards, opening the spoils to his companions. One day I found them jam-packed into the seats with their saliva-smeared faces pressed to the windows. Cupidons they once had been, but were no longer. Like the drip of a faucet, they now registered seepage. Seepage had slowly worn away the topsoil of Jaime García, and some of it was now getting to me. The telephone pole on the corner of Avenida Gutenberg, snapped off shortly after my arrival, still lay jutting into the street like a piece of fallen statuary, its shattered base concealed by weeds. I was getting the message. I read it as a sign to head for the border.

*I*n January my wife flew back to Philadelphia, leaving me in an unaccustomed void, nursing a bad flu. When I had recovered, my depleted batteries would briefly flick my lights, not actually burn them. I would sit at the typewriter, daydreaming, listening to the drip of water in the court. A new infant, on the floor below, found his high decibel range very quickly, and established a predictable howling schedule. I did some reading about the history of the bullfight, but my attention soon wandered.

My landlord could see that I was at loose ends, and suggested a visit to his place in Acapulco. *Acapulco?* The word did not then have the aura it has acquired, but it was destined to have vibrations. His property, he explained, would have five rooms, two with baths, a swimming pool with heated water, a two-car garage—it would have all these things when it was finished. At the moment, it was being constructed. The foundation was poured, and one of the bedrooms, without a bath, had walls and mosquito netting at the window. By now it might even have a door. I was welcome to stay there, if I cared to.

I decided I did care to, for the time being, and suggested to my friend Jaime that he go along with me, but a city without *beisbol* and *futbol* was of limited interest to him. The vibrations to which I responded he did not feel.

On the way down—a steady decline to the edge of the sea—there were numerous detours without signs, or warnings, and one or two that actually lacked an exit. The road, such as it was, simply ended. Unlit lanterns were set about on piles of rocks. The rear of a cow, with the head and glowing eyes just to one side, an apparition in a surreal vision, did not move from the road as I skidded around it, although it was struck by pieces of gravel. Once it was behind me, out of the lights, it disappeared.

On the seaside downgrade of the coastal range the offshore breeze was warm and caressing. The car, however, did not like the sudden change in altitude. The motor misfired, with a series of explosions I thought might blow off the muffler. Coming out of the sierra, I could feel the closeness of the tropical forest. It had not occurred to me that I would come out of the mountains on the west side of the bay, actually facing the east, without the view of the harbor lights I had expected. Widely spaced street lights indicated the coastal highway, and somewhere ahead of my flickering car lights I could hear the wash of the surf. I had been given reasonably explicit directions for a traveler arriving by daylight. In the balmy but black night, the car sputtering, I felt a tingle of terror. How long would it be before anyone missed the American wintering in Mexico? In a month, perhaps, my wife, or my landlord, stopping by for the rent. It did occur to me to pull off the highway and spend the night on the beach, waiting for daylight, but the absence of the racket made by my car would leave an explosive silence. I could see the dim, floating street lights, but nothing of the poles or the street. I had an estimate of how far I should drive to the left, once I reached the coast highway, and I measured it off on the speedometer as I kept the car in second gear. Incredibly, I saw the light bulb, screened off by the trees, and the path that led upward from the highway. I locked the car, and made my way slowly toward the light. Out of the silence, in the gloom to my left, a voice startled me. When I was able to speak, I called out the name of Señor Mendoza, the property's caretaker. A very short man, in a dark sarape—I saw him profiled against the light—took me by the hand, like a child, and led me up the slope to a clearing. In the swing of his lantern I could see the skeletal frame of a structure, like a small cabin on a large raft. White gauze netting hung at one of the windows. Bricks and pails, a shovel in a pile of sand, suggested that the work had stopped at sundown. And Señor Mendoza? He appeared at the rim of the lantern light, at the front of a construction made entirely of netting strung on poles. Invisible through this netting, but audible, I could hear the murmur of voices.

In a hushed voice, I urged the tall, thin man who stood before me to return to his family. To my surprise, without comment, he did. The murmur of the voices inside the netting was like that of a suddenly comforted litter of puppies. I thanked the person with the lantern, man or boy, and pulled back the gauze at the cabin door, to strike a few matches. The flicker of shadowy movement on the walls and ceiling was that of lizards. A cot without bedding occupied one corner. I stood in the faintly luminous darkness and listened to the scurry of creatures. When none attacked me I took courage. With some trembling, I stretched out on the cot, and lay attentive to the voices. Children giggled. A hand slapped a mosquito. In time, a few were buzzing my head, and my perspiring face recorded the fan of their wings as they hovered for a landing. Only then did I become aware of the deafening drone of night music, occasionally pierced by birdlike hoots and cries. I was famished. I was dying of thirst. But what troubled me the most was that I had not brushed my teeth.

Just thirty years later, at my desk in Mill Valley, having typed these words on a sheet of yellow paper, I get up to pace the walk at the side of the house, under the laurels and arching live oaks, so displaced and disjointed in time that I know my wife, Jo, feels the strangeness in my smiling but distracted glance.

Where, she asks, am I off to this time, in my disheveled cloak of light? Neither one place nor the other is free of the tremor of recovery, of transformation, yet there is something in both fictions that is profoundly congenial, time being the most adaptable and immaterial of our imaginings. So I accept the nearness, as well as the remoteness, of Señor Mendoza and his family, behind the mesh of the mosquito netting, even as I feel in this retrieval the poignancy of a real loss. Where now is Señor Mendoza, the slender patrician and professional time-killer, proud of his heritage, his Yucatecan breeding and his considerable gift of gab, and where is the señora, huge as a Mayan idol, bronze black and glistening as she slapped out the tortillas, her five penny-colored clones testifying to her fertility?

That first tropical morning, I was awakened by the noise of birds and chickens. Now and then shadows flashed on the netting draped at my door, where the light seemed trapped. Through the gauze I could make out the movement of creatures. When I bolted upright, they disappeared in a fit of hooting and giggling, but they were soon back. Their sizes were staggered. Was I ever really sure of their number? A tall one, so thin she scarcely cast a shadow, brought me a slice of papaya, dressed with a squeeze of lime.

It puzzled me to note, stepping outside, that the sun seemed to be rising where it should be setting. A slender man, with a pointed gray beard, dressed in the manner of the peons, stood wiping his hands in a fastidious manner on the soiled tail of his blouse. It did not startle him to glance up and see me. On a cord at his front dangled glasses that he raised to examine me more closely.

"Señor Mor-rees?" he inquired. I nodded. In carefully enunciated Spanish, he assured me of the pleasure it gave him to meet me. He was Señor Mendoza. Señora Mendoza . . . He wheeled to face her. A massive woman, the color of fired bronze, she sat at the opening to their shelter. Naked brown children, recognizably boys, ran about with their slices of papaya. All had the full-moon faces and saucer eyes of their

200

mother, with the exception of the slender, vine-like señorita, eyeing me with the boldness of a Lolita. Was I to believe that this old bee continued to pollinate his jungle flower?

Of whom did he remind me? In the manner of a maître d', toying with his glasses, he told me that he was not himself Mexican, but Yucatecan—it came from his lips as if I had urgently asked him—and his wife, Carmen, was from Guatemala. He was voluble, but unhurried. Just in passing, he thought it pertinent to tell me that they would return to Yucatán for the education of their children. He had once served as a lecturer at the university, but political unrest had obliged him to flee the country.

Would he happen to know, I asked him, of a reliable automobile mechanic? That was not what he had expected. He studied me for a moment in silence, his left hand supporting his right elbow, one finger of his right hand pressed to his lips. I believe he had waited so long to be asked to be of service that the actual moment left him confused.

The principal mechanic of Acapulco, he said, choosing his words with care, happened to be an old and personal friend. He would escort me. He was at my service. To his wife—who continued to ignore him—he explained the nature of his mission, the time going and the time coming, the time for the unforeseen, and the time it took him to find the dapper black beret that fit him like a skullcap, his hair in tufts at each side. Of whom did he remind me? Don Quixote de la Mancha. I pondered my resemblance to Sancho Panza.

My car was still there, with its spark plugs and its hubcaps, but the glass in the windows was smeared where the curious had pressed their faces. Señor Mendoza was full of praise for the car, an advanced model he had not seen, and he was greatly impressed with my skill as a driver, the way I managed to keep the car on the road. I was able to puzzle out, as we curved around the bay, why the sun had risen where I thought it should set. Several miles up ahead, in whatever direction, the windows of Acapulco flamed with the sun. It was not as yet the jet set mecca it would soon be but the blaze of light off the sea, the long curved avenue that was fringed on both sides by weeds, put me in mind of ruins, both real and imaginary, involving the image of Cleopatra on her barge of painted silken sails. These unreal places of excessive heat and light stimulated in strangers antique fantasies. Thomas Mann had found it so in Los Angeles, where he would finish his book about Joseph in Egypt. The full length of this avenue, the shadow of the car went along beside us, high as a caboose. The high-rise hotels had not yet risen, so that there was not much to see but the oasis of palms at the fishing pier.

On a side street, in a small lot of junked cars, we found Señor Mendoza's old friend the mechanic. He was in a shallow grease pit, shaded by a car. A sallow, sober man, in a soiled T-shirt, he climbed out of the pit to stand wiping his hands on a wad of rags, his arms already greasy to the elbows. The sight of Señor Mendoza did not lift his spirits. Señor Mendoza had begun his oration in praise of my background, my talents as a driver and my interests as a scholar—at which point he was interrupted.

"What's the trouble?" the mechanic asked me, in good Orange County English.

"It misfires," I said. "It might be the plugs."

He tested the plugs with his screwdriver, the smoke of his cigarette creasing one eye. One plug did not fire at all. Another proved weak. He removed the plugs and gave them to his assistant, a boy about eight or nine years of age. Would I like a good *used* plug, he asked me, or a new one? The used one was four, the new one ten pesos. To clean the remaining plugs was five pesos. I paid him twenty pesos even. "Much obliged," he said. After checking the oil, he advised me to add a quart. Did I want the best used, or *nuevo American*? He liked the sound of it.

Señor Mendoza was silent as we drove away. His humiliation at the hands of a *Mexican* mechanic weighed on him. In an American-style drugstore, open on the street, we sat at the counter and had two Carta Blancas. The overhead fluorescent lights and the number of things to buy cheered him up. He accepted, with dignity, one of my cigarettes, but instead of lighting up he stored it, like a pencil, at his ear. His wife, he confessed, was the smoker in the family, and keeping her supplied was something of a problem. Her consumption might run six to ten cigarettes a day. His income as a house caretaker was not large, but on those holidays the Indians came out of the mountains, he set himself up as a scribe in the market, signing documents and writing letters. Was there, perhaps, someone I would like him to write to? There was. I took a postcard from the rack, showing a fish twice the size of the man who had caught it, and Señor Mendoza, with embellishments and curlicues, addressed it to my editor in New York, said I was having a wonderful time and wished he was here. It looked so great I hated to mail it. He, too, liked what he had done, and when I read it aloud he liked the sound of it. While I sat in the shade of the palm trees, facing the pier, he attended to more pressing business.

I should have guessed that he would make a day of it. After my evening meal at a sidewalk café, he appeared in time to join me for a cognac. He had a new string bag stuffed with sliced white bread, a particular passion of the señora. As we followed the curving road around the bay, the sea took fire from the setting sun. With due allowance for the sliced white bread, I thought the life had much to recommend it. I had bought candy for the kids, cigarettes for the señora, and for myself an ointment to repel insects. In the dusk, the sky remained a banked fire, but there was no perceptible cooling with the evening. Señora Mendoza, considerably deshabille, chain-smoked her windfall of cigarettes and fanned the smoke with a movie magazine. The child of a neighbor, a caramel-colored toddler, appeared with the caps of soft-drink bottles to play a game on the sun-baked surface of the yard. I spied on the children, but understood little. Periodically they all ran about screaming.

It had been a long day for me, but I preferred to recline in the open, swatting and fanning myself with a palm frond, than to take to the windless calm of my private quarters. The beating of a drum, like distant sounds of gunfire, rumbled across the bay. What day was it? Señora Mendoza did not seem to know. She asked her husband, who seemed sure when asked, but the more he thought about it, the less he was certain. Would I like him to go and inquire from a neighbor? No, I thought not. The insect repellent had the suggestion of a fragrance that I remembered from my camping days in Michigan. What had it been? *Citronella!* A marvelous word and not a bad repellent.

One morning—it hardly matters which morning—I stopped for a swim in the misty froth of the sea. I left the car parked off the highway, where I could see it. A mile of open empty beach stretched in both directions. A frieze of cruising pelicans, in military formation, fanning the air in slow motion, sailed by just offshore, low over the shallow water, their primitive wings flapping like sails. One of them suddenly dropped like a stone, to reappear with a fish in its scoop-like gullet. The small button eye of the bird unnerved me. As a youth of twenty in the Carlsbad Caverns, I had seen time itself drip from the ceiling, and rise from the floor, as if to finish off time at the point of their meeting. Hot as it was, watching these birds I felt the tingle of a primitive chill.

I had left my pants, shoes and T-shirt within a few feet of the sea and thrashed about for a few moments, then came up for air. On the white sand of the beach I could see the flashing pelican shadows. Otherwise nothing. To my surprise, I found I was standing in waist-deep water. When I glanced back to the beach, my clothes were gone. Short tracks led down to the beach where a stream passed under the highway through a metal culvert. The stream was shallow, and a not so small boy could have easily crawled the length of the culvert. I was out a pair of pants, about 230 pesos, and a coveted pair of crepe-soled sandals. My traveler's checks, luckily, were in the jacket locked in the car.

One of Señor Mendoza's older boys was able to crawl through the floorboards and open one of the doors. In the car I had a second set of keys, and a pair of old pants wrapped around a jack that rattled. It could have been much worse. The three of us drove into Acapulco together and had a huevos rancheros breakfast. I cashed one of the checks, and bought a pair of huaraches made from an old tire casing, although I knew they would soon give me blisters. On our way back, taking a bit of a ride to that point where the coast road ended, we passed two Indian boys who appeared to be working on a parked car. They were not trying to start it, as I first thought, but had the hood up and were trying to strip the engine. That was not easy, since their tools were limited to a pair of pliers. The car had a shiny new California license. They had managed to remove the seats and the dashboard, but the wheels and the engine confronted them with problems. When we stopped, both boys looked up, ready to run but inwardly triumphant. As an upcoming victim, I was of two minds.

We drove on up the street to where the pavement ended and several goats were grazing. A small boy, wearing a cap with a slowly revolving pinwheel, stood slapping one of the goats with a stick, as if beating a rug. I thought Señor Mendoza left the car to speak to him, but he stooped to gather up handfuls of the bank grass, filling the hamper he had made of the tails of his shirt. The boys working on the car popped up to wave at us as we passed. It occurred to me that the peculiar way I was feeling might be caused by the heat and the shimmering light, but it was also more of an upper than a downer, and in time I might grow to like it.

All four wheels were gone. The rear end of the car was still on the boxes they had used to hoist it. The nose of the car was in the ditch as if trying to hide. We stood there beside it, shading our eyes, but the glare from the paint made it hard to look at.

Mac said, "What'll they do with just the wheels?"

"Sell them back to us," I replied. (Love Among the Cannibals, *1957*)

A week or ten days later, it might have been eight, I was still there. In the morning I would stroll along the beach all the way into Acapulco, taking dips when I felt like it. I was soon well known to the beach photographers, most of whom had little to do. They took pictures of me for nothing, just to keep their hand in. Postcard snaps of me, in a variety of poses, were tucked into their hatbands and ornamented their cameras. We all agreed the early morning was the best light. Given time, it seemed to me, I might shape up into a pretty good beach bum.

After my usual breakfast, at the drugstore counter, I'd loaf

on the beach until the late afternoon, and the first of the fish-
ermen came in with their catch. I could never believe that the
people I saw going out would manage to catch anything. I
saw these plump-type matrons in baseball hats, wearing
Mickey Mouse watches and unlaced tennis sneakers, go out
like they'd never before been in a boat, and come back with a
marlin weighing four or five hundred pounds. I was asked to
stand in some of the pictures, to show the scale of the fish.

In the early evening I would have some food, then walk
along the firm sand—the tide being out—all the way back to
the Mendozas. At the end of that walk, when I took my dip, I
smelled like flint that had just been struck. A mongrel yellow-
eyed dog that liked to walk along with me often licked my
hands for the taste of the salt.

Later, in the dusky twilight, I would sit with the Mendoza
family while the huge señora sprawled on the hammock,
waiting for the dance music on her battery radio. It would
play loud for five or ten minutes, then begin to fade. The new
batteries I had bought her in Acapulco proved to be deader
than the old ones. What I wanted to hear about was the romance between the Yucatán scholar, and public scribe, and
the massive maiden from Guatemala, who after dining in the
evening inclined on her side propped on one flipper, like a sea
lion. Between two black fingers, she held one of her treasured
Old Gold cigarettes, like a piece of chalk. It had been idle for
me to explain that she was not actually smoking old gold. Periodically, and slightly, she coughed. Small as it was, it shook
her. It was hardly an attention-getting cough, but it soon got
mine. How could something so small create such a tremor in
something so large? Not to miss the pleasure of the last few
puffs, she used a bit of toothpick to hold the crackling butt to
her lips. So nothing would be lost, the pinch of tobacco in the
butt was stored in a snuff tin, and rerolled. In the morning,
after a night of deprivation, she would light up and inhale
with a crackle of tobacco like a miniature brush fire. Her need
was so great it made her self-conscious. Now and then she
would glance at me, shamefaced. Not Señora Mendoza, nor
her budding nymphet, but the impudent gringo from Mexico
City had brought to her attention that she was a helpless, vul-

nerable creature. I was not proud of it. It did us both good when I left.

I was both drawn and repelled by the cult of the primitive, the stripping away of endless inessentials, but the great earth mother Carmen Mendoza, squatted in the shade as she probed for lice on the heads of her children, unswatted flies crawling about on her mounds of flesh, put me in mind of the great sow of Schloss Ranna, with her long fluttering lashes, her squirming litter of mini-piglets, pink and hairless as baby mice. I had loved the way she grunted softly when I spoke to her, like a happy dreamer. I had surely set my eyes on contentment that exceeded expectations, but to what extent could I say the lady was conscious?

Señora Mendoza's pleasure—wherever it was centered in her great mound of flesh—was to look for and find the all but invisible lice in the gleaming, honey-hued hair of her daughter. By the hour, she washed, combed and brushed it to shine like wire. The girl sat before her, facing away, her lips parted and her eyes dreamy, as if being stroked by a lover. A full-blown nymphet at ten. What scent would she give off at twelve? If seated at my side, she would idly play with my fingers; she could not catch my glance without flirting. Her scalp was scoured to shine like a pan, but not her neck. In moments of delight, her long arms would twine around her body and wag the fingers at me from both sides. Was this the knowledge that flew the pelicans in stately formation, to drop like bombs on moving targets, trickling along the nerves that itched to play with my fingers?

Murky thoughts might come to me at night under the ceiling of flickering lizards. Hearing sounds like those of a kitten lapping up something, I beamed my flashlight into the corner. A double apparition, both substance and shadow, thrust its gruesome head toward the light. Rainbow-hued and irides-cent, the iguana was a small-scale model for a dragon. I lacked the will to turn away my gaze, or switch off the light. The large head swayed from side to side, to get a bead on me. Under one taloned dragon's claw squirmed whatever he was eating. In her tent of netting, the señora coughed as the crea-ture shuffled off.

207

All of Mexico, at the moment when my wide eyes stared into the darkness, appeared to me like an appendix that would soon rupture, unaware of its own existence. The non-conscious, the semiconscious, the slowly coming into consciousness, for which D. H. Lawrence had such an unearthly instinct, I accepted as part of the mystique of the "exotic." In the long horizontal structures at Mitla, and in the fermenting juices in the jungles, vegetable and mineral, the orderly and the aimless, achieved a plant-like resignation. At what point did the stripping down to basics strip away the civilized essentials? Piecemeal, the smiling wreckers at work on the highway would make out of the whole a sum of useless parts. The reverse side of the tourist was this dim apprehension that no distinction of importance existed between the diving pelican, cruising the beach, and the smiling scavenger on the highway.

On my last day, we all went for a ride into Acapulco. The señora, her huge feet bare, wore a lime-green shift, flowers braided in her hair. She sat with me in the front, a draped monument. What instinct had led her to choose lime green? Under the fans in the drugstore she gave off vibrations. We sat in two booths, sucking ice cream sodas through straws. Not the pots and pans, the shelves of glasses and dishes, but the smell of wrapped soap held her attention. Eyes lidded as she sniffed the wrappers, she stored away this vital information.

From Acapulco we rode to where the pavement ended and found the abandoned car stripped of its tires, but not its wheels. The windshield, the steering wheel, the generator, the carburetor, the lights, the muffler and the radiator were gone. With a little help, Señor Mendoza suggested, what was left might be carried up the slope and installed in the yard for the children. I saw no reason, at the moment, that the house might not be built around it.

I had come to Acapulco to break ties, but I would leave with troubling attachments. Señor Mendoza had bought, from one of the beach photographers, a snapshot of the gringo as a beachcomber. The child Carmelita studied it soberly, the tip of her pink tongue between her lips. Señor Mendoza rode with me to the turnoff for Mexico City. He had been there. He felt no great desire to return. Months later I would send him the snapshots I had taken of all the Mendozas, in particular the señora, a monument grooming her daughter, which would take its place at the edge of her mirror with that beach shot of myself. In the snapshots Señor Mendoza did not put me in mind of Don Quixote. Perhaps the windmills were missing. But in profile, in his beret, he did look very scholarly.

On my last evening in Mexico City, Jaime García and I took in a movie (I've no idea what it was), then had a late dinner at Sanborns that lasted far into the morning. We both sipped black coffee, and I smoked cigars. Time and time again we said that next time we would go to Veracruz, to Orizaba, to Mérida. With a friend who had a jeep we would go to Guatemala! Why not? All of that was next time. Shortly before dawn, I made room in the front seat (the others were packed with baskets, blankets and numerous pairs of the stirrup-heel boots I could not resist) and drove him to his place. We had an emotional parting. My loss was aggravated by the ao ourance that for him it would be much worse. It relieved him to savor my freedom. We felt for each other a deep affection. For months he had saved for me his best Mexican jokes.

Out of Toluca, at dawn, a narrow blacktop road took me north through a spectral landscape, but I was too saddened to appreciate it. In the midafternoon heat I pulled off the road in a setting appropriate for Pancho Villa. I spread one of my new blankets out on the sand, and lay with a straw hat shading my face. Even then, lights seemed to flash on the lids of my eyes. Perhaps I dozed. The sound I heard was like a distant crackling fire. In an instant a horse and rider loomed theatrically above me, the blue lips of the horse flecked with blood from the tooth-edge bit. He snorted wildly through dilated nostrils. That horseman who had for so long come riding, riding, over the purple moor and over plain and pampas had finally stumbled on me. Was my number up? The dark horseman was armed like a bandit; a cartridge belt circled his waist and crossed his broad chest. The heavy butt of a pistol thrust out of the holster. Would he shoot me, like a rattler, or simply let the horse trample me? Whatever, whichever it was to be, Mexico had well prepared me for the script. But the horseman himself seemed undecided how to follow up his advantage. I sprawled out on the sand before him. What a windfall for a fearless bandit! How his amigos would admire him! But this occasion had been thrust upon him without adequate preparation. The horse wheeled slowly, pawing up the sand, then the rider, in frustration, suddenly hooted as he dug in the spurs, and off they went. I sat up to dizzily watch the cloud of dust trail along behind them. Far up ahead, a gray smear of smoke indicated the city of Chihuahua, where I would soon take a seat at the bar and study my windburned face in the mirror. Just like in the movies, I took my tequila straight, with a chaser of salt.

On the highway leading west out of El Paso, I stopped for a double cheeseburger and three ice-cold glasses of milk.

"Where you get a tan like that?" the girl asked me.

I replied, "Acapulco."

The word did not ring a bell. A run-of-the-mill Texas-border-type waitress, she had spots on her scalp, scratched with her pencil. I would think of her almost twenty years later, when I saw the movie *Bonnie and Clyde*. On being asked what he planned to do, Clyde replied, "Rob a bank." That was a very good scene. The one with me and the waitress was pretty good too, with the fan whining, the radio squawking, and me lighting up a black-paper cigarette. I forget what brand it was, but it had a sweet taste and a smooth white ash.

During one of our spring vacations at Pomona College, my friend Ed Lundberg and I hitched up the coast to Robinson Jeffers's country, where we slept on the beach at Carmel and made our coffee in a can over a fire of driftwood. The staggering beauty of the coast would leave on me an impression from which Italy would never recover. We saw something of Point Sur, Big Sur and Point Lobos, but it did not cross either of our sun-baked minds to go on to San Francisco or Berkeley, doomed to give birth to the Beat Generation. Nor did I trouble to cross the Bay Bridge when I visited Mark Schorer in Berkeley in March of 1955. I think of that when I feel about on my wrist for the pulse of my time.

Mark Schorer was a scholar, a gifted writer of fiction, and a critic of generous impulses. He had spoken up for books of mine, and I was grateful. Schorer's wife, Ruth, to my astonishment, had been in Vienna the winter I had been there, and at the Studenten Klub we had friends in common. This did not impress her, as it did me, with the inscrutable powers that shape our ends. In the brief time we had together, I felt that Schorer, like D. H. Lawrence, was a man of intuitive judgments. I was not a good reader of my contemporaries—I seemed to like only what I might have written myself—and Schorer's empathy for what he was reading alerted me to the narrowness of my own practice. I had brought with me several unfinished manuscripts, one of them dealing with Gordon Boyd's walk on water, but I was more eager to have his impression of a bizarre piece I called "Babe Ruth's Pocket." This novel-length fiction consisted of characters from my own largely unread novels. It testified to my ongoing preoccupation with fact and fiction, with what is real-seeming in the world I perceive around me, and the fiction we produce to mirror that world. "Babe Ruth's Pocket" perceived the characters of my novels to be more real-seeming, less shadow and more substance, than the actual people with whom they mingled, and on whom they were based. I was perhaps right in thinking that only in Schorer would such an experiment find a sympathetic reader. He not only read it, he liked it. He would later be so rash as to recommend that the University of California Press publish it. Cooler heads prevailed, but I cite this incident as an example of Schorer's ability to read the book the author believed he had written. My novel was not without interest, but it was not an interest shared by the general reader. Schorer quickly grasped the writer's obsession, found it of interest, and enjoyed the performance. It is one of a quantity of my manuscripts that now reside in the Bancroft Library in Berkeley, thanks to James D. Hart's continued advocacy of the author of *My Uncle Dudley*.

Jim Hart had been one of my readers since that book was published, and had persuaded me, just a year or two before, to deposit my accumulating manuscripts in Bancroft. At the home of Jim and Ruth Hart, where I spent several nights, and heard some fine early Bing Crosby recordings, I met a generous sampling of local literary people, including Henry Nash Smith, George Stewart, the visiting celebrity C. S. Forester, and *San Francisco Chronicle* book critic Joseph Henry Jackson, who had spoken up clearly for my first novel. Did it cross my mind that a writer would be fortunate, indeed, to make his home in such surroundings? It did indeed. Some six or seven years, however, would pass before Walter van Tilburg Clark would ask me to take his place on the faculty of San Francisco State College, just across the bay. In those six years a new generation would stream out of the old American woodwork to make bonfires along North Beach, make trouble, make poems, and make love while putting off war. Of all this the finger on my pulse did not record one beat.

On my way east, at Schorer's suggestion, I stopped to visit with Howard and Dorothy Baker on their orange ranch near Fresno. I thought her novel, *Young Man with a Horn*, masterly. I had not read Howard Baker's poetry, but few Western poets I had heard of were more highly respected. I liked them both immensely, but I felt that Howard Baker especially suffered the torment of those committed, on the one hand, to the good life, and on the other, to great art. I left, soberly swearing I would soon return—a vow that has frequently come back to haunt me. The fault is always mine. I do not take the trouble, in the interests of fraternity, to go out of my way.

From the Bakers' I drove southwest to Death Valley, where I took out my unused Leica and stared about me, like a tourist in Eden who had forgotten his film. Again I made a vow to return that I did not keep. On a cold, clear night I stopped in Santa Fe long enough to warm up in the La Fonda lobby, and splurge on several Navajo blankets. Would the cargo of fleas that I knew that I was carrying in the Mexican blankets welcome these new prospects? I think they did.

The great and intricate secret of the open road—but it must be open, not clouded with smog and clotted with traffic—is the way it provokes and sustains image-making, the supreme form of daydreaming. The road should be a blacktop, to escape the whine, the deadening rhythm of the divisions in the concrete, the line down the center reeling in at the front what it reels out, even faster, at the rear, the car in its own inscrutable flight pattern, perfectly scaled to the world we live in, the heart lifting to see the horizon approach, then registering the loss as it vanishes behind us. What dreams seem to do for so many others, a long car trip does for me. I get startling glimpses of what lies ahead, I feel the stretch and pull of what recedes behind me. At unpredictable, miraculous moments, like the sound of blowing music, loose ends of my thinking come together. Most of it is as unreal as fiction, and as permanent.

Somewhere just east of Tucumcari, where the plains begin, a good breakfast under my belt and a following tail wind, the stalled tumblers in my story of Gordon Boyd began to stir and fall into place. I saw that his failure, the quirky and screwball delight he savored in it, was not an old American botchery but a new one, with its own sweetly rancid flavor. This side of his nature needed the special cultivation it would never get from his old friends in Nebraska. He wanted someone to further provoke and challenge him, someone more outrageous than he was. Who else but someone who had managed—in his fashion—to walk on water? Strange to relate, I actually had this person, filed away for this particular occasion.

In the material I had cut from *The Works of Love* was a macabre winter scene in Chicago. I had come upon the news report, in a magazine, of how, in the late spring thaw, an unclaimed body had been found beneath one of the snowdrifts. It was taken to the morgue, and from there to the dissecting room of a medical school. From the pail of severed hands available, one of the students selected one that he recognized as the hand of his missing father. Not long after, this young man also proved to be missing. He would reappear in my fiction as a cleaning woman in a manuscript I had not published, and he was now in the wings waiting to play a key role, as Paula Kahler, companion to Dr. Lehmann, in *The Field of Vision*. Unable to change an impossible world, Paul Kahler had settled for changing himself.

As I rolled eastward across Kansas and Missouri, the white strip down the center luring me onward, it occurred to me that this bizarre assembly of oddballs, dreamers and failures might naturally come together in one place only—the bullring of Mexico City! This least likely of all likelihoods was appropriate to this unlikely gathering: McKee, his wife and their grandson, the boy's great-grandfather Scanlon, the maverick Gordon Boyd with his Viennese companion Dr.

214

Lehmann, a student of madness, Mozart, and the transcendent Paula Kahler. I saw it all in a quick preview flicker, as I thumped my cold feet on the floorboards. In Missouri an attack of sciatica (I learned the name for it later) compelled me to spend some hours in bed, where I was able to make a few notes. Two days later I honked for my wife, who appeared in the carport with our black cat, Sour Mash.

"Why, you've still got your Acapulco tan!" she said. This I admitted, but I was mum about the imported life in the blankets. Sour Mash loved the smell, but as I recall, he was the first one to scratch.

Before I had settled down to get on with my book, Granville Hicks asked me to do a critical piece on the state of the contemporary novel, for a book he was editing. Eight or ten young novelists had been asked, and agreed to make contributions. I welcomed the encouragement to put in order some of the opinions I had been voicing, and impressions I had been pondering. American writers continued to be both productive and innovative, but our major figures, it seemed to me, were subject to a common and disabling disorder. The past cast its spell over the present. The territory ahead—in the American imagination—proved to be somewhere behind us when we sat down to write.

I was myself a case in point. Was this common affliction seldom, if ever, suffered by writers elsewhere? Were Americans compelled to reconsider their past before they could really deal with the present? How much of this was *self*-recovery—as I recognized it in my own preoccupations? I found the central issue beautifully anticipated by the writer who had first suffered from it. At the close of *Huckleberry Finn*, Mark Twain put it like this:

But I reckon I got to light out for the territory ahead of the rest, because Aunt Sally she's going to adopt me and sivilize me, and I can't stand it. I been there before.

For Twain, this territory would be embalmed in his childhood, a moveable feast to which he could turn again and again. One of its great thralldoms was that this past had no

215

truck with the future. To the widow of a childhood friend, Mark Twain wrote:

I should like to call back Will Bowen & John Garth & others, & live the life, and be as we were, & make holiday until 15, then all drown together.

The extraordinary blackness of this judgment is stupefying. Could an American writer of such magnitude, of such world-wide renown and expectations, actually have believed in what he was saying? That it comes in such a context, and at such a moment, gives it the force of a confession. Not merely the past, but the private preserve of a lost boyhood, was defined as the Great Good Place. Out of this compost would sprout the myths that millions of Americans still find congenial, and that Norman Rockwell would sanction with his *Saturday Evening Post* covers. This made it official that these sentiments were a matter of history and policy. On the one hand, the uncorrupt world of sanctified elders, pets and children, and on the other, the mess we were making of the present. Faulkner, too, preferred to locate himself in this semi-savage wilderness and Eden, where David Hogganbeck and Ikkemotubbe eternally pursued Herman Basket's sister, the primal and receding vision of womanly loveliness.

But Mark Twain died before the Great War, and had little precognition of the world that was emerging, to which he had personally contributed not a little cupidity and avarice. Colors that he thought to be of the deepest black—as the century wore on—would prove to be pastel shades of decorator gray.

I saw two deeply rooted native dispositions affecting the direction of the American novel: the first a deep distrust of the "intellectual," the old quarrel between the small-town hick and the urban sophisticate, but with the novel's future at stake; the second a preference for raw material, the less digested and tampered with the better. In each case, what we wanted and what we would get was the writer who was as broad and deep as our rivers, and as high and majestic as our mountains—not a writer in the bookish sense at all, but one of great natural forces. Mark Twain, of course, was such a figure, appropriately identified with the Mississippi River, and

Thomas Wolfe, looking homeward, would prove to be another, a writer and a man so out of scale he symbolized our vast resources of both sentiments and raw materials. The large bulk of Wolfe's *Of Time and the River* far outweighed Fitzgerald's *Tender Is the Night*. There was not a lack of craft-conscious writers, who read, criticized and challenged each other, but the public was held in thrall by a writer so singular I overlooked him. Between the two wars, Sinclair Lewis would be the read and world-recognized writer, his energy and his talent mingling the gross and the native, the intellectual and the hick, in just the right proportions. At the summit of his success a Nobel Prize winner, he was on the verge of a long decline, the price of his "success" being both failure and self-destruction.

At that very moment, in *The Field of Vision*, Gordon Boyd was celebrating, with appropriate self-abasement, his long-anticipated failure as a writer. The parallel to Sinclair Lewis was so obvious it had been lost on me. Lewis, indeed, was one of the writers neither mentioned nor discussed in *The Territory Ahead*.

From Hawthorne to Faulkner the mythic past has generated what is memorable in our literature—but what is not so memorable, what is often crippling, we have conspired to overlook. This is the tendency, long prevailing, to start well then peter out. . . . The writer's genius is unique, but in his tendency to fail he shares a common tradition.

For more than a century the territory ahead has been the world that lies somewhere behind us, a world that has become, in the last few decades, a nostalgic myth. . . . It is the myth that now cripples the imagination, rather than the dark and brooding immensity of the continent. It is the territory ahead that defeats our writers of genius, not America. (1958)

Exactly twenty years later, in a preface to the Bison Edition, I had some second thoughts.

. . . The role of nostalgia in our literature has dwindled as our great expectations have diminished. The backward look, the consuming longing, is no longer a crippling preoccupation

217

of the writer. The national purpose, the national conscience, are currently pressured from other quarters. I am now more inclined to a nostalgic view of nostalgia itself. What a passion it was for those possessed by it. Americans did not invent this torment, but surely we have made the most of its follies, a passion that was crippling to Thomas Wolfe but liberating to the mind of Faulkner. Without a mythic and alluring past American writers of genius, with few exceptions, had little to fuel their imaginations. It gave substance to their dreams of national purpose, and faith to sustain their personal visions. On such evidence the virtues of nostalgia more than compensate for its foibles. It would appear to have generated what was essential to a young nation's boundless and soaring expectations, uninhibited by, and often indifferent to, the obvious.

While I was working on these essays I was seeing a lot of Kitty Bowen. She had little time for novel reading—caught up as she was in the research on Sir Edward Coke—but I did what I could to introduce her to a few novels of mine. For those who liked Kitty, and she in turn liked, her vitality was contagious; for others, her assurance and detachment were unmistakably regal and distant. Who did she think she was, Elizabeth the first? I rather hope so. No woman I have known seemed so naturally born to rule.

My new novel, *The Field of Vision*, had progressed to where I knew that *time present*, all of it, would take place on a single afternoon in the bullring, the past materializing in flashback:

What a crazy goddam world, Boyd was thinking—and so made room for himself. Also for Dr. Lehmann, the celebrated quack, with nothing to recommend him but his cures, and Paula Kahler, the only sort of failure he could afford. Also for old man Scanlon, the living fossil, for McKee, the co-inventor of the dust bowl, for his wife, the deep-freeze, and her grandson who would live it all over again. Here gathered at a bullfight. The sanded navel of the world. Gazing at this fleshy button, each man had the eyes to see only himself. This crisp sabbath afternoon forty thousand pairs of eyes would gaze down on forty thousand separate bullfights, seeing it all very

clearly, missing only the one that was said to take place.
Forty thousand latent heroes, as many gorings, so many
artful dodges it beggared description, two hundred thousand
bulls, horses, mules and monsters half man, half beast. In all
this zoo, this bloody constellation, only two men and six bulls
would be missing. Those in the bullring. Those they would see
with their very own eyes.

"So you haf tudge boddom?" Dr. Lehmann had asked,
beaming on Boyd with his early-man smile. Then he had
added, "Wich boddom?"

For both Gordon Boyd and the author, "the boddom of the
boddom" was simply not part of their expectations. It would
recede beneath them, and their talent, if they had one, would
prove to lie in another direction.

I had thought the name *Yaddo* spoke for the flying strands of Far Eastern philosophy in the thinking, or the intent, of the founders, but the facts were not so complicated. A much-loved child, accustomed to play in the groves of trees near the house, the ground dappled and alive with the play of shadows, had sometimes run about crying, "Yaddos! Yaddos!"

I soon came to like almost everything about Yaddo, an artists' retreat near Saratoga Springs, including that story. Perhaps the many-gabled Victorian manse, a cluttered maze of rooms and niches, like the one built in Hartford for Mark Twain, somehow approximated the American dream of each man's house as his castle.

My day started with a crackling wood fire to take the chill off the cabin, and with the far roar of the crowd at the nearby racetrack. I loved the sweeping vista eastward, toward the White Mountains, the excellence of the food, the welcome book talk and gossip, and the presence of the handsome, imposing woman, Elizabeth Ames, who had set the tone for

Yaddo from its beginning. The aura of a war-blighted romance did much to enhance the role she played as a Jamesian culture figure. Since I had come to Yaddo primed for work, this tone suited me perfectly.

As I worked, I sometimes wondered if I still had a publisher. Marshall Best had read and rejected the manuscript recommended by Mark Schorer (this did not surprise me), but I was more than reluctant to test him with another commercially suspect novel. An assembly of tourists from the dust bowl gathered in a bullring in Mexico City? What would I think of next? My experience had been—and it was becoming extensive—that a publisher would hustle for the first book, but rest the oars in the locks with the second. With the completed manuscript of *The Field of Vision* I drove east through a landscape beautiful beyond description and twice stopped to wade about in the flaming leaves. Even James had referred to this Arcadia, and the way it resisted human usage, challenging the appreciative outsider to do more *with it* than the natives. But what? It had persisted because it resisted both use and abuse. There it all was, only more so, the cornucopia of riches that defied accounting, and that would be how I found it, and left it. To get beyond appearances was an old American story, but I was fortunate in having Granville and Dorothy Hicks to relate Arcadia to the chronic water shortage in Grafton and to a writer from the Platte Valley of Nebraska. I had come to pay a visit, to talk about Mexico, and to listen to the advice and encouragement of friends who were having a new coat of red paint put on their house. We all thought it looked great.

Granville liked the new manuscript, gave me some helpful criticism, but agreed that it would not be wise to confront Marshall Best with my bullring fable. How was the publisher, or the reader, to get a bead on such a writer? In ten years, no two consecutive novels established or defined my "territory." Some readers had been impressed with my strong sense of "place"; others regretted that this place proved to be where it was. The plains had briefly been the property of Willa Cather, who had soon, and sensibly, turned to other landscapes. Let the writer come from the plains, if he must, but be smart enough to leave them behind him. About that predicament, I was of two minds. *The Field of Vision* displayed a disarray of landscapes, characters and events that mirrored the conscience of the writer, but did not deceive him into thinking that the preoccupations revealed in his writing were shared by his contemporaries: neither what he created, out of reasonably whole cloth, nor the friends and colleagues with whom he shared the status of a writer and a reader. In a really quite tiresome way, he appeared to be a throwback to those "loners" who emerge out of a fabric of fact and fiction, compelled to do what we find them doing, compelled to make a limited model of the world out of an excess of impressions. In this perspective, *The Field of Vision* is coherent, and sometimes successful. The familiar ingredients are present—even the fabled receding past—and the writer's affection for the characters he is also obliged to pillory. A very characteristic performance, in a very unpredictable setting. I went back to my friend Harry Ford, who passed the book on to his friend Jerry Gross, a new editor at Harcourt, Brace, and to my great relief Harcourt, Brace contracted to publish it.

For some time, as part of *The Territory Ahead*, I had been pondering Norman Rockwell's America. His portraits of the presidential candidates Eisenhower and Stevenson, widely displayed in a series of posters, had aroused renewed interest in his work. My own taste and sentiments had been shaped by Rockwell quite beyond my grasp or the telling of it, and this knowledge gave edge and persistence to my reactions. What a bill of goods he had sold me—and I had bought! That barefoot boy with cheek of tan, his feet sticky with roofing tar, his face smeared with the pie still cooling at the pantry window, had also leaped from the bridge into the quicksand, and turned from there to try his hand at walking on water.

No cliché has been evaded; every cliché alters the actual image of the past in the interests of the sentiments of the present. To what end? Had the actual past been so bad that the memory of it had been suppressed? To what end would one diminish the truly memorable moment in the interests of a sham sentimentality? Was it a failure of nerve (a fashionable phrase at the time) or of memory itself? Was it feebleness

223

of taste, or intelligence, that would lead us to prefer the spurious to the genuine? Calendar pictures of romantically nuzzling horses (a movie innovation) to the realities of the farmyard? Americans who had searing memories of poverty and hardship, of sickness and death, of real losses without imaginary gains, had put it all behind them with the first calendar pictures of mixed litters of kittens and puppies, steamboats rounding the bend, and amber waving fields of grain. On the graves of what had been both forgotten and suppressed, Rockwell assembled a fiction that was pleasant to remember, and made us all feel good. Including myself. My *Boys' Life* mind had been honed and buffed by the *Saturday Evening Post* covers that celebrated so much I seemed to have forgotten. What access did I have to the real past? Where might it be said to be located? It was my first dim perception that *history* was not a volume of authorized texts, to which, in time of doubt, I would always have access, but rather a landscape of immense and cloudy horizons peopled with figures of my own imagination. The past to which I had access was a film that flickered on my own eyeballs. I might well buff it up, and add to or subtract from it (as I had just done in *The Field of Vision*), but I would never find it on those maps nailed to the walls of railroad stations. Norman Rockwell had his version—the gentle, white-haired old lady (a negotiable image, in the absence of an icon) and the decent small boy, "snapped" at the moment of prayerful silence as they say grace in a "rough" railroad café—and I would eventually prove to have mine if I insisted on writing about it. At the extremities of our lives, youth and age, we had established two durable fictions, but even as I prepared to mock them, I was aware they were receding. I, too, was receding, unobserved by myself, on a belt of time external to my perceptions, about which I sometimes felt quite superior. Hadn't I learned, as a fiction writer, how to run it both forward and reverse? The flashback, that bit of craft cunning, permitted me to conjure up a time of my own, all the while concealing from myself the time in which I was captive. I would get a glimpse of a larger time in those first photographs from space, where planet earth, a sort of timepiece, ticked away like a pocket watch. I would never long be free, however, of the tricks time would play on such an observer as myself, able to stop time in such a way the blur in the film indicated its passage, a happening to which I bore elaborate witness.

This elusive, ineluctable time had become a commonplace property of fiction. Katherine Anne Porter's story "Old Mortality" closes with Miranda's reflections on her entrapment in time past, but her high hopes for time future.

. . . I can't live in their world any longer, she told herself, listening to the voices back of her. Let them tell their stories to each other. Let them go on explaining how things happened. I don't care. At least I can know the truth about what happens to me, she assured herself silently, making a promise to herself, in her hopefulness, her ignorance.

As a young, and not so young, man, I felt that the conjunction of time and place—in particular, place—that left on me such a memorable impression was a property of the place and the time rather than of an event that took place within me. I also felt that such impressions of time and place were commonplace. Anyone (I felt) with a past would share them. The passage of time, indeed, had given rise to these impressions.

After a lifetime of being time's fool, and observing my own peculiar behavior, I conclude that my response to the time-place syndrome is not as widespread as I had imagined. Ingredients are present in nostalgia, but they are like shavings that have not taken fire. I know these feelings, and I feel such ties, but that is not what I am describing. Many, if not all, writers share it, since it is part of their purpose to recover losses, but the parallel I feel to be more exact is what many feel for "holy" places. That is my feeling, once I allow for a profoundly different orientation. Had I been bred or trained to religious observance, or sentiments, I would have been more than open to religious vibrations, to unearthly perceptions, to "seeing" the appropriate manifestations. Rather than merely open, I would have been eager. Between me and these "places" there is a pact that is earthly enough, in its origins, but with a bit of cultivation gives off its palpable aura. Henry

James has captured both its earthly and its unearthly trappings.

To be at all critically, or as we have been fond of calling it, analytically minded—over and beyond an inherent love of the general many-colored picture of things—is to be subject to the superstition that objects and places, coherently grouped, disposed for human use and addressed to it, must have a sense of their own, a mystic meaning proper to themselves to give out: to give out, that is, to the participant at once so interested and so detached as to be moved to a report of the matter.

That remarkably accommodates the sensations I have been evoking, and a lifetime of considering their complexity. I would add to this the exposed but uncritical soul of the child—or any person, such as myself, who accepted the world before he analyzed it, and accumulated a large, ticking store of impressions saturated with their own mystic meaning to give out. I became, as if on a higher order, the participant so interested and so detached that I was moved to a report on the matter.

On such a participant as myself, actual events, casual or dramatic, are of relative unimportance. They might be likened to the blurs in a photograph, indicating time's passage. If my training had been religious, my participation would surely have spoken of "voices," of visitations, of materializations, and called on the resources of the "séance" to give substance to my sensations. The space beneath the porch, or some other concealment, provides the child with his own magical trappings, and I am impressed—as a restless analyst—with how closely they resemble the more orthodox holy places. In Chicago, grown too large for concealment, I attributed qualities to everything at hand, and to routines that emphasized recurrence. The streetcar ride from the Loop: the platform of this car became for me a "place" of ritual observation, with the smell of the track sand as incense, and the view down the streets to the east, the vista over the lake, a prospect of life enhancement. Chicago, indeed, mystically collaborated with a naive but highly conscious young man whose inner voices required a cultivation of more outward forms. I was perhaps overripe for the picking, the quick transplant to Eden, the California oasis that mingled the groves of academe with those of lemons and oranges. In such wise I was approaching that moment, as a participant, when the mystic meanings to which I had been exposed, and it was proper of things to give out, would begin to elicit from me a lifelong response.

This clarified for me why, on my return from Europe, and before I had written a line of fiction, I found myself evoking in words these epiphanal images from my boyhood, those objects and places, coherently grouped, disposed for human use and addressed to it. In terms of what was given, I had been destined to be such a participant.

*I*n the winter of 1956, I applied for a stay at the Huntington Hartford Foundation, a colony for writers, painters and composers, in Santa Monica canyon just north of Bel Air. In the middle of March I headed west, by car, in my familiar flight pattern. My expectations as a writer were on the rise, but so was my discontent with my personal life.

Throughout our married life, my wife often felt the need for the companionship of older women. With such a self-preoccupied husband, this was perhaps understandable. Her need for such companionship had its origin in the unusual nature—or denature—of her mother. Deprived of this affection and nurture, my wife had learned to find it in the context of her teaching, and a shared love of music. To keep my mind on my work, I would wangle ways to be gone. So in the middle of March, I made another of my welcome escapes.

Somewhere near McCook, Nebraska, in a seasonable blizzard, I left the car in a rising drift and walked along a fence to a gas station. A dozen or more stranded travelers were huddled around an electric heater. There we spent the night, swapping stories, sipping quantities of instant coffee. By midmorning, however, it was warming and sunny and the road to the west had been opened. Just a few miles ahead, in a defile where cattle had huddled out of the winds, the blowing snow had covered them over to a depth of fifteen feet. More than three hundred had suffocated. Following close upon the plow that opened the road, I could see the white-faced Herefords, still propped upright, a frieze of bodies in the low relief of the snowbank. Twenty minutes down the road, there was not enough snow to conceal the grain stubble, and I did not discuss the blizzard, or the snow-buried cattle, with the travelers from the west in the next diner. This was known to be a country of remarkable liars and farfetched tales.

Two days later, northwest of Santa Fe, I looked for the adobe house with the beautiful doorway I had photographed in 1940, for *The Inhabitants*. I didn't find it, but I sat for several hours, my back against a sun-baked wall, in a silence that seemed an inaudible music, the dazzle of the light penetrating my eyelids. Another time, this moment would have been sufficient, but I wanted other company than my own. To bear the occasion in mind I bought a small Navajo rug, of traditional patterns and colors, to be there on the wall in whatever room I might wake up in.

A few days later, on a narrow dirt road winding above a dry firetrap of an arroyo, I got out of the car at a huge iron gate to announce my arrival. This was done by a phone call to the lodge, where a button was pressed and the gate swung open. As I made my windy descent into the canyon, I caught glimpses of the lodge, the skylights of the studios assigned to painters, and in the clearing below me a pattern of tiles in a swimming pool emptied of water. Someone was playing Gershwin's *Rhapsody in Blue*, repeating and repeating the same opening chords.

Among the Hartford residents that season was Edward Hopper, who rose from where he was seated, it seemed to me, in sections, a structure in the process of assemblage, to stand towering solemnly above his petite and pert wife. (He lowered himself to his seat in a similar manner, collapsing behind the posts of his knees.) I would often exchange with Hopper a series of uncoded, inscrutable glances as I listened to the gossip of his wife who was enjoying a holiday among talkers. An original splinter from early Yankee floor planking, Hopper, it was clear, preferred total social deprivation to what passed for social contact. I liked as much of him as I got to know, and often saw that he got his second cup of coffee.

Sam Kaner, an attractive, companionable young artist from New York, who had lived in Paris after the war, among other respectable distinctions had read one of my books. This put him in the class by himself. We began our friendship discussing that book, *Man and Boy*, for which he had a keen and experienced appreciation in his role as a husband and a father. His very pretty Danish wife, with their daughter, made her home with her family in Copenhagen, a topic that inspired the bohemian Sam Kaner to artful passages of self-mockery. We would often begin our talk at the lunch hour, with the sandwiches brought to our cabins, then continue it under the fog that usually veiled the beach where Sunset Boulevard met the sea. This shroud of fog was deceptive since it intensified, rather than diminished, the sun's glare. By mid-afternoon, when it burned away, many of the paler mermaids were already parboiled, iced with gobs of Noxzema. Sam and I would spread our towels just back from the sand edging the water, with a critic's view of the day's offerings.

This chick, with her sun-tan oil, her beach towel, her rubber volleyball, and her radio, came along the beach at the edge of the water where the sand was firm. Soft sand shortens the legs and reduces their charms, as you may know. This one pitched her camp where the sand was dry, slipped on one of these caps with the simulated hair, smoked her cigarette, then went in for a dip. Nothing particular, just a run-of-the-mill sort of chick. (Love Among the Cannibals, 1957)

We were usually back at the Foundation for dinner, where the food was good and the company congenial. The mix of personalities was continually changing and restoring the bottomless well of gossip. Max Eastman, vital, handsome, and a source of some apprehension for his plump, blond Russian wife, was instrumental in getting the pool filled with water, and the first to bounce the clanking diving board. One Sunday, Gérard Philippe—as if part of a tour—added real Hollywood luster to our retreat, and I liked him both as a person and an actor. His beautiful French wife seemed to feel the burden of a husband so disarmingly captivating. A few years later, when I learned of his death, I felt a keen personal loss.

On rare occasions, such as a good foreign film, some of us made the long drive into Westwood. As we returned to the Foundation, dipping into and out of the series of canyons along the palisades, the white lights streaming toward us, the red taillights receding, the ineffable sense of adventure that is part of movement, that cunningly enhances romantic expectations, would be so palpable it shamed me to feel it. With the sun's rise these sentiments would burn off, like the fog, but they would return, undiminished, with the evening. If there was appropriate music on the radio, or the appropriate girl in the seat beside you, these moments, however delusive, would prove memorable.

One evening we were invited to a party in the exclusive Bel Air enclave just north of UCLA. There the son of a prominent Midwestern meat packer had bought a mansion. He fancied himself a jazz musician, and had married a Hollywood starlet. In the Hollywood fashion, clusters of partygoers, strangers to each other, milled about for a while and then left. I was captivated by the host's widowed mother, one of the long-suffering agents of mercy and terror I believed I had patented, and she seemed to recognize in me one of her lost prodigal sons. All evening she shared with me her nostalgia for what had been, her anxiety for the future. I sat with several albums of Minnesota photographs, including a leather-bound volume in which her husband was praised as a founder and pillar of the community. I studied his portrait. Toil-worn and thickened hands were placed on his meaty thighs; a chain looped across his wrinkled vest. How many days of his life had he wondered where the time he wound on his watch had gone? Her fingers moved across the photograph for the reassurance her eyes failed to give her. Her hand resting on my arm, she acknowledged that after each party many things were missing. A silver-backed brush from her dresser. Could I explain it? Would guests invited to her home actually steal things? I imagined that in the purse she clutched to her lap she kept her jewels. She was eager for me to read about her husband, born on a farm thirty-one miles north of Oslo, a good, decent, half-conscious man dead at the summit of his career, his name on the best-selling bacon in the supermarkets. I was what she needed, she took the trouble to tell me, not just to advise her son but to be an example to him (I a young man from the same unpopulated landscape, who had come to California and not married a starlet), and I said, yes, yes, of course I would be back, but I knew I would not. One window of her new home offered a view of the cloudland irresistible to starlets, star-makers and such incurable pipe-dreamers as myself, so that the bathos of our mutual pipe dream no longer struck me as amusing. In Joyce's story "The Dead," the character Gabriel, at a moment of deep emotion, catches a glimpse of his reflection in the cheval glass, his face with the expression that always puzzled him when he saw it in a mirror. So I, too, saw myself as a ludicrous, fatuous figure. Only a touch more consciousness was necessary to see that in this tableau I was the most bathetic, since my pretenses were the least defensible. As an observer, I had caught my reflection in the mirror I so often held up to others.

In Brentwood, just a few blocks north of Sunset, Leon Howard lived in a spacious Mediterranean villa happily out of fashion at the time he had bought it. Both Leon and his wife loved parties, and they had found the ideal house to accommodate them. On my frequent visits I would sometimes meet scholars from Europe or Japan who enjoyed, as I did, the Howard hospitality. Leon's book on Melville had just been published, and the Melville scholar Jay Leyda might be on hand.

I had written a short, once-over-lightly piece on Melville, for *The Territory Ahead*, which I was not eager to show to Leon, but I had brought along with me several others, including one on Hemingway, that I wanted his opinion on. To my great relief, he liked it, and thought it said something fresh on a very tired subject. That was high praise from Leon, and on the strength of it I brought over the Faulkner piece. A departmental party was in session, and a young woman introduced herself to me as she brought me a drink. A handsome blond Rhine maiden, with a peeling tan, she had read two of my books, and she wanted to talk. I had to rock back on my heels to keep my eyes on her level. A woman who likes men, and knows herself to be attractive, need have little concern with the usual preliminaries. She wrote her number on a matchbook cover, but cautioned me not to call her during meal hours. She cooked and child-sat for a family of six in Brentwood, out from New York for a California summer. The young man who had brought her, pleased with his role as an escort, took no offense at her expanding interests.

"I paint," she said to me in parting. "I'd like to paint you."

I said something or other about my lack of time, and caught the glance of Leon, across the room from us. His gaze was so absorbed and direct he seemed unaware that I was looking at him. Did he clearly perceive, in this casual encounter, so much more than I did? In his gaze I felt the detachment necessary for appraising the possible results. Later we talked about Faulkner, and about the teaching I might do at USC the following summer, but he did not allude, at that time or later, to my first meeting with the Greek, the name she would bear in *Love Among the Cannibals*.

As willing as she seemed to be, the Greek found it hard to fit me into her schedule. She had several classes at UCLA. On occasion we discussed her reading on the telephone. I usually met her near the Brentwood residence, where she lived in. On occasion she might run late, and I would catch up on a little of my own back reading. She was usually still in her maid's white outfit, which went well with her figure and her tan. We might drive to the beach, near Malibu, or to the deli lunchroom in Brentwood where she liked the pie and I liked iced tea made with mini ice cubes. These were unpredictable encounters. She might be moved to throw her arms around me—a hazard not to be dealt with lightly—or would sit chewing gum and reading Conrad. Her taste in literature I judged to be good, since she liked us both. Another time, we might discuss the

young man in Colorado who wanted her to marry him and sent
her money. Would she like Colorado? Had I been there? Knowing her as I did, did I *think* she would like it? The thought of
horseback riding brought out the Valkyrie in her nature. To
please me—only me?—she changed her bra style to one less
revealing and uplifting. In due time—which proved to be considerable—I perceived that her features were remarkably common. But little I cared. I was hooked on her vitality, and the
desire she could bring to her eyes.

Late one afternoon, she called me to say that she would
have the house to herself that evening. Just at dusk, I parked
in the street below, and made my way up the driveway to this
assignation. I found her sprawled out on her cot in the small
maid's room, watching TV and eating a bowl of sliced
peaches. Her interest seemed to have drifted to other matters.
We sat there watching TV together. I was prepared to be a
patient seducer and sipped warm beer until the movie ended.
We both needed a shower, and she took one. Somewhere upstairs I could hear the water drumming, and above it the
sound of an approaching car. Lights flashed at the window. I
heard the shrill, high-pitched squeals of the returning children. One of them ran into the house, shrieking her name.
She had told me how the children loved her! I had just time
to roll from the bed, and skid beneath it, before the door
pushed open. The child ran up to the bed—I saw bobby-
socked feet—turned to look around, then ran out. I lay there
as the house filled with the inhabitants. There was talk in the
kitchen. I heard her chatting with the children. Some time
later she entered the room, closed the door. She took a seat on
the bed, her broad flat feet on the carpet. I could smell the
warmth of her showered body, the fragrance of the soap. The
springs began to creak and bounce with her laughter. When
she sprawled out wheezing on her back, I gave her a good
thump from below with my knees. That set her to gasping
hoarsely. Half an hour might have passed while I waited for
the first floor to empty of children. She made a place for me
on the rim of her cot. My rage was less at her than at the
clown, smeared with floor dirt, who sat there watching her set
her hair in curlers. The painted nails of her toes were like

crushed grapeskins. It did not flatter her figure to be propped up in bed, like a piece of soft chocolate. Quite beyond conception was the fact that I had panted with desire as I came up the driveway.

Finished with her curlers, she smoked my Delicados and seemed to take pains not to intrude on my reflections. On the walls of her room were photographs of boys chasing her into the sea, leaping with her from diving boards, packed with her into the seats of convertibles. At the foot of her bed loomed a poster of the mad King Ludwig's fairy castle in Liechtenstein. That gave me the last smile, if not the last laugh. She was called upstairs to tuck her kiddies in bed, and I was able to make my escape down the driveway. I drove around for quite a while, up the coast as far as the Trancas restaurant, where I stopped for a cup of coffee, and listened to a rehearsal, in the adjoining booth, of the Hollywood and Vine art of seduction. I deserved every word of it. Driving back through Malibu, where the surf was pounding under the cabins, I caught a glimpse, through one of the open doorways, of the high-fish-net style of the interior, just as a Romeo of mature vintage escorted his Rhine maiden to the car. I've no idea why, but she carried her shoes. This would provide me with the image that was true to the Greek and Horter, and to which I owed my quick recovery from the events of the evening. It is the girl who kicked off her shoes that I still bear in mind.

I never saw my Rhine maiden again, not that I didn't try. When I called the residence, a woman's voice said, "You the one who was crazy about her? She just left. You can just be grateful if you don't find her. She's a willful woman. She just takes what she wants."

I had been smitten by a real enough dream girl, with toenails like crushed grapeskins, but the one to seduce me had kicked off her shoes as she entered a Malibu cabin. Losses and gains were equally shared.

It was my good luck that we had in residence, at the Foundation, a flesh-and-blood jazz pianist, a self-described poet of the black keys. One or two of his tunes, played on Broadway, had trickled down to the jukeboxes. One hundred and eighty pounds of heart, he was a wonderful man to watch. For my condition, he was just what the doctor ordered.

"Listen to this one, man," he would say, and play something that sounded familiar. It was always familiar. But that, indeed, was its virtue. Mac—as I chose to call him—saw a great future for both of us. For one of his new tunes I coined these lyrics:

> *What next?*
> *The life of love I knew*
> *No longer loves the things I do.*
> *What next?*

I felt that once I had the appropriate voice, the casting would come easy.

If you have sometimes wondered who really wears the two-tone ensembles that set the new car styling, Mac is your man. That's why I keep him down at the beach. He's quite a sight in his Hawaiian shorts, made of coconut fiber, a cerise jacket with a bunny-fur texture, a sea-green beret, and something like an ascot looped at his throat. . . .

To get away from the raw material—the virus of suggestion threatened to kill me—I left the Foundation and headed for Philadelphia before my period of residence had ended. During the long drive back, I often pulled off the road to make notes on the maps, or anything handy. In my eagerness to hold the wind in my kite, I kept up a flow of two-way dialogue, featuring Mac, Horter and one Billy Harcum, a Southern belle, appropriate to the occasion. On arriving in Wayne, I went to my study before I unpacked the car. The great pleasure of this enterprise was that of a romance without hang-ups. I worked the long, hot days, and got up at night to take dictation from voices that did not sleep. By early October I had the first draft of *Love Among the Cannibals.*

Just as I had hungered for the sea and the sun when I had left in the spring, the dense, lush growth of a Main Line summer now had a soothing effect on me. For the first time in my career, I believed the book I was writing would find me many

237

new readers. A young friend, David Hawke, to whom I read many of the chapters, assured me that *The Cannibals* had the verve, the pace, and above all the *appetite* that would seize the reader and hold him. We spent much of our time wheezing with laughter. The book had also emerged, as if on order, to cut the ties, real and imaginary, that I had developed with the past in my recent fiction. *The Cannibals* explicitly cut such ties, as if with the intention of cutting the author adrift. There are few readers of fiction who trouble to distinguish between the "I" of the narrating voice and the author, a confusion of identities they find too agreeable to either surrender or examine. Even my friend Kitty Bowen, once the book had been published, sometimes glanced at me with Elizabethan misgiving, curious as to what extent she might have misjudged my nature. Kitty had a new book of her own going to press, and my wife was busy with the galleys of *The Lion and the Throne*. Sometimes we stayed on for a buffet supper in the patio, listening to music. These occasions approximated the good life (I repeatedly felt the urge to say so) in so far as I was able to participate in it, or to judge it—good food and good companionship—yet a strand of dis-ease, not quite discontent but a twitching, febrile need to be somewhere *else*, to be someone *else*, to become rather than to merely be, faintly stirred the humid air we all breathed with such satisfaction. *What next?* That chord, tiresomely plucked, drifting in on the breeze, then drifting away, was as present in this civilized, cultivated garden of plenty, within sight and almost sound of similar occasions, as to Nick Carraway at West Egg gazing toward the lights of Gatsby's mansion. What next? Would it be my rendition of "Just One More Chance"?

In November I put aside *The Cannibals* to do a piece for *Holiday* magazine on the plains. I turned to this assignment with the appetite of a man long deprived of his soul food. As a writer who had thought to put all that behind him, this was somewhat puzzling. My editor at *Holiday* liked the piece, and urged me to do others for them. Such as? What about the cars in my life? He had read enough of my fiction to know that cars had played both leading and subordinate roles. One of my childhood memories was of car lights, smoking like torches, crossing the yard as if to enter the house. My father had bought the car in Columbus, a distance of forty miles, and driven it the forty miles in second gear rather than risk the crisis of shifting. That car, an Overland, would soon be followed by a Willys Knight, famed for its sleeve-valve motor and soft blue exhaust. That gave way to a Big Six Studebaker with fold-away seats and flapping side curtains. A Liberty sedan, with plush velour upholstery and a vase for flowers on the doorposts, gave way, briefly, to a Reo Flying Cloud, and for about two hundred miles, an Essex Coach.

The writer who had just symbolically cut his ties with the past spent most of the Christmas season splicing new ties. These cars were links in a chain that led me back to the winter of 1927, when I had arrived in California with my father in the sidecar of a Harley Davidson motorcycle. The sun shone, pigeons wheeled, and the open cars came down Sunset, with the good-looking women holding on to their hats. A young man had just swum to Catalina Island, winning a lot of William Wrigley's money, and he could be seen, covered with lard, on the front page of the newspapers. In a used-car lot on Sixth Street, a Marmon touring car, with wire wheels and a patented Liberty airplane engine, was waiting to begin its eastward passage with a carload of idlers, a fox terrier, and three passengers on the fold-away seats, one of them my father. Some five weeks later, that car would be abandoned, at high noon, in Lake Village, Arkansas, at the moment the levee broke a few miles to the north, and it had always been my secret, inscrutable intent to one day return and see if it was still there.

How does a boy seventeen years of age, and healthy, having long admitted to such ties, cut them? He eventually writes a tie-cutting book. He writes a tie-splicing book. It's hard to do malice to a great nation where the cutting of ties, the splicing of ties, the staunching, securing and sealing of ties, the rupturing, the breaching, the dissolving of ties, is the passion that binds us, one to the other, the fast and the slow bleeders, shoring up with Band-Aids our accumulating arrears.

Holiday found "The Cars in My Life" amusing, but felt I

should turn to something more substantial. In *The Field of Vision* I had written about Mexico. How about a piece on Mexico? This suggestion greatly appealed to me, since it would finance my return, and oblige me to see more of the country. For Christmas, from Acapulco, Señor Mendoza sent a family portrait taken by one of the beach photographers. There sat the massive señora, spread wide as a melting idol, with her tribe assembled about her, and Señor Mendoza, in his beret, holding the hand of the wide-eyed Carmelita. I looked to the side and behind these figures for Mac and Horter, for the Greek and Billy Harcum, who were more real to me than the pile of sand from which the shovel handle still protruded. Having lived for months with the scene I had invented, Mac and Billy Harcum, Horter and the Greek, the day-by-day disassembling of the car on the highway, I had perplexing feelings about the real Acapulco. Was it a tie to reestablish, or to relinquish? In the light of the fiction I had just written, the real seemed unreal. This was disturbing to my sense of facts, my love of things as they were, my respect for memory and the emotion, both of which, in the play of my imagination, had been freely altered and corrupted. I wanted the real world, with its affections, and the adornments of the imagination. Yet I felt that the *real* had been curiously diminished. Was this loss the expense of the imaginary gain? The real had not as yet become the phantom that recedes as we approach it, peeling away like the layers of an onion, but was a commonly perceived state of nature confirmed by observation. I would wait several years for Wittgenstein's comment "My aim is to teach you to pass from a piece of disguised nonsense to something that is patent nonsense" to momentarily locate myself in an orbit subject to predictable corrections, including the train that waited for the arrival of the station.

A writer's life is not entirely lacking in drama. On a midwinter trip to New York, as I waited, on my publisher's floor, for the arrival of an elevator, I was joined by a graying but vital woman who paced up and down the foyer, pushing the buttons. A handsome woman, with a brisk professional manner, she proved to be unaware that her bloomers had drooped, to hang like a harem costume below her skirt. Here, indeed, was a moment of truth and I met it. We were alone, but as I stepped forward I hoarsely whispered the necessary information.

"Young man," she said to me, "speak up! I can't hear you!"

So I spoke up. I also threw in a few pointed gestures. She tilted forward to check, saw the problem, and walked from me to the limits of the foyer, where she stooped and hoisted the bloomers. We descended to the street in the same elevator. Some weeks later, I was able to verify that the lady was Dorothy Canfield Fisher.

That incident may have had something to do with a stop I made in the used-book department of Brentano's, on Fifth Avenue. Waiting there for me, after a search of many years, at a price that was plainly a blunder, was the Oxford edition of John Keats's letters, in the orange buckram with the paper labels on the spine. All but a few pages of the introduction were still uncut. I had coveted these volumes since I had first set eyes on them in the library of Pomona College. I was certain that the clerk would note the mistake in the price, but he was engrossed in expressing his own love of Keats. Two hours later, safely home in Wayne, I called my friend Eiseley to announce my triumph, and point out that the pages were still uncut. A still further refinement, with me in mind, was that the English printer, John Johnson, had bound into each volume an extra paper label for the spine. My excitement about this coup led me to forget, for the moment, my encounter with Mrs. Canfield Fisher, a literary incident calculated to please the ladies.

In mid-February, shortly after midnight, we were awakened by the phone's clatter. My editor, Jerry Gross, was calling from his home. "Prepare yourself," he said to me. I self-prepared. *The Field of Vision* had won the National Book Award for fiction. He explained that there would be no public announcement until the award ceremony, late in March, more than five weeks away.

My wife and I discussed this windfall briefly, then lay

awake most of the night with the aftertremors. Surely this would enhance the public reception of *Love Among the Cannibals*, a manuscript I had postponed submitting. I did not want a publisher disappointed by *The Field of Vision* pondering the "problems" of *The Cannibals*. The effects of this on the author were to be seen, and heard, in the buzz given off by the aroused expectations, none of which he was free to discuss. To our friends it perhaps seemed obvious, and to at least one of them it was a pain.

"For heaven's sakes, Wrighty," Kitty Bowen said to me, "I'm sure you deserve it, but stop acting like a ninny."

Once I had been exposed to classical music, I had come to rely on it for both pleasure and relaxation. We loved good jazz, from Dixie to Benny Goodman, but most of the records we bought were of chamber music. Our first extravagant purchase, after the war, had been the London Gramophone record player, the size of a small piano, capable of an unearthly fidelity. With this example in mind, I had become a high-fidelity addict. Recently, to accommodate my wanderings, I wanted a sound system that would travel. I found it in the Ampex tape recorders and amplifiers built into sturdy, compact pieces of luggage. The book award money made it possible for me to own this equipment. Most of March and April, I spent hours of each day transferring our record library to tapes. For several years, the money we had once reserved for books had been channeled to collecting records that would not soon find their way to the new LPs. We were great for Casals, unaccompanied, playing Bach, Landowska on the harpsichord, the Budapest Quartet, and early albums of chamber music with the Victor Red Seal label. Purcell's Trumpet Voluntary, played on our London Gramophone, ceremoniously opened most of our social occasions. I often relied on Ralph Ellison's tips for cigars—the new leaf coming in from the Canaries and from Honduras—and it was Ralph who called to my attention a new album of flamenco music from Spain.

My publishers had an apartment in the East Fifties made available to visiting bigwigs, and for a few days in March I would be one. I went to the city in advance, to bask in the reflection I saw in shopwindows. My friend Sam Kaner was a good man to meet at such a time, with his own private blend of affection and sarcasm. Sam had applied for a fellowship that would take him to Venice for a year, and we talked about that promise as we strolled around the city.

Award ceremonies are seldom moments of drama, but I contrived to make this one a bit unusual. When called to the podium by the master of ceremonies, I made the ascent without trouble, read my acceptance comments, then scooped *all* of the papers from the podium and made my escape. The cries I heard swelling behind me I accepted as part of the applause. I had reached the center aisle before the MC caught me, sorted his own notes from those that I clutched, then returned to the platform in waves of applause! As my wife said, and a few friends confirmed, the moment was unforgettable.

In interviews with the press the following day, I was frequently asked to what I attributed my memory for details of the past. What details? A few were quickly mentioned. Take, for example, the way the front wheel of a bike will continue to spin when the rider spills it on its side in the yard. Or take the way keys for tightening up skate clamps were invariably bent. It pleased me to be thought so clever, but there was nothing unusual in a bent skate key. Nor would any small, frozen-fingered boy soon forget the battle he had to tighten the clamps. As for that twirling bike wheel, I saw it clearly enough, but I would not say that I remembered it, *then* wrote it. More than memory was at work in what I remembered. The effort and act of memory enabled me to see what I had often both observed, and ignored, until that moment when I actually described it. Thanks to the questions I was asked, I began to ask myself what I actually *remembered*, and what seemed to appear at the moment of writing—like the voices and actions in a séance.

"Reading your book brought it all back!" one reader said, as if he saw it captured like the fly in amber, embalmed in time until someone's memory brought it back.

* * *

243

One reason I see it all so clearly is that I have so often put it into writing. Perhaps it is the writing I remember, the vibrant image I have made of the memory impression. . . . Image-making is indivisibly a part of remembering.

If I attempt to distinguish between fiction and memory, and press my nose to memory's glass to see more clearly, the remembered image grows more illusive, like the details in a Pointillist painting. I recognize it, more than I see it. The recognition is a fabric of emotion, as immaterial as music. In this defect of memory do we have the emergence of imagination? If we remembered both vibrantly and accurately—a documentary image rather than an impression—the imaginative faculty would be blocked, lacking the stimulus necessary to fill in what is empty or create what is missing. . . . Precisely where memory is frail and emotion is strong, imagination takes fire. (Earthly Delights, Unearthly Adornments, 1978)

I stayed on in the city for several days, breathing air that seemed a bit bubbly with oxygen. One day, I was seated alone in my editor's office, sipping coffee as I peered into an adjoining office. Several Harcourt, Brace executives—I had met them briefly—were crouched about the chair of one of their number, who had lowered his head to read from a manuscript in his lap. He spoke in an excited whisper. Occasionally he glanced up to share his appreciation. As he went on reading, I caught fragments of sentences that sounded familiar.

. . . My room was dark, but the door to the bathroom was open, and this little girl with her glass of ice water stood facing the mirror. I watched her empty the water into the sink, but retain the ice. She put the loose cubes in a face towel, whacked them on the edge of the sink until she had crushed them, then took the crushed ice, a handful of it, and slipped it into the cups of her halter. All the ice she had; then she cupped it to her breasts. I saw her face reflected in the mirror, the eyes closed in a grimace of pain, the teeth clamped down on her lower lip till it turned white. (Love Among the Cannibals)

The pleasure shared by the reader and his listeners was interrupted with loud guffaws and thigh slapping. At the ap-

244

pearance of a secretary, the manuscript was slipped into a drawer of his desk. His colleagues made a quick departure. Sometime later, walking the streets, I marveled less at boys being boys than I did at the naiveté of the author. It had been a delight to write that scene, but I would not read it again without the appropriate grimace.

Fortunately for my unsettled state of mind, I had made arrangements to teach a course at the USC summer school. Just before I left, the painter Ynez Johnston, whom I had met at the Hartford Foundation, wrote to tell me I should call her good friend Jo Kantor, an art collector and dealer, in Beverly Hills. I thought it unlikely I would—I had lectures to prepare, but I put the number that would change my future where I could find it if I wanted it.

I left for California in early May, and my wife, to have a visit with her mother, rode along with me as far as Cleveland. Mother had given up the house and moved to an apartment in Shaker Heights. We spent the night in a motel, where, again about midnight, we had our second surprise from my editor. New American Library had bought the paperback rights to *Love Among the Cannibals* for twenty thousand dollars. As part of this agreement they would also publish *The Field of Vision*. This was the largest advance I had ever received. I thought it would surely ruin my sleep, but after a short and practical discussion with my wife, my half share of this vast sum of money did not weigh heavily on me, and I was soon asleep.

In the morning, after one of Mother's calorie-coded, one-egg breakfasts, I drove back to the freeway, dimly aware of tremors in a part of my nature previously unheard from, and conscious that tumblers were falling before I had turned the key in the lock. I liked the sensation. By late afternoon, in Indiana, riding the tailwind of my rising expectations, I decided to drive right through the night to see if I could pick up some music from Mexico on the airwaves. Whatever else might turn up in my future, I also had an agreement with *Holiday* magazine that Mexico would be in it, and soon. And that I liked.

Between Needles and Los Angeles, even early in May, I drove with wet towels at the car windows and cooled my windburned face with swipes of lip ice. In the shade of gas station awnings, the horizon shimmered like cooling ashes. The wavering line at the center of the highway seemed to reel me backward to the safaris of my boyhood: the flapping side curtains, thumping tires, the ascending hiss of the steam on the inclines, and the spouting geyser of rust-colored water when I unscrewed the radiator cap.

Long after sunset, the car interior cooling like an oven, I stopped at a lunchstand in Claremont, where I had once waited on tables. A fan droned, stirring the paper napkins. The cook, a heat- and light-bleached cockney from Liverpool, leaned on his padded elbows at the food slot window, a cigarette between his lips. I had stopped to have a milkshake and a cheeseburger before confessing my ties with the establishment, a vital, freckle-faced, bird-eyed woman and her tottering singer of snatches of cockney ballads, who greeted me with "How's tricks, matey?" My ties with his past had eroded.

He cooked my cheeseburger braced on a crutch. His legs were shot. Even in the dim past his wife had referred to him as im-*po*-tent. "Besides, he's im-*po*-tent," she would assure me, a calamity I could judge for myself, if I had the nerve.

On my return from Europe, in the fall of 1934, I had waited on tables for Ma and Pa Slade for one "hot meal" a day. When I appeared with my girl one weekend—pleased to share her radiant bloom and uncommon beauty—Ma Slade remained in the kitchen while Pa Slade hobbled about in his carpet slippers. She was there to take my money at the register, however, and kept me waiting while she checked my meal ticket. "Don't you trouble to come back," she said to me with a smile, "if you're going to bring *her*."

Just short of two in the morning, I arrived at the Howard home in Brentwood. The front door was unlocked, and a desk lamp burned in the study. On the desk, the floor and the seats of the chairs were the term papers Leon had been reading. I used the shower in his study, then cooled my windburned face by lying in the draft from the patio. In a neighboring house, the white ceiling lit up when the refrigerator door was opened. I heard the clatter when a glass was added to the dishes in the sink.

A letter from Benjamin DeMott, of Amherst, had been forwarded from Wayne. He wanted me to come to Amherst for a week in October, meet with a few classes, give two lectures. For this I would receive fifteen hundred dollars.

I discussed this with Leon while he fried us some eggs and I burned the toast. He thought that I should do what I could to enhance my standing in the academic community. One day I might need it. Speaking for himself, he thought the life of a teacher, with all its maddening frustrations, was still the most civilized and gratifying of vocations. It impressed me to hear this from a teacher and scholar who gave of himself freely, and daily suffered the familiar academic abuses. With a fresh pack of cigarettes and a new pot of coffee, he returned to the papers in his study.

I had worn out the front tires on the trip west, and drove over to Sears in Santa Monica to check on prices. On my way

248

back, driving east on West Pico and passing a large car lot with wind-flapped banners, I glanced up to see a green Jaguar coupe with the price finger-painted on the windshield: $1,795. I proceeded several miles down the street before what I had seen registered, and it dawned on me, after a lifetime of rejecting, that I could now buy some of the things I wanted, if I wanted them badly enough. I wheeled around to drive back to the car lot; I parked where I could get the bloom of the aristocratic profile. Was it a lizard, a leopard, or a green dragon? It was down in the books as an XK-120, well known to Jaguar fanciers. Sensing my vulnerable state of mind, the salesman was charitable about my Studie, a car that I could brake by dragging my feet. After a spin on a side street, the gears gnashing, the pavement as close as in a toboggan, the Jag was almost all mine for $1,095, a good price for such a great folly. As I drove away, my mind would not hold the point of the matter steady. I had taken the step to West Egg. How far up ahead was the green light on Daisy's dock?

Lacking the panache that went along with the car, I spent several days, and long evenings, explaining why it was that I had bought it, I, of all people, when it was apparent to my friends that I had struck it rich, having written a best seller. Why didn't I play the role that was thrust upon me, life- and dream-enhancing as everybody found it? I was an ignoramus. In explaining my folly to others I hoped to explain it to myself.

On a June Sunday morning, a week or two later, the air along Amalfi Drive already misty with sprinklers, I headed for the beach with an attractive poetess of "middle years," who liked to sit on her feet in cars with bucket seats. As we cruised along Sunset toward the sea, she put her hands to her face as if weeping. The problem? The shame she felt that I— this now famous author—tooling westward toward the Malibu cloudland, had in the seat at my side not one of these ravishing starlets, lonely and captive in the houses we were passing, but an almost old woman of thirty-nine!

Were women *actually* crazy, as well as seeming to be? In answer to the question What did they want?: They wanted what they didn't have; they wanted what was missing. This "aging" woman got something of what she was missing in the attention I gave her to ease her sorrow, to compensate for her losses, bringing plates of French fries and deep containers of Coke (fetched from much too far, with the tide sloshing) to where she sat hugging her knees, with her not so pretty feet buried in the sand. Later I drove her to Trancas, and sat at a table near a Hollywood mogul seducing a starlet who (in her opinion) should have been mine.

What is the case but pitiless in its ferocity?

Seeing this starlet in the flesh, exposed as it was, confirmed the fantasy my companion had brought with her from Kansas, and knowing that we shared this knowledge made us good friends.

When the galleys of *The Territory Ahead* arrived, she offered to help me with them. Why did I prove so reluctant? Thanks to her, I had the feeling that *The Cannibals* had picked up from where I had left it, and was still going on. Any day now, surely, as I cruised down Wilshire, or made the seductive curves on Amalfi, I would run into the Greek, with that smile on her lips, or catch a glimpse of Mac and Horter, in their XK-120, paused at Wilshire and Westwood, waiting for the green light.

On the morning after I had bought the car, I called my wife in Wayne, confessing my guilt. On the spur of the occasion I suggested that she might fly out, later in the summer, and drive back with me. In her silence I sensed more than surprise. This would interrupt her summer with Trudy Caspar, the good and loyal companion who I felt meant the most to her, and a few days later she wrote to tell me that Trudy hoped to be flying out with her, to visit old friends in Beverly Hills.

My teaching went so well that I knew there would be more in my future. I welcomed any excuse to talk about writers and writing. I had written to Ben DeMott suggesting that I would like to talk about the works of Morris—a subject in which I had more interest than the public. Could I publicly discuss novels so few people had read? In a few months *The Territory Ahead* would be published—surely marking the end or the beginning of something—and the author of so many unread novels was eager to take a look rearward at his own works. Since 1942 I had published ten novels, two books of photo-text, and one volume of criticism. What was it—in the absence of readers and, up until that spring, in the absence of money—that egged me on? Had I made myself into this creature that found both food and pleasure in the act of writing? Was it through writing that I made sense out of the non-sense outside my study window, and perceptibly diminished the quiet desperation common to those who were not writers? I accepted my calling as a form of living necessary to my own nature, requiring no more reason or persuasion than the flowers on bushes, or the leaves on trees. It did take some doing, but what I was doing came naturally. To cease to do it seemed an unnatural, destructive act. In May of 1958 I saw that I was one of those determined to persist in his folly. At the moment, of course, I was feeling the confirmation of a writer who had made ten thousand dollars, and had been repeatedly identified as the debauched author of a coming best seller.

Late in June I made a call to Josephine Kantor, the friend of Ynez Johnston, and she suggested I come by for a drink. She was busy packing several bags for Europe, and partially packed bags occupied the couches and chairs. We talked about where she planned to live—she was thinking she might live in Paris—as I noted the tapered beauty of her hands. Had I never before been captivated by a woman's hands? One held her cigarette, the other toyed—in the way of women—with a lock of her hair, a graceful movement of her fingers as if they played on keys. With each puff of her cigarette, one hand led my gaze back to her oval face. Of whom was I reminded? Could I—on first meeting a woman who now planned to live in Paris—afford to be reminded of more than that? What did I actually know about her? That I did not at all like her hairstyle. It was the hairdo, in fact, that blocked my urgent sense of recognition. The American male, young or old, has a skimpy repertoire of examples to provide him with models of beauty. Fortunate the man who has the image of a mother, a sister, a surpassing fiction, to blot out the image of the starlet, the blond bombshell, the movie siren. This young woman had no kinship with these models, but my sense of recognition was haunting. Where had I met or seen her? This would tantalize and confound me in the months of her absence, to that moment when, as we left the steamer in Dubrovnik (we were on our way to Venice), several young men lounging on the pier cried out, "Gioconda! Gioconda!" and blew her kisses. In such wise did the hands of my love finally sketch in her face.

I had borne the imprint of this classic oval face, painted by two hundred years of Italian masters, since my long afternoons at the magic lantern in Mrs. Josephare's History of Art class in Chicago. And now, at long last, I had found her. In time, I was able to persuade her to wear her dark hair in the classical manner, drawn back to a bun at the base of her neck, a spectacle that intercepted countless forks of spaghetti during our stay in Venice. The European, especially the Southern European, with his tradition of madonnas and icons, has been bred on images of art and responds instinctively. Nor was it only the men. Jo's classic beauty caught the eyes of the women, selling their vegetables, and the eyes of the boys, hawking their strings of beads, in an instinctive act of homage. To hang strings of beads about the neck of my signora was one of the pleasures of the peddlers of Venice. Mamma mia! Kisses blown from the tips of the fingers. The disinterested pleasure taken by the women (not all! not all!) was for me a special enhancement. In time I learned to be at ease with the bold appreciative stares of the men. I will never forget the signal that I saw passed from waiter to barman, and from barman to waiter, as Jo entered or left a café. The thumb and first finger form a circle, as the other three stand up like feathers. *Bellissima.* What compared with the gift of beauty as the gift of life?

But I am still in the room with partially packed bags, inquiring about her plans. In ten days she would take a train to New York, and from there she would sail to France. So I had a week? Did that perhaps work to my advantage? It did make me bold. After our third or fourth evening together, in my worst literary manner I asked her to come live with me and be my love—for the remaining five days. At that time Jo Kantor, née Josephine Mary Rossler, was about to escape from the marriage ties that had bound her, and she was not eager for a new involvement. I had so little to offer, it made me reckless. What did she say when I called to ask her? She said yes.

Jo's talents were many, but none was so unexpected, so unexampled, as her laughter. An explosive cawing honk, or honking caw, unmistakably bird-like, was still like no bird previously heard from. The release of this blast was so life-enhancing, it was cause for celebration among her friends, of whom I was now one.

I had rented an apartment in Malibu, out near the pier, and we moved in with our toothbrushes. When the tide was out we did a lot of walking. We ate a lot of her scrambled eggs and my cottage cheese salads. Out of the wisdom of almost a week together I concluded she was my kind of woman. Might she, in time, be in the market for my kind of man? I was old, ripe and wise enough not to ask her, but when I stood in her doorway, thinking I might lose her, I said I was coming to Paris. I asked her to write to me, and she said she would.

At the time we met Jo was reading Albert Camus. I had been a fan of Camus since the first line of his novel, *The Stranger* "Mother died today. Or, maybe, yesterday; I can't be sure."—a matchless summation of modern alienation. One writer I was eager for Jo to read was Wright Morris. Her intelligence, her ear for the voice of the writer in all that he writes, confirmed my feeling that this young woman was my future, and the sooner the better.

In July, I found that I took to teaching and, to my relief, that most of the students took to me. In early August, joined by my wife, I drove north to a writers' conference in Portland, Oregon, along the way mashing in the beautiful nose of the Jaguar. Eleven days of the twelve we were in Portland were taken up with the repairs. I remember little, fortunately, of the long, grueling drive east. My wife's relief to arrive home alive was inexpressible. That same day I packed a bag for Europe, and two days later sailed from New York for Le Havre. I wore a natty new corduroy cruising cap, and my face was still windburned from the drive east. In the fall of 1933, twenty-five years in the past, I had sailed on a freighter for Antwerp, and in so far as I could judge them, there was little changed in my expectations. I was now a fool confirmed in the folly that must make him either wise or lucky. In the meager, skimpy annals of my life as a writer, it had been a good year. Waiting for me in Paris (I hoped) was the woman who would give my life safe harbor, as I faced Gordon Boyd's old dilemma of making success out of failure. That would be one book I would give her to read, when we found time for reading, with a marker inserted at the point where Boyd fancies he can walk on water, just as I was doing at this moment.

*T*he *Île de France* docked at Le Havre in the late afternoon. I stood in line in the salon to have my papers checked. I glanced up to see a woman, smartly dressed in black, enter a side door on the left and cross the room to exit through a door on the right. She clutched a purse. I could hear the sharp clack of her heels. "Jo?" I called out, but too late. Many doors, in the next fifteen minutes, closed behind her, to be opened by me. Each time, however, thanks to the bag I carried, I lost ground. I saw her like a suspect in a Hitchcock movie, forever receding down corridors, through doorways, never glancing to the right, left or rear. Could I be sure it was her? I only saw her from the rear. I had written to tell her when the boat would dock, but it had never crossed my mind she would meet it. Unmistakably *her*, it seemed to me, was the intent, purposive way she descended stairs, entered or left rooms, without a pause in the crisp heel-clacking.

From the deck, where I inhaled the fresh air, I saw her sidewise, descending the gangplank. *That* would be her. "Jo!" I bellowed. She paused to glance skyward. Dark glasses gave her the aspect of a movie star traveling incognito. She waved, then returned up the gangplank. Moments later she found me, seized my hand, and led me back through the ship, down to the pier, where the train was about to leave for Paris. There would always be this apprehension about the departing train. We found an empty compartment, took seats at the window, and in its light I saw her face. The exercise had flushed it like that of a schoolgirl. She removed her sunglasses to powder her nose. My delight and excitement were so keen I did not speak. Out the window, the landscape slowly darkened. I gripped the small hand I was holding, and for once in my life my emotions were in keeping with my extravagant expectations. What did I say? What did she say? I have no idea.

In the Madison Hotel, just off the Place St. Germain, the young clerk examined me rather than my passport, with unconcealed distaste. Could it have been for *me* she had been waiting? He leaned over the counter to peer at my luggage. Nor could he pronounce my first name. As he paused to clean the lenses of his glasses, he gazed with sympathy at the young woman beside me. I made the mistake of saying a few words in French. Would I please write it down? He provided a pencil and a pad of paper. My humiliation was brief, however, since I was the one with the girl. The art nouveau cage of the elevator provided a balloonist's view of the lobby. On the top floor, holding a tray of glasses, the *femme du chambre* stepped back to get a less obstructed view of me. Her eyes rolled, but she quickly recovered. What hadn't she seen in her years of service! A bed and a wardrobe crowded the room (one of Jo's partially *un*packed bags occupied the chair), but there was space enough for us to stand, at the doors to the balcony, with our arms around each other. Was I right in feeling that she had filled out a bit? I was right.

The French doors opened out on a view of the city at night. Parts of it glowed with Minister Malraux's new spectacular lighting, with the dazzle of a world's fair, but the city was still scaled to the bustling life of the sidewalks and the hooting horns of the traffic. We were both starved. The clerk was relieved to see us back in the lobby so quickly, and we went off to the Café Royal, close by. In the café, my bad French was much appreciated. Had I acquired it during the war? No, I had been *entre les guerres*. In those days, the waiter, about my age, would have been setting up his first tables. I recall eating fried eggs still sizzling in the pan. All Paris seemed eager for our attention, but we went back to the Madison, where I told the clerk that he need not call us in the morning. We exchanged glances of understanding. His upward-straining gaze, as we rose from the lobby, assured me that I was truly ascending.

At the American Express, I had a letter from Sam Kaner, who was now living in Venice. Why didn't I—why didn't *we*—pay him a visit? He didn't know about Jo, but how often we had discussed bolting to Ronda, or to Paris if that seemed more convenient. As it had. While we went here and there, or sat in taxis, or at a table at Les Deux Magots, or while we lay awake watching the lights on the ceiling, we discussed what we should be doing. I had about three weeks. *Mon dieu*, how long and short that seemed! In October I had lectures to give at Amherst, and in November I would go to Mexico for the *Holiday* piece.

We would make a sort of tour, we decided, our first stop being Venice, full of paintings she must see, then Vienna, from where we would drive out to Schloss Ranna, to reassure myself, after twenty-five years, that it was actually there. From Ranna we would go to Munich, where one of my novels was about to be published, visit with my friends Jack and Leslie Aldridge, then return to Paris.

The man Jo knew at the American Express seemed relieved to note that he and I were about the same age—he may have felt this to be part of *his* problem—but in making out our wagon-lit reservations, and noting our separate passports, his agitation may have led him to reserve accommodations on the right train but for the wrong night. Some hours out of Paris, we were notified that our reservations were not in order, and that we had no sleeping accommodations. We could leave the train at its next stop and spend the night in a hotel, or we could sit it out in the coach compartment.

Jo would have preferred the hotel, in Lyon, but I was for sitting it out. One night in a coach? Were we so feeble? Most of my life, that was how I had traveled. In retrospect it didn't seem to be all that bad. I didn't know, of course, that the train would spend most of the night winding and creaking through the Alps in numerous short and long tunnels, past flashing warning lights and clanging bells, while we rocked and tilted one way, then another.

After the stop at Lyon, several men entered our compartment. One, gripping a string-wrapped parcel, appeared to be a clerk, so weary his head drooped the moment he was seated. At his side, his head so large his features appeared shrunken, a short-legged but powerful man held his huge torso erect by spreading his thighs, like props. He wore an expensive suit, with a silky, iridescent sheen, the material stretched tight across his bulging lap. Fresh food stains spotted his unbuttoned vest. On his small feet, light-tan oxfords with pointed tips had their laces untied. About his small, puckered mouth, beneath the tuft of moustache, smears of grease gleamed like perspiration. Several rings, with large stones, were embedded in the plump fingers that rested on his paunch, just the tips of the fingers touching. The large head, with its close-cropped pelt, tilted from side to side as the coach swayed. In homage to Balzac, I examined him carefully. An archetypical provincial figure, sharpened and honed by centuries of French life and writers, adorned with the fashionable attire of the moment for this night of orgiastic dining. It seemed I could hear his digestive juices percolating. A monumental vision of imperfect, bourgeois felicity.

At first I thought he dozed, but his small piggy eyes peered at us through his brown lashes. We contributed, indeed, to the dessert of his banquet, a strange pair of illicit lovers passing a miserable night in a train seat. To the taste of the peach Melba still on his lips we added the refinement of the flaming cognac, the touch of sin that had been lacking. To enhance his pleasure, I stretched out with my head in Jo's lap.

In Milan, in the late morning, we shared a coach jammed with Italian families, all of them with their parcels of bread, cheese and salami, slurping from bottles of Chianti in their

258

raffia wrapping. Between choking gulps of food, the children stared at my shoes from Mexico, my tan from California, my turquoise ring from Arizona. In their charmed presence I slowly recovered from a ghastly night. The black-clad women, clutching their string bags, solemnly gazed at my companion. What speculation she would provide them! This madonna traveling with the bleary-eyed stranger.

The coach partially emptied at Verona, and as the train approached Venice I got whiffs of the sea-tanged air. Where was Venice? The glass-hooded railroad station proved to be new. I lowered the window, to see Sam Kaner smiling and waving. How glad I was to see him! Our bags were passed through the window, and Sam went ahead of us after staring, with some disbelief, at my companion. Had I actually *bolted*? The thought pleased and amused him. "Well, Dad," he would say when he could speak, and beam appreciatively.

We pushed through the last doors to step out on a stage that would have tested Shakespeare's imagination. Unreal but fabulous city! On the choppy canal a *vaporetto* tacked about for the pier. Water slapped the stone steps. The peeling walls of Venice, an outdoor museum of art, held Jo's speechless attention. Sam had gone ahead to get our *vaporetto* tickets. I stood there troubled by what seemed to be missing. There were no cars. There were no wheels! The *vaporetto* coughed wetly as we boarded. "Well?" said Sam to me, his eyes gleaming, seeing in our astonished faces something of what he had already forgotten. This city was like nothing. It could only be experienced and compared with itself.

The mind-boggling gift of Venice is that it has escaped the tyranny of wheels. The motor launch coughs, the exhaust pollutes the air, but man walks—*he does not run for his life. Only time will accustom us to a fact so profoundly bizarre. Of all unreal cities, this is the one that has its roots deepest in the imagination. Men dreamed it up, and now it is sinking into the ooze that will preserve it. Venice submerged may well prove to be stranger than Venice preserved. The gondolas in the Piazza are merely a reminder that this city was born of illusion, and that what man takes from the sea, the sea will*

repossess. As if it were sugared, the smog-polluted air crum-
bles the stones, discolors the marble, and adds the final refine-
ment to our taste for mutilations, our love for man-made
ruins. (Love Affair: A Venetian Journal, *1972)*

We stayed with Sam Kaner and his wife, but we had most
of our meals at the Locanda Montin, just off the Zattere and
the Rio San Trovaso. A family establishment (as were most in
Venice), with a cat-haunted garden at the rear (a choice between the cats and the rats from the canals), it numbered a
group of painters among its clientele, a few of them Americans, most of whom found places to live on Giudecca, some
with a view across the water to the piazza of San Marco and
the Doge's Palace. What could a modern painter do with this
museum of six centuries of masterpieces? Those ignorant of
or indifferent to this aesthetic dilemma might do pretty well
selling their productions to tourists.

Sam and his blond wife, Ruth, whose almost white hair excited the younger males to hoots and whistling, occupied the
top floor, a sort of Venetian penthouse with a view of the Zattere. It was fine October weather, but what would they do in
January? Sam had already survived one winter in Venice, and
described a world of mist and fog, like that of London, with
such apparitions as snow-frosted gondolas. In the cafés, especially the Locanda Montin, with everyone crowded inside,
there was much talk and fellowship.

I retained my doubts about January, but October in Venice
had us captivated. Would it be possible to find an apartment?
The few available were in demand by Venetians. But Sam
Kaner happened to know of a choice modern apartment on a
walled garden, with steam heat, plumbing and barred windows. The bars were a must if it was on the lower floors. Life
was safe enough in Venice, but not easily portable property.

At the moment, this apartment was occupied by Sylvia
Brown, a young woman from California, who had lived in
Venice for years. We had met Sylvia at Montin's, where her
manner, her slow, deliberate way of speaking, was that of
someone accustomed to teaching, or to teachers. She was also
fluent in Italian and French, and was planning a trip to Spain

to improve her Spanish. The apartment she was in, just off the Rio San Trovaso, was very select in every respect, but it was on the first floor and never warmed by sunlight. There was also the problem that the large shuttered windows, with bars but no glass, were terra cognita to the neighborhood cats. People fond of cats might actually like it, but she did not like cats. We did, we thought, like cats, so we made a visit to the garden, from where we had a chat with Sylvia Brown through the closed shutters. She was at that moment about to leave for Paris, and closing up. Discussing this problem through the shutters is one of my very special Venetian impressions (I was never free of the feeling that she was captive, and lying to us at sword point), but we did seem to agree that if she could move to higher and sunnier accommodations, the apartment she occupied would be ours. That was enough for me. (I put little faith in what I was hearing or saying, or what was happening, but I did feel confident about the future.)

On each of our five days in Venice we walked around and around, hoping to get irrevocably lost. Time and again we were mysteriously back where we had started, and paused for an espresso before going on. In the sunny *campos* we watched people, the plump-kneed boys hooting as they played their ball game, and in the dim chill of the Accademia museum we stared at Bellini, Carpaccio and Giorgione. Surely the sense of such abundance would pass, and we would go, like the natives, about our own business, stirring up the pigeons and pausing to stroke or feed an occasional cat. If that were possible, was it a condition to aspire to? We had five days; four of them started with eggs that should not have been boiled, and if boiled never opened. In five days, that was one thing we learned. On the evening of the sixth day, we took the *vaporetto*, with Sam Kaner, up the Grand Canal to the railroad station, where the bottle of champagne he had reserved for the occasion fell from the bag and shattered on the platform. That one was for Venice! He ran back to fetch another one for ourselves.

Would we be back? Sipping the champagne, we made a promise. In the spring, I swore, but I didn't believe it. It was just not possible that the key tumblers in my life would fall

261

again as they fell to bring us to Venice. In our wagon-lit compartment I spelled out for Jo how, twenty-five years in the past, I had been cycling in the reverse direction after my winter at Schloss Ranna. Many people returned to places they had once visited, but I was compelled to return to those where I was still captive. This was at the heart of my agitation. I might indeed find Schloss Ranna, even the Meister, but would I find that young man who had never escaped—who had left part of his life in that bizarre province? Once a place had taken root in my imagination, it had for me an aura of enchantment. I could not explain it, but I knew that it generated the cycle of returns in my writing. A disinterested observer, pondering my behavior, might say of me that the function of the present was to confirm the nature of the past, and by a commodious vicus of recirculation the reality of the present.

Some years back, on a stop in Chicago, I had driven to Menomonee Street, where it began at Clark Street and Lincoln Park. My father and I had lived in rooms over a delicatessen. Bottles of milk had cooled on the windowsill, and in the winter pushed their caps up as the milk froze. I could sometimes hear the ice cracking up on the lake. In the summer I heard the roar of the crowd at Wrigley Field if someone hit a home run. Right beside this delicatessen, on the east, was a ruin that might have survived the Chicago fire. Weeds and crawlers had taken it over. For years, summer and winter, I had walked by it without the memory of having *seen* it. How was that possible? I did not then understand my feelings, but I considered this a loss that had to be salvaged. I sat in the car, the motor idling, staring at it. With certain objects and places I shared both gains and losses. Why had I felt compelled to confirm it as a loss?

One night in Paris, I had awakened Jo to tell her of my strange adventure at Schloss Ranna, and something about the people and the past preserved there. I think she heard it and accepted it as one of my fictions (I seemed to be full of them), but it was not as a fiction that it held me. It was crucial to me that I be able to confirm the reality of my early impressions, since I had failed (in my own opinion) to give them imaginative confirmation. *My* Schloss Ranna was an unacceptable loss—like those that bombs had reduced to rubble—until I had reaffirmed its existence, and given substance to my impressions.

Vienna was still war-scarred. On Florianigasse, the building from which I had peered into the *blind Garten* had vanished. The matronly woman who rented us a car concealed her cracked red hands in the sleeves of her sweater. I was tempted to ask her about Frau Unger, with her flashing eyes and swinging earrings. In the chill garage basement I felt her vibrations. How did the air itself accommodate such losses? Whitman had thought that it bathed the globe, but it was little more than the skin of a bubble. How did it absorb the cries and the shrieks, the deafening, atom-splitting clamor of one unholy, tumultuous day on earth? Was it possible to speak of this congested ether as thin air?

We drove west to Krems, then followed the road along the Danube to Spitz. There we had lunch in the garden behind the hotel, the gravel paths sloping down toward the river. I made it a point to have a carafo of the *neue Wein* I had heard so much about but never tasted. We both thought it sweet as ambrosia. Might the waiter—a black stud at the throat of his collarless shirt, the moist sad eyes of my friend Hermann Unger—have been a child in Spitz when I came down from Ranna to get a haircut? Was the Meister still at Schloss Ranna? I asked him, with the assurance of an escaped inmate. "For certain!" he replied, curious that I might doubt it. And how was he? He temporized, rocking the hand he extended with the palm turned down. He was old. He studied me before saying, "He has remarried." This had the effect he had hoped for. He brought us cups of coffee, then continued. During the war the Meister had been imprisoned. When he returned to Schloss Ranna, it had been with his new wife, a German woman. More than that he was reluctant to say, being a man of discretion. I had thought to ask him if *Ranna* was still there, but lacked the nerve. From the movies, I had gathered that old castles were sometimes used to provide elite quarters for military personnel, but the memorable lack of "civilized" comforts might have spared Ranna.

Where the road turned north to follow the canyon to Muhldorf, we stopped to watch a steamer make the bend in the river, her paddle wheels slapping the water. Travelers standing on the deck waved to us, and we waved in return. I remembered thinking how I had been struck, in the past, with what a remarkable custom that proved to be, even more remarkable after the intervention of the second war. As we approached Muhldorf, I looked for and saw the mill wheel that corked one side of the canyon, but without the ice and snow, the shimmering winter silence, the slanting rays of the sun on the buttressed walls, what I saw on the slope that rose behind the village was a disappointment. How shabby it looked! The field below the walls had not been cultivated, nor had the walls of the inner Schloss been whitewashed.

"Just you wait," I said to Jo, making the turn to Ober Muhldorf, a lane with weeds growing at its center, and we followed it to pass the church, with its onion dome, and the shrine along the trail where we had gathered for the midnight hunt, then passed the vacant, abandoned outbuildings to curve up through the orchard of dead and dying trees. As we approached the gate, I stopped the car and got out. "Come," I said, and led her to the wall that fenced the moat. In my absence it had aged, but not shrunken. Deep in the dry moat, shrubs were growing. At that instant, as I glanced upward, I felt a tremor of the chill that had seized me upon my first hearing the bell rung by that madman, Antone, from the top of the tower. Not this time. The weather vane tilted, ready to fall. Not a sound from the deep moat, the inner Schloss, or the canyon behind it. It relieved me to note that Jo stepped back from the sheer fall, just as I had.

I drove the car through the arch, along the rutted ramp to where it narrowed. There we sat as I reflected on the impulses that had brought me back to Ranna. If the Meister was there, what would he remember? More to the point, what did he care to remember, after the war? Impulsively, I put my hand to the horn. It was not at all the right sound for the silence. We sat there, apprehensive, until one of the small windows opened. I made out the broad face of a woman.

"Herr Deleglise?" I called out. "I have come to see him." She made no comment. "Tell him Herr Morris is here to see him."

"Who?" she inquired. I repeated my name. "Tell him the young American. He will remember!"

She left, but was soon back. "Come in!" she cried, and thrust out her forearm toward the entrance. I led Jo into the corridor, dark as a cave since the door at the far end was shut. The door to the inner court stood ajar, and we crossed it to mount the stairs to the landing. A stout, matronly woman, both broad and deep, the sleeves of her dress turned back on her plump forearms, beckoned to us from a doorway. We saw little but her broad back as she led us down a hallway. Loose floorboards sagged and creaked. Slits of light burned at the base of closed doors. She led us directly to the room I knew to be the Meister's, where we found him propped up in his bunk. The familiar grimacing smile parted his lips; toward me extended his frail claw-like hand. "Not well, not well," he piped, but I thought he looked more the same than altered. The high brow a little higher, the moustache a little grayer, the mother-of-pearl teeth still mother-of-pearl. Also unchanged was his amiable disinterest. Why had I come?

I said that I had long wanted to return to Ranna, and that my friend, Josephine, had been eager to see it. The name Josephine pleased him. He studied her with interest.

"Italian, yes?" he queried. "Madame Deleglise was also Italian."

That I well remembered. Did he see a likeness between my swan and his ugly duckling? He explained to the woman who I was. He described me as an artist from California. This both pleased her and made her bristle. In a fluent German, the text so familiar I could follow where it was leading, she spoke of the barbarous bombing of Dresden. When did we expect to pay reparations? All of her property destroyed. For ten years she had been waiting. Using the cane stretched at his side, the Meister tapped on the wall, like a professor on a blackboard. She fell silent. He spoke to her again, suggesting that we stay for dinner. This caused her the greatest discomfort. In a scene of classic matronly woe, she gathered up and clutched the folds of her skirt. Was she about to weep?

"No! No!" I intervened. "We will take you to dinner. We will go to Krems!"

There were good cafés in Krems, but I felt certain she would decline the invitation. Not so. On the instant, it aroused her. She turned to persuade the Meister, adjusting his position—his left arm clung to his side, the hand deep in the jacket pocket. "*Nein! Nein! Nein!*" he repeated, but she ignored his complaint as if he were a child she was tending. From a hook on the wall she took a long wool scarf, several yards in length, and opened his jacket to wrap it around him. He was soon resigned. His eyes eluded mine, but behind his tantrum I could sense his satisfaction. He was in good hands. She would do with all of us as she would.

We had just finished lunch, but no matter. It would take us an hour or more to get to Krems, and it might be a half hour before we started. A contented, clucking hen, the woman went off with Jo, and I sat with the Meister, smoking. He took deep drags of the Camel cigarette, reluctant to exhale; his eyes were hooded. "And Mizi?" I asked him. She had married. A widower to the west. One of her sons now worked in Spitz. "And Antone?"—the father of his country. A blacksmith in Ottenschlag. Many children. Joseph an *Obermensch* in Krems. I would have heard much the same on a visit to the Home Place. Time marches on. We were silent for a moment, then he asked me:

"Josephine is your wife?"

"Not just yet," I replied. He looked at me with a concern that puzzled me.

"My wife—" he began, stopped.

"We'll stay in Spitz," I said. "There's a *Gasthaus* in Spitz."

He sighed with relief and reached to grip my hand. The good German hausfrau was doing what she could, in a disorderly world, to reestablish order, and reaffirm good, decent German morals. "Frau Deleglise—" he said to me, and we exchanged a reaffirming glance of male understanding.

266

*   *   *

On the drive back to Schloss Ranna, seeing it emerge dim
and ghostly out of the darkness, an ark beached by the receding flood (my impression was that it seemed to be tilting),
there revived in me much that I had feared to be lost, having
looked in the wrong place for it. A young man from the new
world, an older man and a dog of mythic proportions—one
could hardly improve on the combination—had slodged
through the snow to that point in the canyon where the
Schloss appeared to be ascending to heaven, on the froth of a
wave, or at the least the cloudland in the glass ball on all
sewing machines west of the Missouri. The Meister himself
had been the first to come down with the virus, and he had
spent his life passing it on to others. Had it taken with any
others as it had with me? Had there ever been a canvas better
prepared for what was to be painted on it? But even I had
failed to imagine the frame that Frau Deleglise had provided:
a last stand for *Kultur* in a crumbling ruin pending the arrival
of just reparations. She had her plans. Buses of tourists, from
Vienna and Salzburg, would stop at Ranna for the night, then
proceed elsewhere. Others would come by paddle boat from
Budapest and Innsbruck. During the night it had crossed her
mind that Americans, too, should come to Schloss Ranna, as I
had. Might it not interest me—once she had the reparations—to conduct a tour? I regretted that my work would
keep me in California. Frau Deleglise had surprised us with
an invitation to spend the night at Ranna. She had made up
separate rooms. After a *Butterbrot Frühstück*, and excellent
Schokolade, we had an almost tearful parting out on the ramp.
The Meister wagged his cane from his balcony doorway. I
don't know what I was thinking as we drove back to Spitz,
and stopped where the road came out on the Danube. A boat,
a steamer with big paddle-wheel fenders, was drifting with
the current around the curve at Spitz. On the fender, with the
hyphen, were the words BUDA-PEST.

*In that cold air, veiled with the smoke of our breathing, I
seemed to see Richard the Lion-Hearted, on whom I had once
written a term paper, cold and clammy in his suit of clanking*

armor, only his black eyes glinting at the visor of his helmet,
weary in mind and aching in body, eaten alive by lice and
gnawed with fear and suspicion, uncertain of friend and foe
and whether he would ever get back to his homeland, with a
large pack of vassals and hangers-on to account for, along
with numerous baying dogs, thieves and beggars, pause for a
moment right where we were standing to peer down at the
black, alien river he would never see again—not a great fig-
ure in history, carrying a shield, but a flesh-and-blood bully
who was saddle-sore and homesick. Far to the east, where the
sun was still shining, the landscape was like a painting on
glass through which I could see back to where I had come
from. . . . How Richard the Lion-Hearted had felt was not
strange to me. (Solo: An American Dreamer in Europe:
1933–34, *1983*)

In Munich we met Susi Hofstadt, an editor for Henry
Goverts, whom she had persuaded to publish two of my
books. Goverts shared my love of Rilke's *Notebooks of Malte*
Laurids Brigge, and we talked of little else at dinner. We had
some time with Jack and Leslie Aldridge, and an afternoon
with Hedda Soellner, who had just translated *The Huge Sea-*
son for Goverts. On the train to Strasbourg I was served a
bowl of cherries, in a compote, that I have never forgotten.
Back at the Hotel Madison, in Paris, the clerk appraised Jo for
signs of ennui, of blighted expectations, but reached no reassuring conclusions.

The painter Emerson Woelffer and his wife, Dina, came up
from Ischia to see Jo, and meet her new companion. If they
were still in Ischia in the spring, Jo said, we would stop and
see them on our way to Venice. That unsolicited support, at
that moment, did much to solidify my future plans.

Later I took Jo past the Cinema Montparnasse, where I had
first seen Disney's *Three Little Pigs*, then I walked her up the
Rue de la Gaîté to the Hotel Duguesclin, to point out the front
window from which I had leaned to watch the landlord's
beautiful daughters cry, *"Me voici! Me voici!"* From there I
walked her back to the Boulevard Raspail (she was starving)
for a bowl of borscht at Dominique's, served to us at a table

with napkins. Monsieur Dominique (he put me in mind of Stravinsky) admired my companion, and claimed to remember the young American who took more rolls from the basket at the counter than he paid for—but all that in the spirit of the times, and meaning no offense.

I was up at six to catch the boat train to Le Havre and send my love a *pneumatique* from the railroad station: "Here's one for my baby, and one for the road."

I was at once elated and deprived, coming off a great high, yet I remember nothing—*nothing*—of my three cabin companions; I know we had a stormy passage. I was in Wayne, packing a bag for Amherst, when I had a letter from Jo telling me that she had fallen ill a few days after my departure, and had been taken to the American Hospital. What distressed me—now that she had recovered—were the comforting fictions I had borne in mind assuring me of her well-being. This discrepancy in time between our infrequent letters would trouble me most in Mexico, where I had little confidence in what I sent off and virtually none in what she mailed from Paris. It would have much to do, once I reached Mexico City, with my heartfelt plea that I needed her with me, right there at my side, no longer at the whim of gaps in our correspondence—I needed the real voice, the glance from real eyes, the warmth and assurance of the real person to be felt and touched. Was it possible something was wrong with me? Yes; I was in love.

I drove the Jaguar to Amherst, leaving the freeway to get the bloom of the flaming fall colors. I was put up at the inn, much beloved by the alumni, in a room bringing to mind traditions of whaling, a cubicle that required caution in getting in and out of its small berth. At the time of my stay, Robert Frost was making his yearly visit. The first morning, as I pondered my impressions, he sat alone along one wall of the dining room, I alone along another. A bit of tinkle and slurp disturbed the silence. He had his second, and his third, cup of coffee, waiting for me to pick up the signal. As I passed by, his mariner's glance caught me directly and I took a seat at his table. He gave me his splotched farmer's hand, what was left of his pot of coffee. Frost was eighty-four at that time, a hunkered-down, bear-like figure with his white icing, and the creaky manner of a valued, but seldom used, antique. He also wanted company. He told a good story, and feigned real interest in my own. Former times. How different, we agreed, for both of us.

The week I was at the inn we had breakfast together, and

271

as a rule I got his bacon. He explained to me that if I sat at his table, strangers were less likely to intrude on him. That was true enough, but also something of a problem, since most of these intrusions were his pleasure. The monument receiving due homage. He liked especially to hear it from the young. Parents, receiving mutual reinforcement, after a period of nervous, coffee-cooling indecision, might approach the great man to speak of his importance to the past, the present, and of course the future. What a pity they had found so little time for poetry themselves! Frost played this role with true rustic charm, and just a touch of humility. He referred to me as his "young friend," and so I was. That I was headed for Mexico greatly intrigued him. What was it like? I tried to tell him. In these glimpses up ahead, into the lives of the young, he hoped to do his living. Would I write to him? he asked. I said I would. "Dear Bob," I would write, being his friend, as he had said.

The meetings he had with the students I thought less happy, the students too much alert to the occasions' importance. One comment I made drew us together. The waitresses at the inn bore resemblance to stuffed historical figures, repeating roles that were duly recorded. They were less matronly than fraternal, a family of kinfolk, male and female, in which the sensual element was totally lacking. I could not imagine a rogue bold enough to pinch or goose one of them. How in God's name did Yankee lust, I asked him, persist in reproducing the species? That he liked. Perhaps only Frost, and only the New England campus, with its swinging birches and unmended fences, would provide on the eve of his canonization a rustic figure still suitable for framing.

I had come to Amherst to meet with the students and lecture on "The Origin of a Species," this being the figures of my own fiction. An ill-advised enterprise, but it had interested me, and I had come prepared to make the best of it. Ben De-Mott gave me all the encouragement I needed, and the students were both respectful and responsive. One of them was a young writer named Pete Howe. I met with him occasionally, and I saw and felt in him many of the traits of my better self. One day I found him standing beside my Jaguar, a car he greatly admired. I suggested that we take a spin, but at that moment he lacked the time. I thought Pete Howe a very attractive young man, and a "promising" fiction writer. I suggested he might write to me, if and when he cared to. He was there the morning I drove away, and when I arrived in Mexico City, many weeks later, I would find a letter from Amherst about him. Shortly after my departure, he had been killed in a car accident. In his memory a small volume of his writing would be published, to which I was asked to contribute. To his parents I managed to write a few words, but it shamed me to feel my impotence in this loss. At the head of my list of losses that mocked imaginary gains was the name of Pete Howe.

Did I see myself at the wheel of the Jaguar, cruising along the coast of Mexico to Mazatlán? I did indeed. And there I was. The car purred without knocking. The oil was cheaper. I passed miles of fields under irrigation, and stopped to drink iced beer at the fishing stations. Approaching Mazatlán, I slowed to join a line of traffic made up of trucks, tourists, and carts pulled by donkeys.

An American from Covina, California, had built a new motel just back from the surf. It was so new the beds had not yet been delivered, but the cot in the room seemed acceptable. I stepped from the shower to see a large iguana scooting across the floor like a toy dragon. That his panic was greater than mine calmed me. I stood on the cot, calling for help, until a Mexican youth came to the door. He opened the screen, gave the iguana a boost as it scrambled out. When I asked him if they were dangerous, he shrugged.

The checkered tablecloths had not yet arrived for the tables, but real American T-bone steaks had just been shipped in by air, frozen. I had one, with French fries and a bottle of Dos Equis, and knew that I was among my own people. I learned from the proprietor that the fishing was great. The problem was—and I was listening, what with my piece on Mexico to write—that the plumbing fixtures installed in his new showers twisted off in the hands of the husky American tourists, who didn't know their own strength. The *problem* was, once that had happened, it took time to replace what had been broken. Maybe three, maybe six, maybe eight or nine months. Americans who had been driving for eight or ten hours, or had been fishing for five or six hours, and looked forward to a refreshing shower, were seldom long on understanding. They peered into the showers, looked at the twisted pipes, and took off. His wife, who served as the café hostess, and had designed the menus, the size of newspapers, had never been able to get a really good tan back in Covina, but after seven weeks in Mazatlán he told her some of the tourists thought she was colored, and that settled that.

The second night, I woke up to hear the cries of mariachi singers, and see the lights of a Ferris wheel far down the beach. I walked to where they were having a carnival, with thousands of the Indians in from the country. I loved the way the beautiful children accounted for each other, an older one linked to a younger to where the links gave out. As I mingled with them, sharing their excitement, I was troubled by the suspicion that I was an impostor. I felt that eyes I could not see both saw and judged me. Whose eyes were they? Was I growing wise to myself? At what point did my pleasure in the child carrying a child become a symbol for the situation? If the exotic was stripped away, what would the visitor be left with? Had I fallen into thinking that this many-ringed circus was staged for my fleeting benefit?

It troubled me to have these scruples at the start of my journey, but leaving Mazatlán, I felt better. In the late afternoon, approaching a larger city, I joined a line of trucks and campers moving slowly toward a river. In moments of quiet I could hear the rush of the water. Too late, making the descent toward the river, I saw that the bridge was missing. Parts of the collapsed structure were there, at each end, but the bridge consisted of vehicles, bumper to bumper, moving slowly through water above the hubcaps. In the Jag that would be halfway up the door, and high on the motor. Nor was there any way for me to turn off, or to turn back. It occurred to me—and there proved to be time to reflect on occurrences—that if I should drown here, my love, in Paris, might

274

well *never* learn about it. What would she think? I had no choice but to survive.

In my rearview mirror I saw the lights of a truck, looming high behind me, flash me a signal. What did he have in mind? The Jag's motor had stopped the moment I entered the river. Some part of the front end of the truck behind me—the bumper appeared to be as high as my rear window—contacted the rear bumper on the Jag and he pushed me ahead of him like a half-submerged boat. It took some time, but it was not quite long enough to despair. On the far side he pushed me up the slope to the street, clouded with dust, a confusion of vehicles like that of an army fording a stream, and I leaned out of the cab to watch my benefactor, his teeth gleaming in a villain's dark, smiling face, wave at me as he passed. I sat there for some time before I noticed that my feet were ankle deep in water, and I opened the door to let it out.

It seemed idle to trouble to look at the motor, but I wanted to confirm that it was still there. The top of the block, still hot, hissed and steamed like a simmering pot. Water had pooled in the plug sockets, and I used my T-shirt to sop it up. The ignition wiring had been soaked, and I put in my time fussing with it. At my side the traffic clamored as in a scene of wartime panic. I had survived. The woman in Paris would not be puzzled by my disappearance. One day—preferably not in Mazatlán; Venice would be more appropriate—I would attempt to describe my crossing of the Hellespont.

Some of my previous cars had been reluctant to start on those chill mornings when there was mist in the air, so I was not such a fool as to think that this submerged, lifeless mechanical corpse would spring to coughing life when I turned the key. But that was what it did. I sat there too stupefied to believe it. Quickly it choked and died. But it had actually *run*! Was that what it meant to be British? Knowing that the spark of life was there, I went back under the hood, did more sopping and wiping, did more praying, and on the third try it sputtered and ran. One plug was not firing, but I was able to buck along in second gear, like an injured animal at the edge of the pack.

There was still light in the sky, although it was already dark under the trees. One of the features of the city—I had found it in my tour book—was a new and elegant motel, overlooking the sea, approached by a winding, ascending ramp, along which I was escorted by hooting small fry. The car made its bucking entrance without comment from two valets in caps and white jackets. Not being familiar with Jaguars, they accepted what they heard and saw as normal. I let the motor run, fearing that if stopped, it would never start. The high water had left a ring on the sides of the car. The hot motor gave off a fishy odor. I let it continue to run while I had my dinner—I got up frequently to check on it—and after an hour and a half of idling, the firing was almost normal. I stopped the motor, wiped the car with my T-shirt—and discussed with a tourist from Minnesota some of the hazards of Mexican travel. He was glad to get it from a tourist who spoke with authority.

I felt such an adventure augured so well for the future that I spent several days in Guadalajara, drying my wet clothes and making a few notes. I drove out for another look at Ajijic, where Lawrence and Frieda had left their spore; it was now ornamented with American women with mannish hairdos, peasant blouses, Hopi jewelry and hand-loomed Navajo skirts.

In Mexico City I had a reunion with Jaime García, but after a few hours together I felt his reluctance to repeat the past. Here I was again, full of myself and my plans, and in a few weeks or months I would be gone. On Jaime's lips, when he was silent, I could see the words *Todo pasa*. The burden of our friendship weighed on him. Whatever we had together I would take away with me. We went to a ball game, we walked on the Paseo, we dined and sipped the mild gin at Sanborns, but all we were doing was passing the time, passing the time. . . .

I spent more than a week looking for the right apartment, which I found just down the street from the old one. Described as a "penthouse," it seemed to be on a level with the smog that now veiled the city. It did offer a fine view, how-

The Osborn Family,
Chapman, Nebraska, circa 1900
Winona, Violet, Dwight,
Marion, Myron, and Grace

Grace Osborn Morris,
Wright's mother

The Morris Family,
near Zanesville, Ohio, circa 1895

On photo safari, Manhattan, Kansas, 1939

Self-portrait, the Home Place, 1947

Mexico City, 1954

Mary Ellen Morris, 1952

On the beach at Acapulco, winter 1954

Wright and Jo in Paris, fall 1958

Jo, on our way to New York, 1959

Wright on the Zattere, Venice, 1959

*Wright and Jo
in San Miguel de Allende,
Mexico, 1959*

Jo in Venice, Corfu and Mexico City, 1959

Wright and Jo at home in Pacific Palisades, 1960

In Pacific Palisades, 1961

ever, of the roofs of the houses where the Indian girls came to wash, sun and brush their gleaming black hair. I felt that would please Jo. Waiting for me had been a letter from Paris, for which I was grateful, but of the sort a woman writes with too many other things on her mind. She was seeing friends. She might go to England. She hoped to visit her friends in Ischia. If she went to Italy, should it be Rome or Florence? The thought of her being there *without* me brought me to a decision.

Before leaving for Oaxaca, I wrote Jo a letter with the emphasis on my recent losses. Besides her, what had they been? I cited my new and young friend, Pete Howe. I touched on my loneliness in a strange country. I may have said I did not want to go on without her, an extravagant admission for a lad with my background. I not only said many of these things, but I mailed the letter off. I also managed to mention the new penthouse apartment, the excellent food at Sanborns, the sun and the view from the roof, and the aroma of the broiled chickens on the deli rotisserie on the corner. I overlooked reference to the fleas and the bedbugs in the furniture. I had originally planned that Jo would drive with me to Oaxaca, with side trips to Cuernavaca, Taxco, even Acapulco, but just a few days in my empty penthouse had clarified my priorities.

Early in December I drove south to Acatlán, noting that the Jag purred its smoothest at the lower altitudes. In the dusty patio of the café, one of the resident chickens, light as a feather duster, hopped to my lap and ate out of my soup plate. A small bantam hen with frazzled tail feathers, but with the bold assurance of a street-tough urchin, she had the bald behind of the hens that had scratched up my Aunt Clara's farmyard. With piercing glances at me and at the mongrel yellow-eyed dog who observed her from a safe distance, she plucked the peas, the corn and the gravel from my soup.

In Oaxaca, the California tourists were gathering for the white man's Christmas festival. I spent the cool mornings in the plaza, pondering its enchantment, my evenings at the bar in the motel, sipping the mild Mexican gin. The barman, a handsome young fellow with the hair and the eyes of an Arab,

277

was quick to light my cigarette, to replace my drink, and to see that the dish of olives was at my elbow. Our exchanges were little more than glances and nods. He had the best job in the place, a white shirt, a bow tie, a cummerbund with a sash, and black American patent-leather oxfords. Was he content? He seemed happiest when he was waiting on me. When he learned I was leaving, he spoke to me like a suitor, a short formal speech, not all of which I followed, then he stepped forward to place his hands on my shoulders and gaze into my eyes. Speechless, we confronted each other. The sober formality of his manner testified to the seriousness of this gesture. On my belt I wore a chain of silver, attached to a silver cigar cutter (I had always had a weakness for Mexican silver), and I unhooked it from my belt and gave it to him. In the early morning, as the Jag warmed up, he ran to embrace me in the Mexican manner, then took off. This brief but intense (for him) friendship reminded me how, here in Mexico, old men strolled about the streets holding hands like children.

I may have been thinking of my friend, several hours later, when I rounded a sharp curve north of Acatlán, the road ahead concealed by the cliffside, to find the highway strewn with boulders the size of basketballs. Dodging one, I hit another, then another, and felt the motor shift and rock on the frame as the steering wheel vibrated. Through the window on my side, which was open, I saw an Indian crouched on the cliffside, his head resting on his arms, taking his siesta. A stick with a red warning flag attached to it lay across his lap. He raised his head to gaze at me with sleep-drugged eyes, but he saw nothing. I could hear the car's hot metal pinging, and catch glimpses, in the rearview mirror, of the smear of oil that darkened the street. My hands seemed to be locked to the car's steering wheel. When they loosened, I walked back around the curve to flag my arms at an approaching car. A young man and his girl were crouched behind the wheel of a two-toned Chevy. I pointed ahead to the boulders, the film of oil on the pavement, and it took him a moment to make the connections. His girl eased out of his arms to check on her lipstick, but lucky for me she was there. Without her, he would have had no shortage of excuses—his old car, bad tires, an urgent appointment—but he was a decent fellow, with the sad, knowing eyes of my friend Jaime. He walked with me to look at the Jag. Depressed as he was, he could not suppress the sympathy he felt for the car's owner. Never before had he seen such a car. Two, three times, he circled it slowly. He tracked through the oil smear to admire the dashboard. A pair of miniature huaraches hung by a string from the mirror, showing my Mexican connections. He kneeled on the pavement to see what could be seen from below, and I did the same. A hole bigger than my fist had been poked in the oil pan. My good samaritan had one last ray of hope.

"I have no rope," he said.

How did it happen that I had a rope? After the crash in Oregon, the mechanic had sold me a length of heavy rope in case I might have to be towed to Portland. This coil of rope, still wet from the river, was found in the rear. Neither of us knew much about knots in rope, but with some labor, mostly his, we got it attached. Would it work? Not without some practice. We stopped every ten or twenty miles for water, bringing it back in five-gallon oil cans. I had to buy these cans, then leave them beside the road. Twice the rope broke, sawing through on the frame, and I watched his car leap away to what I assumed would be his freedom—but each time he came back. We did not speak or joke. He had reached that point of no return that asked of me only silence. I was silent. Often I thumped him so hard from the rear I could see both of their heads bob.

The town of Matamoros—I do not know where it is, but I know that it is there, somewhere—we entered late on that Sunday afternoon, the streets empty and in shadow. Barefooted boys ran along beside me, happily beaming. They, too, had not before seen a Jaguar. Some blocks down the street, huge doors stood open on a courtyard crowded with junked cars. Under one of them a youth was working. My companion explained what had happened. Both gazed at me with sympathy. Could they fix it? *Sí, como no?* Of course they could fix it. He spoke at length about how he would fix it. *Muy bueno*, I replied. The Jag was pushed—a platoon of boys had gathered in the courtyard—over an oil pit, from where the young man assured me it was nothing. He would need a few things, but it was nothing. How much oil did it take? He admired its consumption. What a car it must be to take fifteen quarts of oil! One of the others, seated behind the wheel, found that the gears would no longer shift—but that, too, was nothing. How long would it take? All agreed it would take a bit of time.

The good samaritan who had towed me for miles, and surely won the girl with the sallow complexion, rejected my questionable offer of money for gains of a more spiritual nature. I wished him well. We embraced. Not for the first time, I was reassured that I was among my own people, even in Matamoros. Everything is a matter of time and place—boulders in the street, and short lengths of rope—and I have described the gist of the matter that Sunday in Matamoros. Somewhere along the way, I had gained in stature, but lost my French beret.

I asked the young mechanic if he would recommend a place for the night. He led me into the street to point it out. A building with a balcony, just beyond the cantina. To eat also? No; for eating, since it happened to be Sunday, I would have to go to the railroad station. One of the boys led me. It proved to be quite a walk. A station like one seen in movies graphically depicting South American wars of rebellion, it glowed with the rosy light of sunset. A child appeared to ask me if I wanted *la comida*? It was served by an elderly, shrunken woman with one blind eye. Probing with the fork, I saw that I had been served *frijoles* many times *refritos*. In the past I had been fool enough to eat it. Would I repeat this folly? I did—no more than two or three bites—drank the beer to squelch the fire, and left.

Those towns that provide tombs for the living, Matamoros being one of their number, have about them a funereal aura of ruin that is biblical and timeless. No dogs barked or chickens cackled. I thought of Guanajuato, where the dead were available for discussion. Somewhere a Roman writer, and a good one, speaks of entering a city where the corpses of the dead could be seen walking the streets. He puts it better than that, at greater length, and I remembered it at that moment. My room in the hotel featured the balcony, a view of

280

the plaza, and a toilet bowl at the back that lacked a seat. Through the arched doorway to the balcony I could see the stopped hands of the clock on the bell tower. That detail I liked, and it would prove memorable. Some hours later, I awoke in a sweat and the assurance that I had come to Matamoros to die. *Matamoros!* How could a writer of fiction improve on something like that?

. . . Two pariah dogs, with unmatched eyes, their bodies like racks for drying skins, cringed at a distance determined by an alert, tailless bantam rooster, their noses pitted with the pecks from his corn-tipped beak. Did not that symbolize something? Too much. Much too much. But in Matamoros everything was a symbol, nothing was its simple, visible self. The square with its tree of India, draped as if with mourning, the fountain that dripped and smelled like an illness, the bright tile benches that managed to be too hot in the sun, too cool in the shade, and the clock in the bell tower that tolled no recognizable hour.

A species of canary, Cowie's first impression had been that it was an object, made of cork and pipe cleaners. Artful, perhaps. No question it was horrible. There were quills, but no feathers, below the neck. The head with its lidded eyes was elevated on the neck like a lampshade. The legs and claws were twisted bits of wire. Cowie took it as an example of the Mexican taste for the macabre: the skull-and-bone cookies eaten by children, the fantastic birds and animals made out of paper. When he glanced up to see it headless, he simply thought the head had dropped off. But no. Nothing lay in the bottom of the cage. The head, with its knife-like beak, had been tucked under the quills of one wing. Fly it could not, lacking the feathers. Sing it would not. But on occasion it hopped. (One Day, 1965)

I did not die, but my living proved to be like the hands of the clock. The landlady lived in the front apartment, with a window on the street, where she sat and sewed, a plump, matronly, sorrowing woman, surrounded by a large assortment of paintings of saints and religious objects, many lit up at night by the glow of candles. I was struck by how often she made the sign of the cross at what she found herself thinking, or feeling. Her black-haired daughter had her mother's large, moist eyes, but a disfiguring acne that she concealed with a heavy cream paste. At night, if she thought me asleep, she might come to the archway and peer in at me.

An Indian girl, Dolores, her broad face pitted like the moon's surface, the mouth wide as a slice of melon, took care of such things as spooning him food and the daily nightmare of the bedpan. That she seemed to feel no disgust herself helped Cowie some, but not much. She came to him fresh from her own eating, her mouth greasy, her breath scented with chili, and went about her business while loudly sucking air through her teeth.

Every morning, Dolores mopped the upstairs hall, and swabbed down the tile stairs that she was the only one to use. She brought me food without a discernible trace of interest in my condition. I observed in her face an unscrupulous cunning she made no effort to conceal. Her coarse brownish hair was like that of a dog's pelt, the back of her head a smooth slope to her hunched shoulders. I listened to her comments with some amazement that she could speak. Taking my own arm by the wrist, like a handle, she would hold it to her ear to hear my watch tick. She admired the watch so openly—a Swiss chronograph—I acknowledged that she might poison me to get it. Did her boyfriends—she reported on several— feel the quality of her nature as I did? She seemed to me a human to whom it had not occurred that a distinction existed between kindness and indifference. I had seen her lips curl with contempt when her mistress kneeled in prayer.

On what proved to be a Friday, I was able to get up and walk to where I had left the car. A boy with a pail of water swabbed it down with newspapers. Would it run? Would it shift? I looked around the courtyard for the mechanic, found him under one of the wrecked cars. He crawled from beneath to accept one of my cigarettes.

How had I liked Matamoros?

Fine, I replied. He thought that a sensible comment. It led me to add that I had found the food a bit of a problem. Ha! he

282

cried. The tourist problem! I thought he must mean *turista*, but no, he meant tourists. They found the food different than it was where they had come from, wherever that was. If I stayed in Matamoros, I would soon grow accustomed to the food.

And the Jaguar? It was *muy bueno*. He took his place at the wheel and started the motor. He shifted from low to second, and from second to high, but into reverse was a bit of a problem. If it could be avoided, I should not reverse. I might get it there, then not get it out. In Mexico City they could make a finer adjustment. Until Mexico City I should just go forward.

My bill, scrawled on a piece of wrapping paper, was $26 for labor, $4.80 for parts. The fourteen quarts of oil would be extra. Would he accept my traveler's checks? He would. I gave him forty dollars, with my blessings. He walked along beside me as I drove back to the hotel, where he made an adjustment in the gas mixture.

I let the motor run while I collected my razor, and the pajamas that Dolores had just washed. Her broad, grubby palm, like an animal track, clutched the wad of pesos that I gave her. In her grin I saw nothing but greedy pleasure. The landlady urged me (from the balcony) to send her daughter a postcard from El Paso. She collected stamps.

I drove slowly toward Puebla, my lips dry, almost at ease with the folly of it, seeing on the far horizon the snow-capped peak of Ixtacihuatl, the sleeping woman, my sense of having escaped with my life so fragile I knew that I was not yet fully recovered. I drove as Jo had advised me to drive, like an old man. In Puebla I sat in the café on the plaza as it was being hosed down by the waiters, happy as children to be playing with the sparkling water, water being what is green and Go in Mexico.

While waiting for a letter from Jo, I worked on the *Holiday* piece. What did I *know* about Mexico, an immense darkness lit up by fireworks and candles? On several occasions I had passed through it as a bird flies through a tunnel, coming in at one end and flying out the other. On me Montezuma had taken his revenge in Matamoros, in Acapulco, in Guadalajara and elsewhere. I had had numerous glimpses through the chinks of time that lured the unwary traveler out of his depth, and I had dimly felt—not for the first time—the folly of all such enterprises. A piece on Mexico? A quick reading of the disguises I had adopted for my travels. *Me voici* in my Jaguar, in a flooding river, pushed from behind by a villain who smiled like Pancho Villa.

In recording my adventures I somehow assured the reader that if he just hung in there—in Matamoros, in Acapulco, in a place unmentioned, near Irapuato—it would be all right. On my way south to Puebla I had driven through a surreal landscape of streetlamps without streets, thousands of them, streets without houses, without people, and I had said to my-self, *How like Mexico!* What was meant by that? Perhaps I meant the sudden appearance, and the instant collapse, of such decent, well-meaning, hard-earned, good intentions. The real-life fiction of a people who were learning to live with their own arrears, their own prebuilt ruins. But how long would it be before this affliction appeared in epidemic form north of the border?

On the new escalators in Radio City, from where I caught glimpses of skaters on the ice rink, I had once felt the pre-scient chill of crowded tombs waiting to be plundered. How much, or how little, did it take? One degree of change in any direction would be enough to set the tumblers of change in motion. The *keeping up* was what would get them in Mexico, and it could be seen catching up with us, the inertia of ma-chinery slowly grinding to a stop.

The more exotic and bizarre the surface of a culture—Mex-ico, Brazil, Saudi Arabia—the more fundamental and basic we judged the mask of life behind it. Was that its charm? The dirt, the squalor, the women and the children, the animals, and the survival. From my window at night I could see the glow and spit of the fire where an Indian girl sat on the curb-ing, slapping out tortillas for her family, her hands shining like polished brass. She accepted my charity with a glance, but without a smile.

After delays—she had been to England—I heard from Jo. As soon as she could pack, and arrange her affairs, she would fly to Mexico. My relief was so great I saw my situation clearly. If she had not come to me, I would have gone to her. In the airport—I was there at noon, for an 8 P.M. flight from Paris—I watched the plane staffed by Frenchmen who clearly represented a superior order, the big things that came in small packages. I stared at them with admiration as they passed, like gods, through the disorder of the customs office. My girl was there, frantically waving! Once more her brisk, clicking heels reassured me that I was headed in the right direction. What a relief I found it that her first view of the city was at night.

Jo liked Mexico moderately well, but it did not often excite her favorably. After a few weeks, our discussions soon veered back to Venice. A letter was sent off, pronto, to Sam Kaner, inquiring about Sylvia Brown's apartment. Would it be vacant by April? Our plans were to drive to New York—as soon as the weather permitted—and make the arrangements to sail from New York to Venice. This was more of a cruise than a passage, requiring almost three weeks at sea, with stops at all of those places on the walls of the travel bureaus. Mallorca, for example, had haunted me all these years I had failed to make it on my *Wanderjahr* in the mid-thirties. There was also Greece, and Dubrovnik, on the Adriatic, facts I had determined on a quick stop at the Italian tourist office in Manhattan. So what were we doing in Mexico City? We were packing our bags.

I've no idea who it was that first mentioned Rancho Atascadero, in San Miguel Allende. We would make a stop there on our way to the border, and check on the weather they were having in the Midwest. After the inspired repairs made in Matamoros, I had had the Jag checked over by the British Motors shop in Mexico City, but with Jo in the bucket seat beside me, I did feel an occasional tremor of apprehension.

The great roads for Jaguar cruising are those of blacktop, full of dips and curves, but they have to be relatively free of potholes. We had such a road to Querétaro, where an assembly of *muchachos*, in the plaza, washed and polished the car while we were having lunch in the hotel. Querétaro had been designed, it seemed to me, from impressions I had received in the forties, to be discovered by intrepid British females—than whom there are none more intrepid—who had previously exhausted Spain, Morocco, Doughty's Arabia Deserta, but retained their appreciative eye for vanishing colonial empires. We lunched that day with several, refugees from both Santa Fe and Bloomsbury, keenly observant of our illicit romance, as well as of the elderly Indian, with the face of a Chinese sage, who had appeared in the lobby with a brace of turkeys dangling head down from a rope about his neck. While he bartered with the clerk at the desk, the turkeys fastened on

287

me their gimlet eyes. Turkey, alas, was what I was eating, or had been eating up to that moment.

Rancho Atascadero offered no heated swimming pool (at that time), but had extensive resort accommodations, an attractive bar lounge and excellent food. Attractively literate and illiterate vagrants seemed to feel at their ease there, one reason being that ten dollars a day covered all expenses, including a few martinis. San Miguel itself, staggeringly picturesque, created with the tourist and his camera in mind, had an art school, but otherwise had been suitably embalmed by the altitude, like Guanajuato, for the visitors of the future. After our season in Venice, why didn't we return here? The weather seemed perfect. The accommodations were handsome and spacious. We left with the understanding that we would be back in November, just ahead of the Venetian winter. Had we managed to stumble on the best of two worlds? Our only complaint was the number of sand fleas we picked up on our walks.

This firm prospect to return in November did much to lift my spirits on the long drive east. It proved to be a strain for Jo, who was more of a night owl than a meadowlark, and had to adapt to my barbarous on-the-road travel rituals—the worst being my dawn starts, with our first cup of coffee at sunrise.

Incredibly, the Jaguar gave us no trouble until our arrival in suburban Philadelphia, where I had the good sense, and the luck, to turn it in on a new car for my wife. A letter from Sam Kaner was waiting for me in Wayne, and he reported that Sylvia Brown now planned to move from her garden apartment into the one Sam was just leaving. He had found a studio on Giudecca. These moves would be made, he assured me, by the time of our arrival in late April.

Jo found a suite in a hotel off Madison Avenue in New York, and she had already begun our travel arrangements with a clerk at American Express. A tall, handsome and cultivated Britisher, he was greatly appreciative of Jo, and intrigued by the details of our romantic involvement. (How tenderly he handled the passports!) His discovery that I was a *published* writer inflamed his imagination; he saw two of my books in a window! He came to the hotel to discuss steamer accommodations with Jo. Passage on the *Vulcania,* from New York to Venice, making stops at Barcelona, Naples, Palermo, Dubrovnik, a cruise of almost three weeks, cost about $250 each.

My wife's new car did not long distract her from the time I was spending in New York.

I had described Jo as an assistant to my editor. Why did all the details prove to be so threadbare? My wife quickly determined that Jo was not in the publishing business, and she confronted me, in the classic manner, when I came back from New York. There is little that is new in these ancient deceptions. She had not meant to force me to a decision, but in the heat of our spat she could not help it. I had to assure her that I was leaving. With control that I admired, at the time, she used the word *separation*, avoiding the dreaded term *divorce*. For several hours this admission released much of the tension; she asked where we were going, and I told her. We were, as was said, civilized about it. I had hoped to spare her anguish. At that moment it was hell for one of us; but if I compromised, it would be hell for us both.

I packed my bags and took a train for New York. It was apparent to Jo, when she opened the door, that the die had been cast, and that from now on we would be forging ties that would test our affections and our natures. A few days later we sailed on the *Vulcania*. We had the pleasure of stops in Barcelona and Mallorca—Barcelona and the Gaudís we liked so much we thought we might come back, if Venice failed us. A friend wired to say that my wife had not been well, but she was now back at her teaching, and seemed much better.

The turn of events had brought Jo and me closer together, and the ties we were making had been tested. We lived well together. Living together suited us fine. Jo would prove to be a very independent young woman, with absolutely minimal needs for entertainment and distractions. We could sit or stroll for hours, people-watching. I had begun to make some notes for my new work, and it did not occur to her that this was competition. Her observing eyes were often keener than mine, and there was more to be seen than we could absorb. Jo soon became the first reader of my manuscripts, and reader of the proofs.

An old boat, relatively speaking, the *Vulcania* had about it a riper sense of leisure, of elegance and of service than I had experienced. The clatter of plates and cutlery was common, but voices seemed to be subdued. There was also a relaxing ease between the server and the well-served. We loved it.

Perhaps every cruise ship is a ship of fools. Circumstance has selected them from the millions who are still at home, going about their business, and it is not easy to be long out of this world in such an exposed and vulnerable manner. Some dim image of Shangri-la looms far up ahead—it is never the port where you are anchored—and some haunting image of the past hovers in the darkness behind. A big steamer is a remarkable refuge from both the up ahead and what is behind. Each day there was a new menu to be mastered; each night, the horseplay and the dancing. The dancing could be great! "Arrivederci Roma" was a new and catchy tune.

One of the passengers, a well-curved young woman, traveling with her cat in a large hamper, was in the process of divorcing a husband of fourteen months. "And every one of them was hell," she told us. It was for this hell he was now paying. Having heard that I was a writer, she asked what it was I had written. She was a reader. How was it she had not heard of me, or of my books? This depressed her long day in Barcelona, until the truth of the matter dawned on her. I was an impostor, passing myself off as a writer. This discovery—shared with the passengers—proved to be exhilarating, and preoccupied her as far as Naples, where she disembarked. In a marvelous passage, the Swiss writer Max Frisch speaks of the great things about dogs—you either love them or you needn't have them—and this is also true of cats. Her cat was much loved, and lapped cream from her saucer when she was having tea.

We made a brief stop in Greece, which the movies had prepared us for, the simple village life that seemed to be on hold until the arrival and whir of the cameras. The sense of unreality—I realized later—testified to what was actually real about it. A pause seemed to have occurred, with the boat's arrival, in whatever it was that was going on. The sun shone. We sat at a teetering table waiting for the stopped time to start up.

When, at the pier in Dubrovnik, on seeing Jo, several of the young men cried "Gioconda! Gioconda!" it was a moment in my life that still gives me pleasure. The steamer's approach to Venice—the dawn sea becalmed, abandoned dwellings on islands that seemed to be drifting—was so gradual, with the engines silenced, it seemed to diminish what was actually happening. We had arrived! With Lawrence, I could cry, "Look! We have come through!" I had a glimpse up the Grand Canal before tugs towed us to where we seemed to dock in Lilliputia, a miniature city when seen from the steamer's deck.

I had brought along a stock of Marsh-Wheeling stogies, which I nervously escorted through customs, then found a porter to cart our many bags to the Locanda Montin. There we received the welcome we very much needed, in the absence of Sam Kaner, whose wife was having a baby. Sylvia Brown was actually in the process of moving from her garden apartment the fifty yards to Sam Kaner's penthouse, but there were formalities to be settled before we could take possession. What sort of occupants were we? How long did we plan to stay? The apartment was hung with many bad Venetian paintings, of the sort the owners get so fond of, was furnished with fragile "antiques"; the bookshelves sagged with mildewed books. An itemized list of these valuables covered more than twenty pages. As tenants, we were responsible for them. We met with one of the owners, an elderly *avvocato* of such reticence, distinction and good breeding that speech of any kind was not in order. He proved to be, once out of his chair, six feet five inches tall; at the table where we assembled in the Locanda Montin, he was compelled to sit with his knees in the aisle. There was not much in the way of communication. We eagerly agreed with everything. Ten days later we were given occupancy. The floor of crushed marble, spotted with throw rugs, seemed designed to conceal the scorpions that came in from the garden, but all of that was in our future. In the immediate and pressing present there was a tub, a shower attachment, hot water, real plumbing, and gas. One of the low tables, and a mound of art books, supported my portable electric typewriter. Would it run on the local current? I had come supplied with a transformer. After all, I was a modern traveler—how would I shave?

I had also come to Venice to work, and I was in a fever to get started. I had brought with me (of all things!) the opening chapter of *Ceremony in Lone Tree*, the driest of enterprises for a city built on islands. Just down the path to the entrance, we could see the canal barges passing, with their cases of Campari and Coca-Cola, the boatman leaning on the tiller as he gave us a few arias from Verdi.

More than ten years later, after Jo and I had returned to Venice, I wrote *Love Affair: A Venetian Journal*.

Accustomed to the bizarre, our friend from California has come to see for himself if we are living in Venice. We assure him that we are. A lease has been signed to ensure our exile. Already my wife Jo has been lost and found. Bells are ringing. The light seems to vibrate with their clamor. Our friend impatiently waits for this unaccustomed racket to stop. Through the gate at the entrance he has left open we watch a barge drift past, we hear the lap of water, we note the cases of Campari, Punt e Mes, and Coca-Cola. The man at the tiller—he leans on it like a fence rail—wears a striped T-shirt, the smile of a happy pirate. To Jo he waves. She is popular with pirates from the way she goes up and down the city's bridges. He is there and gone. There are shouts like a street brawl as he greets his friends.

Right there on both sides of the Rio San Trovaso was everything we needed for housekeeping: a bar with the bottled water, the brandy, the wine (all delivered in a hamper, with a cash discount); a baker with whole-wheat bread (on certain days; on others, a Venetian shrug); several vegetable stands, run by the ladies, with the assistance of a lout who sat on the

292

cartons, reading comic books; a shop with butter, cream to be spooned, and a basket of Russian-roulette eggs (refunds to Jo, a trusted consumer); and just a sprint or a stroll to the south, the promenade of the Zattere, the Montparnasse of Venice, with the decks of tables bobbing on the water as the *vaporettos* skied in for the stop. We soon had our café, and our waiter:

The happy few in Venice have a window on a garden. We are among the happy few, but our happiness is clouded. Venetian cats pad in and out of the window at night, transporting kittens, live bait, and the heads of fish. At the foot of our bed, on which they land with a plop, they launder and dry clean the family pelts, check on gains and losses, practice cat witchery. Their motors hum like refrigerators. There is one with one eye: it winks and flares like the flame of a match. We are cat people, and they seem to know it. The word has spread. By the light of morning we examine saucers tongue-buffed to gleam like enamel. Cat tracks on the table, cat hairs on the chairs, cat smears on my papers, but no visible cats. They are night strollers. During the day they go about masked. A carpenter has come to put a screen at the window, but the idea is novel and will take much reflection. While it is under advisement our new friends pad in and out.

Was there anything like it on the planet? An Italian or a Greek steamer might be docked there, about to depart for Cythera! The Adriatica liners, white and gleaming as yachts, with a crew of villains visible at the portholes, went to such places as Cairo and Istanbul, with travelers long abandoned by Conrad. Week after week we thought about it, but they were not our favorite places. We were holding out for Corfu, Athens and the isles of Greece. There was also—for a month at a time—a battered freighter undergoing repairs that required jackhammers, docked for these repairs on Giudecca, so that each sound carried across the water. But we were, after all, still *on* the planet. For seven cents we could ride, from where we were seated, down the canal and across the bay to the Piazza San Marco, a stage with the world's players on it, the air above it a swirl of color as the local pigeons zoomed in for a landing. What could one do with all this grandeur?

Her name is Dora. She acquired us in an involved transaction concerned with the washing of two bed sheets. The sheets are large, the color and weight of sailcloth, deliberately constructed to outlast the sleeper. But they are not easily washed. To be used as sheets, rather than a shroud, they have to be ironed. The first takes water, which is not in short supply; the second takes electric current that is sold by the drip, like maple syrup. We persuaded a lady in the Campo Santa Margherita (we saw her, Vermeer-like, ironing at an open window) to wash and iron our two sheets for 950 lire. That's a dollar and fifty cents, and it took her a week. This led to a discussion with the baker's wife on the curious scarcity of laundries in Venice. She had not heard about laundries. Anything that gets dirty is washed by a maid. Pillows are fluffed, rugs are beaten, children are watched and scolded by a housemaid. If one had a house, what one had to have next was a maid. Dora Rizzoli, a Rossellini-type woman, long accustomed to making crucial decisions, proved to be willing to wash and iron our sheets, and thereby acquired us.

Jo sleeps. One arm lies at her side, the palm up, as if she floated on the quilt pattern beneath her. Her head is turned to the light, her lips slightly parted, her right hand bent at the wrist like a drooping flower.

Where is she off to, here in Venice?

My breathing is hushed, as if I might hear.

We found we could look at it, and its strolling players, for several hours most days, and another stroll in the evening, when the soft glow of the lamps transformed the real into a surreal canvas. Do you tire of this hyperbole, reader? People are not lacking who *hate* Venice, some of whom have actually been there. When it rains, we are of that number. Or on any one of those hot days of summer, the fetid air smelling of the slued-up garbage, or of a nearby canal that is being cleaned,

294

just a whiff of the stench suffocating. The human folly of having built such a city in the first place, then leaving people to live in a ruin that resists burial but does not resist reminding you of it.

The unsigned murals of Venice, hung in plein air, compete favorably with those displayed at the Biennale. They are old in subject but modern in taste, avant-garde in their harmony of color and texture. The instinct for the ready-made and labeled object comprehends the ready-made and framed abstraction. Walls, doorways and windows, patterns of bricks and mortar, peeling strips of plaster with the gloss of leather, colors blended by time and mixed by the weather, graffiti and collages, the assembly of devices, emblems and symbols in the gondola, seem to be lacking nothing but the signature of the artist. If everyone is an artist—a currently fashionable notion—Venice provides everyone with his own ready-made work of art.

We surely had all the best of it, the weather so unseasonable we came away with a dreamer's notion of summer in Venice—hardly a day of the stupefying sirocco, the languor that drugs all senses. In its place we had showers, dramatic blasts of thunder that seemed to roll right out of the paintings, with crisp, scoured skies, whitecaps on the bay, and even happy surprises from the butcher. (The beast lies there, but you have to point out, or divine, what part of it you would like to be eating.) There is no Gorgonzola anywhere like what we ate that summer—and that is why: we ate it all. I drank the local Merlot like water, and reserved the Brolio Chianti for heavy dining. I found and bought some good pipes, tinned English tobacco, but I did not light up a smokable cigar, other than my Marsh-Wheeling stogies.

To top it off, even my work went well, and I had a finished manuscript early in September. I shipped it off—not without some apprehension—to Hiram Haydn, of the new firm of Atheneum. To celebrate this occasion, Jo and I took off for Rome, which we found was not a great place for the walkers we had learned to be in Venice. The world of wheels and smog soon had us wheezing, so we went north to Assisi, the landscape one unfolding vibrant painting. We saw the Pieros in Arezzo, then went on for several good days in Florence and the memorable confrontation with Botticelli's *Primavera*. Nothing prepares the viewer for such a marvel but the painting itself. I was dazzled by its matchless imaginative power, as I would be by Bosch's *Garden of Earthly Delights*. How did the modern painter, beholding such works, make peace with his own shrinking talents? And how else describe them? I had not been in Florence since Lorne Ward and I had sat pondering the octopus in our soup, as we exchanged our less than fearless glances. Jo was able to persuade me to buy for myself an elegant tobacco pouch, just what I needed, and we bought for her a very swanky handbag, much admired by the ladies in the second-class train coach to Bologna.

Every time we saw one of the white, gleaming boats of the Adriatica Line, at the dock or headed seaward, we spoke of going to Greece. Occasionally we saw a loose pack of *Wandervögel*, in their lederhosen and rucksacks, their hair sun-bleached, go clomping by in their heavy hiking boots. Where were they going? How? We never actually saw them on one of the boats.

I finally determined, after a week of asking questions, that a Greek boat, the *Philippos*—once said to be a Thames river steamer—sailed from Venice to Piraeus, the port of Athens, and then to Mykonos and other Greek islands. That was for us. But what did this boat look like? I was told I would see that on the day it sailed.

This proved to be in mid-October—a fine time, we were assured, for our sea adventure. The *Philippos* was docked some distance down the Zattere, where the scene was cluttered, an unpainted, peeling hulk less than half the size I had fancied. The cabins proved to be inspired makeshifts for trapping the passengers below deck. I thought of Conrad. I tried, unsuccessfully, to put it out of my mind. I clearly received and recorded the signal that this boat was more than a calculated risk. So what did I do? I calmly began unpacking our bags. On an upper level, there were five or six cabins with teak and mahogany doorways and brass fittings, with an area for dining and lounging, but we were down where the galley slaves were chained between bouts of rowing. I reminded myself that Homer's wine-dark sea was just a big pond.

From the sea, Piraeus, the port of Athens, smoldered like the wasteland of the Jersey marshes, or, more poetically speaking, the gates of hell. Undecided, Soby leaned on the rail rather than risk an early commitment. Behind the sulphurous cloud, on good authority, was Greece. A wind smelling of diesel fuel held the ship flags taut as fraternity pennants, puffing the cheeks of Miss Kollwitz with more than words could express. One sleeve of Soby's promised sweater was looped around her neck . . . A babushka, souvenir of Corfu, flapped about her face.
"Look! Look!" she cried. "We are here!"
(What a Way to Go, 1962)

There were no casualties as far as Piraeus, where we were bused to the Acropolis, an experience so out of scale with a schoolboy's impressions I was both staggered and dazzled. It had been true, then? All this time, there had once been giants on the earth. I am also confident that only ruins have this power over the romantic imagination (mine), but I could not people this hallowed ground with real flesh-and-blood figures. Nor can I now. It seemed to have been conceived as a ruin in order to have on me this overwhelming effect. I was awed, and stooped to fondle bits of the shrapnel-like marble that were strewn along the paths.

A Greek schoolboy of such uncommon beauty I simply stared at him, as at a clever restoration, held our attention as he reeled off a litany of names and dates that meant less to him than they did to me. With his dark, bushy brows, his head of thick curly locks, his bronze skin stretched tight over his bursting flesh, he would live to see (in my opinion) this hallowed place sold to the highest bidder. He was a Greek and a realist (a redundancy), not a sentimental schoolboy who had once made a trireme out of nine boxes of Diamond kitchen matches. Both of us were ignorant of the forces once released on this elevation. I bought postcards from him, and touched the skin of his palm when I gave him the coins. He, too, ignorant though he was, had some of this force pulsing in his veins, and it filled me with awe.

A little after midnight, I was awakened by the rolling and pitching of the boat. At the portholes, the blast of the waves made a luminous froth. Everything trembled as if struck by blows of a hammer. I knew, if I knew anything, that the hour had come. Water sloshed under the berths, and to stay in them we had to brace our feet against the frames. Doors flapped in the hall as if loose on their hinges. I futilely rang for the cabin porter. The occasional buoyant inertness of the boat gave me the feeling that it bobbed, like a cork, on the surface, at the mercy of the next wave. Hearing a bell clang, I thought it must be a signal to abandon ship. How did one do it? Ankle-deep water sloshed in the gangway. The lights blinked off, leaving the cabin in a glow that was phosphorescent. My words were not a comfort to Jo. I made note of this, being a writer.

And then, as if the storm had been turned off with the switch of a button, we were becalmed in a breakwater. I saw a ring of lights, splintered with gusts of rain. Dimly I perceived a few ghostly houses. I heard shouting, the clank of chains, and the *put-put* of an approaching motor. Someone was disembarking. This inspiration came to me too late. I opened the cabin door to see an old man, in his shirttails, calmly urinating into the slosh. He nodded to me, a cigarette dangling at his lip.

"Where are we?" I asked. At the moment, I did not understand his reply. We were at Mykonos, anchored in the small harbor. The gentle rocking of the boat was actually soothing. A sputtering flame of consciousness that fed on my nerves kept me awake for another five or ten minutes, then, seated at the edge of Jo's berth, I lay back with my head in her lap and slept.

What we would do—we were seated at breakfast, our elbows on the soiled tablecloth, a blue-black, white-capped sea sporting like dolphins at the portholes, the light a shimmering dazzle—what we would do would be to go on to Rhodes, and from there *fly* back to Venice. I had never flown, but I could be persuaded to fly for my life.

By noon we were on Rhodes, a picture-postcard fortress lapped by tides of sea and light. We had lunch in the one resort hotel on the beach, the window framing a view of the *Philippos* basking in the sun of the harbor. It looked pretty good. The walled city of Rhodes, thronged with *Wandervögel* (where had they been during the blow?), was as beautiful as the brochure insisted, and only a day's sail from Piraeus. The sea was calm. Had I perhaps exaggerated the crisis? Since the boat was there, and our bags were on it, we sailed peacefully back to Piraeus, from there to Corfu, and from Corfu back to Venice, where it seemed that the dusk came perceptibly sooner, and the shadows on the canals were longer.

These October days we've had barges from Chioggia, painted like banners, moored in the Rio San Trovaso. The men sleep on the decks. We see them plainly at the end of the tunnel that leads to our garden. Lanterns gleam in the hold where they sit eating: they glance at me with the eyes of men sorting booty. These sea dogs are another race from Venetians, they have the air of whalers among city people. Their voices have a deeper register; it pleases me that their speech smacks of faraway places. I think of wandering Greeks, of affluent Phoenicians, of barbarians who raid and loot by water. As the sky cools, the light of dusk enhances the color of their barges. The city before them lies waiting to be ravished, while the leaders discuss the terms of the ransom. The mood is optimistic. A carnival will celebrate the settlement. In the morning, however, I am pleased to find them gone, having sailed at dawn for Byzantium, their holds crowded, their decks jammed with impressions that remain unchallenged. We did not come here to gawk at sea dogs who had lost their bite.

Along the Zattere, most of the tables sat empty; the chairs were being moved back inside. The sound of the water lapping the promenade, slapping the steps of the piazza, gave us a bit of a chill. The light over the city—as one saw it from the crest of the Accademia bridge—was very much as it had been painted by four hundred years of Venetian painters. You could pick your own light, and your own painter, but when we stopped for an espresso we took care to sit in the sun. In the dark, winding alleys we caught the damp whiff and savor of what it would be like in the winter. Snow on the gondolas? We had already seen it in the photographs. How smart we had been to have made the arrangements to be back in San Miguel by December, basking in the Mexican sunshine at Christmas.

Back in the summer, I had received, and accepted, an offer to teach for a year at Los Angeles State College, beginning in the fall of 1960. This would take care of our immediate future, so all we had to deal with was the immediate present. After several days of drizzle, early in November (there is nothing— no, nothing—like a November drizzle in Venice), we made our reservations to sail on the *Columbus* to New York.

Drizzle or no, it proved a painful parting from our friends. Two of our Dora's sons appeared with a barge as wide as a café deck to transport our luggage to the boat. As the drizzle increased, she was encouraged to come up the gangplank for a drink in the bar. She approved of the elegance of the furnishings. It was how, in her opinion, people of Jo's distinction should travel. As we departed, a rising tide lapped the promenade, prophesying, once more, a sea burial for the city. I remember that my sorrow was nicely neutralized by my relief.

Following dinner—our best meal since a marvelous lasagna in Florence—we had our first intimation that the Adriatic also had its surprises. A gale swept the decks. Most of the night, we rolled and tossed. It was somewhat better out of Barcelona—we always meant to get back to Barcelona—but once we had passed through the Strait of Gibraltar, we had an unrelieved winter passage. A dim, mist-filtered light—ideal for paintings of dreams, nightmares and caverns—veiled whatever might be seen in any direction. I looked with longing at a

300

steamer said to be headed for the Canaries. The Canaries! Why hadn't we thought of them sooner?

We had six days of it, the dining room empty (I had the attention of half a dozen waiters at breakfast), but it proved to be the ideal circumstance for my rediscovery of Thomas Mann's *The Magic Mountain*. The small, dimly lit library, no larger than a cabin, the sea rising and falling at the portholes, restored to me the magical shimmer of Hans Castorp's dream in the snow at Davos. In my mind seascape and snowscape are now of a piece, as if I vividly recalled a darkened theater and a film of Castorp's adventure.

At the bar, I had the time to discuss with the barman, in my fractured Italian, the trials of life at sea. He was from Verona, but seldom saw it. He belonged to this boat, to this life, where he worked a long day, slept in a dormitory, and saw the world, if at all, through a porthole. A handsome fellow, Giuseppe, with a Toscanini moustache, flashing eyes, and a gallant manner with the ladies. But where were they? Bundled up in their berths? What a day it was for him when Jo returned to her place. "Enchoy life!" he cried, as we hoisted our glasses, and he exchanged with me glances of affection and envy. How could I not, with such a girl! There was no revelry or horseplay. Mournfully the orchestra tooted "Arrivederci Roma." A pair of diehards grimly hugged each other. Would it never end? Then one night it did; the ceasing of the battle created an ominous vacuum. What next? I got up early to be prepared for it. Far on the horizon, I saw the telltale hint of land. In the dawn, light birds soared. Over there somewhere, beyond where I was looking, but where I had been born, bred and trained to look, was America.

In New York, I spent some time with my editor, Hiram Haydn, who had some suggestions about my new book, but I was eager to buy a car suitable for our trip to Mexico. I had hoped to find one of the classic Thunderbird coupes, but none were available. In the suburbs of Long Island, driven there by a friend, we found a Studebaker Golden Hawk that appealed to my long history with Studebakers. We loaded up with our

301

luggage, some of which we had left in storage, then drove through a winter landscape that looked like home to me for a reunion with Dorothy and Granville Hicks in Grafton. I reminded myself to make sure, before we left Grafton, to check the antifreeze.

This meeting proved to be our first chance to share with friends the many months of our love affair with Venice. Just ten years later, in May of 1969, Jo and I would persuade Dorothy and Granville to visit us. These happy comminglings of people and places that so often seem to be there for the asking, but will somehow prove to be so elusive, had the bloom of an experience that we may have sensed would not be repeated. The cold drive had given me a touch of arthritis in several fingers, and I was persuaded by Dorothy to apply a remedy she had found in an old almanac—a daily dose of vinegar mixed with honey. I gave it a try. It tasted so god-awful I had the assurance it must be good for me.

Once more, to begin a new life, I was headed west. This time my longed-for companion was there beside me, and I had never felt so confident about the future. First we would have our winter in San Miguel Allende—to which we both looked forward—then in the spring we would drive to Southern California and settle in for a year's teaching. Jo and I were in agreement that the Palisades, just west of Bel Air, would be where we would live. *Ceremony in Lone Tree*—that very dry book written in a wet place—was scheduled to be published in September, and gave us a welcome point of focus. Hovering over us both, however, was the looming divorce that could no longer be ignored or evaded. It had been mercifully suspended during our stay in Venice, and for that I was profoundly grateful. Now that we were back, it was the first fact in our life together.

I was fifty years of age, and that was how I looked. Photographs taken by Jo, at Rancho Atascadero, show a man in what might be called his prime, his face in profile, his hands in the pockets of a coveted field jacket, the sun casting a shadow on the wall of a handball court. This shot will appear on the jacket flap of his new book. It would be hard to say to what extent he felt it, but he is at the threshold of a new life, although still clad in his familiar, self-loomed cloak of light.

Jo tells him, as the shutter clicks, that he looks great.

CODA

I had little or no suspicion that my true feelings were precisely those that I would learn to conceal

There is a moment in *Will's Boy* where my father and I, headed for California, are driving south from Chicago through the early winter morning. The first light of dawning seems to bathe the world. Up ahead the narrow road swerves to pass between farm buildings, a frame house with the sun blazing on its windows, a red barn that casts a purple shadow on the powdering of snow. The blaze of sunlight and the deep shadow, the sound made by the car as it whooshed between the buildings, left on me an impression that I would feel compelled to recover. Fifty years after this moment I attempt to recapture the spell of that morning.

Near Springfield the road curved between farm buildings that sit so close to its edge I could see in the windows. We crossed a bridge, the water black beneath it, a big tilted barn dark against the snow, with a deep purple shadow beside it. Nothing special. Just something I would never forget.

Something we never forget, something we repeatedly remember, an impression fleeting as a casual gesture or the unprovoked glance of a stranger.

In her face, like a sunburst, I swear that what I saw was my own salvation . . . as if the window of the car framed my conversion.

A solo performer on the flying trapeze, the writer does not know, as he soars through the air, if or not the safety net is stretched beneath him: addicted to flying, he is held aloft by his cloak of light.